THE EDUCATION OF A DESIGN WRITER

SVA NYC

STEVEN HELLER & MOLLY HEINTZ

ALLWORTH PRESS
NEW YORK

Copyright © 2025 by Steven Heller and Molly Heintz
Essays copyright © by their respective authors according to the proximate dates given

All rights reserved. Copyright under Berne Copyright Convention, Universal Copyright Convention, and Pan American Copyright Convention. No part of this book may be reproduced, stored in a retrieval system, or transmitted in any form, or by any means, electronic, mechanical, photocopying, recording or otherwise, without the express written consent of the publisher, except in the case of brief excerpts in critical reviews or articles. All inquiries should be addressed to Allworth Press, 307 West 36th Street, 11th Floor, New York, NY 10018.

Allworth Press books may be purchased in bulk at special discounts for sales promotion, corporate gifts, fundraising, or educational purposes. Special editions can also be created to specifications. For details, contact the Special Sales Department, Allworth Press, 307 West 36th Street, 11th Floor, New York, NY 10018 or info@skyhorsepublishing.com.

29 28 27 26 25   5 4 3 2 1

Published by Allworth Press, an imprint of Skyhorse Publishing, Inc. 307 West 36th Street, 11th Floor, New York, NY 10018. Allworth Press® is a registered trademark of Skyhorse Publishing, Inc.®, a Delaware corporation.

www.allworth.com

Cover design by Alexandra Mooney
Interior design by Landers Miller Design

Library of Congress Cataloging-in-Publication Data is available on file.

Print ISBN: 978-1-62153-841-7
eBook ISBN: 978-1-62153-842-4

Printed in China

DEDICATION

Ralph Caplan

humorist, critic, historian, orator, and raconteur who brought design and words together in perfect harmony.

Phil Patton

journalist, scholar, historian, teacher, and pioneer of industrial design writing, who revealed that even the smallest object contains a universe.

PREFACE

VI **Writing Is Design**
by Steven Heller

IX **Why I Rite**
By Steven Heller

INTRODUCTION

XII **The Case for
Design Writing**
By Molly Heintz

1
DESIGN NEEDS WORDS

2 **My Manifesto**
By Karrie Jacobs

7 **Thinking Design
Thinking**
By Mark Kingsley

11 **Ode to the
Design Editor**
By Zachary Petit

14 **A Writing +
Design Practice**
By Warren Lehrer

40 **Good Design at
Its Worst**
By Veronique Vienne

48 **If You Are Writing
an Essay or a Thesis**
By Chappell Ellison

51 **The Fine Art of
Loving and Liking:
How to Survive the
Emoji Economy**
By Sarah Boxer

54 **Paris Clichés**
By Ken Carbone

2
WORDS NEED DESIGN

58 **Writing for the Ear**
By Julie Lasky

61 **Writing on the Wall**
By Angelina Lippert

66 **Clutter Is Good for You**
By Rob Walker

70 **Portfolio**
By Rick Griffith

3
THE INTERVIEW

78 **The Art of the Interview
in 10 Short Lessons**
By Adam Harrison Levy

82 **Mark Mothersbaugh**
Interview by Steven Heller

85 **Christopher Long**
Interview by Steven Heller

87 **Deborah Sussman
(1984: An Invasion of
Butterflies)**
Interview by Alissa Walker

102 **Lauren Cantor (A Pinch
of Artificial, a Dollop of
Intelligence)**
Interview by Steven Heller

108 **How to Use Quotes**
By Adam Harrison Levy

4
SHORT FORM

114 **The Real Bambi**
By Steven Heller

116 **Spot Ads**
By Steven Heller

118 **Can Posters Help?**
By Steven Heller

120 **The Evil Eye of Envy**
By Molly Heintz

122 **The Carcaça**
By Frederico Duarte

5
WRITING HISTORY NOW

126 **Typography Cracked
the Voices of Silence**
By Steven Heller

130 **Playing to Type**
By Virginia Postrel

134 **The Almighty Euro**
By Todd Pruzan

139 **The New Visual
Abnormal**
By Colette Gaiter

146 **1990s: End of
the Millennium**
By Steven Heller

151 **Keeping Tabs:
The History of an
Information Age
Metaphor**
By Edward Tenner

154 **The Forgery Market**
By Anne Quito

164 **The Fairytale (Excerpt)**
By Jennifer Kabat

6
WRITING BIOGRAPHY

172 **Linnaea Tillett Often
Finds That Less Is More**
By Akiko Busch

77 **Takenobu Igarashi Pushed the Parameters of Typography**
By Angela Riechers

80 **Victor Moscoso's Hallucinogenic Flashback**
By Steven Heller

7
MAKING IT PERSONAL

184 **Roy McMakin's Overpowering Simplicity**
By Eva Hagberg

189 **What the "Whole Earth Catalog" Taught Me About Building Utopias**
By Anjulie Rao

194 **Blonde and Dangerous**
By Pune Dracker

201 **Toxic Nostalgia**
By Angela Riechers

8
REVIEWS AND CRITIQUES

206 **Giving and Taking Criticism**
By Chappell Ellison

210 **Out of the Shadows: Women Artists and Abstraction at MoMA**
By Ken Carbone

212 **Tourist/Purist**
By Jarrett Fuller

215 **The Legacy of Racism in the Making of Cities and Communities**
By Alicia Olushola Ajayi

219 **Dress Sense: Why Fashion Deserves Its Place in Art Museums**
By Virginia Postrel

223 **There's Too Much Damn Content, and Slick UX Design Is Making It Worse**
By Chappell Ellison

227 **The Canon of Chicago (American) Modernism Examined**
By Steven Heller

230 **Can a Typeface Sell an Idea?**
By Andrew McQuiston

234 **The Rebranding of Air India**
By Roshita Thomas

237 **Heads Together: Weed and the Underground Press Syndicate, 1965–1973**
By Steven Heller

9
WHERE, WHEN, HOW, AND WHY I WRITE:

Writers/Editors/Designers Answer Questionnaires

242 **The Polymath**
Tod Lippy, Founder, Editor, Publisher of ESOPUS

244 **Knowing Your Audience**
Liz Danzico, Lead of AI Microsoft

248 **Every Day Begin Again**
Kim Tidwell, managing editor, www.printmag.com

252 **Oral Traditions**
Michele Y. Washington, writer, critic, historian

254 **On Exploration**
Alan Rapp, editor, book packager, and content curator

256 **A Meteor Crashing Experience**
Colette Gaiter, Professor Emerita in the Departments of Africana Studies and Art & Design at the University of Delaware

261 **Struggling to Find the Right Words**
Ellen Lupton, Chair, MICA Design, Curator Emerita, Cooper Hewitt

264 **Writing and Editing**
Adrian Shaughnessy, designer, writer, and co-founder of Unit Editions

267 **All Roads Led to *Print***
Joyce Rutter Kaye, former editor-in-chief *Print* magazine, Director of Communications, SVA

270 **Chronicling Black American Graphic Design**
Silas Munro, artist, designer, writer, curator, and the founder of Poly-Mode

275 **Starting a Newsletter**
Deroy Peraza, Principal, Hyperakt Design

278 **An Honest Assessment**
Rob Walker, journalist and author of *Significant Objects*

CONTRIBUTORS
280

ACKNOWLEDGMENTS
290

INDEX
291

PREFACE

WRITING IS DESIGN

✲ BY STEVEN HELLER ✲

Writing about design, designers, and designing is as crucial as making design itself—and for some it is equally satisfying. Conceiving and executing a design scheme or object certainly gives immense pleasure to the designer for its functional, aesthetic, and formal attributes—whatever the medium or platform—and the same is true for writing. The act of turning ideas and concepts into sentences and paragraphs that have structure and meaning is no different than any other art or craft. Good design is a translation of thoughtful (and sometimes random) words together to develop concrete outcomes. Good writing is translating those outcomes into mental pictures, either through literal description or poetic interpretation. Design is intended to be used. Writing is intended to be read. Both are interactive experiences. Design can and does often speak for itself, but its rationale is afforded an even greater relevance when it is part of a word and image narrative. Since writing and design must work in harmony, this book will provide insight into the numerous ways by which this is accomplished.

It can be argued that writing is a lot like talking on paper (or screen). Talking is exactly how I began writing. I'd talk to the paper and allow the ink to flow as though it were automatic (a cousin of automatic writing). However, that procedure had limitations. To write well enough so a reader is compelled to follow a train of thought or the arc of a story is a challenge; ad hoc is *bad hoc*. Perhaps if I had paid attention in my high school writing classes I would have figured that out earlier. The same is true with design. I learned to design in a difficult way. Rather than take classes, I looked at what professionals were doing in magazines and books and attempted to copy them. I say "attempted" because not having any serious training in either the tools or rules of design all I could do was, while occasionally interesting, more often poor mimicry of what I saw ("monkey see, monkey do" makes a messy monkey!).

Whether in a long or short form, writing is a discipline. Discipline demands structure. Design is a discipline too. A good design writer must understand how design is made and operates in the world. How an idea is phrased is often as important as what is being said. There are many ways of conveying ideas through the choice of words, tone, and cadence—style and voice. A writer can choose to be didactic or scholarly (the facts and nothing but the facts, no frill or flourishes); journalistic (reporting the facts through as seen through a particular lens); lyrical (prose that has a rhythm where every sentence plays off the preceding one); effusive (where adjectives are excessively used to gild the proverbial lily); critical (where opinion is expressed in the first person); satiric (where wit, humor, sometimes clever sarcasm conveys a message). Writing about design, whether in a scholarly, journalistic, biographical, or whatever form, is more often than not subtly or overtly expressive (putting forth a point of view). But writing about design, like any subject, can be bland or exciting. What we will attempt here is to provide examples that lean toward the latter when appropriate—or at least interesting.

Writing is based on certain rules of grammar, syntax, punctuation, etc. One of the most useful pieces of writing advice (one could call it a "rule") I've received was passed on to me from Sam Tanenhaus, a superb writer and my former editor at *The New York Times Book Review*: "You can't go wrong starting a sentence with 'IT IS' because it is a sentence already. So too with 'It is not.' The trick is to write as many declarative sentences as possible—that is sentences you can stick a period in really early—after just a few words. 'It is'—or 'it was'—can't get shorter than that. It also makes it possible to build on the sentence with more words and complicated clauses—if that's your thinking—because the reader feels on solid ground. Check out long sentences by Norman Mailer, e.g., and you'll see what I mean—how often they begin with a simple declarative statement. I once counted 150 pages in a Don DeLillo novel (*Libra*) in which *every sentence* was declarative."

It is not always as easy as it sounds to make declarative statements. In writing about design, it is not always as essential to declare as to explain. That said, all writing should open the door—it should say "come right in, stay a while, you'll enjoy this!" The duty of the author is to inform while holding the attention of the reader. Presenting information must be accessible, though not necessarily simple. The author cannot do all the work for the reader. It is necessary for the reader to take some responsibility.

Often design writing requires the reader to have previous knowledge. The reader must abide by some prerequisites. Here lies a balancing act.

This is not a textbook devoted to the mechanics of writing, but rather an anthology of individual writer's methods and rationales for writing and editing employing various writing techniques. So, to share my personal motivations for writing, I've adapted the following from a recent essay.

WHY I RITE
★ BY STEVEN HELLER ★

George Orwell, whose novels *1984* and *Animal Farm* I reread after the 2016 election and whose Spanish Civil War memoir, *Homage to Catalonia,* is a favorite of mine. However, I somehow missed out on his brilliantly crafted essays, and especially the inspiring 1946 "Why I Write." With this introductory essay for *The Education of a Design Writer*, now is the perfect time to read it and write a version of my own.

Although I am making no comparisons between me and Orwell other than that we both write in English, I do relate to this: "So long as I remain alive and well I shall continue to feel strongly about prose style . . . take pleasure in solid objects and scraps of useless information. It is no use trying to suppress that side of myself. The job is to reconcile my ingrained likes and dislikes with the essentially public, non-individual activities that this age forces on all of us."

I call this segment "Why I Rite," because for me writing is a daily ritual (also I love puns). I write something, and (now through the curse of digital black magic) I publish just about every day. Most of the time I have an agenda of sorts, sometimes they are random musings. I write because there are issues and themes I compulsively must address, but also I can write with the wide-eyed desire to share and show off new discoveries with an audience.

I did not set out to be a designer. At NYU in 1968–69 I was an English major but never studied English. Instead, I worked as a cartoonist for an underground newspaper: I was okay. So, I left NYU to study illustration at the School of Visual Arts where I was a mediocre artist. Instead, I worked as art director of another underground newspaper. This led me to practice graphic design and then to art director (and sometime illustrator) at *The New York Times* Op-Ed page. Being attached to such a prestigious page triggered my writing about cartoons, illustration, and design. I always wanted to study and write about tumultuous times in history—the American Civil War, the rise of totalitarianism in Europe, etc. I realized a unique way of doing this was through the lens of cartoon, illustration and graphic design. I am insatiably curious and writing and researching became an optimum process of self-learning. Therefore, I write so I can discover and then share what I've discovered with others. I am fortunate to have found many outlets for this indulgence-cum-profession.

I compulsively publish everything I write, sometimes as an end in itself, sometimes as a means to an end. Some of the essays in this book fit this compulsion. Sometimes they are well edited, other times barely so. What I write about varies within the parameters of communication arts, which includes media like graphic design, typography, satiric art, illustration, film and TV; on themes such as politics, technology, commerce; covering political and aesthetic movements, styles, symbols and individual artists and designers. I've written books (large and small), essays, interviews, articles, reviews, prefaces, forewords, afterwords—I've done reportage, scholarship, criticism, and treatments for short documentaries that I have also narrated. I've written professional profiles, analyses, and testimonials, memorials and obituaries of those artists and designers I (or someone I trust) deem important. My favorite assignments have been obituaries for *The New York Times* because the form combines reportage and historical analysis and documents achievement for time immemorial. I've stopped doing them, however.

Why else do I write? Often, I cannot sleep. I cannot sleep because my mind is always racing with ideas for stories, among other concerns. My ideas back up during the day, pouring out when I should be asleep—I write notes and on occasion entire drafts when I should be asleep. Design is my lens; there is always something to write about through this camera obscura. For those who follow my meanderings you will understand, for those who have not, you will.

Writing is a form of intoxication. I hope what Orwell calls "solid objects and scraps of useless information" that I write about on a disciplined basis, sprinkled

I compulsively publish everything I write, sometimes as an end in itself, sometimes as a means to an end.

with my variegated biases (and arcane language), will be of interest to an audience. I write for myself but nonetheless with the reader foremost in my mind.

Now, I will briefly explain "How I Write." I fixate on a subject, then I free-associate based on some personal knowledge or connection, however slight, to said subject. When research is demanded I'll take as much time as necessary to find primary, secondary, and other sources. Where I can think for myself, I write my thoughts and craft them into a collection of hopefully satisfying sentences, paragraphs, and chapters that are usually massaged by wonderful editors (God created editors for the likes of me). Where I have nothing original to say, I quote or paraphrase others from one-on-one interviews or primary and secondary existing sources. I'm at that point right now, so allow me to end with Orwell one more time:

Putting aside the need to earn a living, I think there are four great motives for writing, at any rate for writing prose. They exist in different degrees in every writer, and in any one writer the proportions will vary from time to time, according to the atmosphere in which he is living.

(i) *Sheer egoism.* Desire to seem clever, to be talked about, to be remembered after death, to get your own back on the grown-ups who snubbed you in childhood, etc., etc.

(ii) *Aesthetic enthusiasm.* Perception of beauty in the external world, or, on the other hand, in words and their right arrangement.

(iii) *Historical impulse.* Desire to see things as they are, to find out true facts and store them up for the use of posterity.

(iv) *Political purpose.* Using the word "political" in the widest possible sense. Desire to push the world in a certain direction, to alter other peoples' idea of the kind of society that they should strive after.

I couldn't say it better. Anyway, that's why I write, how I write, and why writing is a rite that I wouldn't give up for anything, regardless of how few or how many are reading my stuff. Thanks George!

INTRODUCTION

THE CASE FOR DESIGN WRITING

∗ BY MOLLY HEINTZ ∗

Many writers will tell you that the beginning is the hardest part of writing any piece—not the snappy opening line that pops into your head in the shower or while crossing the street, but the real beginning of a story that sets up how a narrative unfolds. In the beginning, you, the writer, must convince the reader that you've shown up with the goods and they should follow you around the corner.

Writers, design has you covered.

Design comes fully loaded with great beginnings. And, conveniently, design is everywhere, ready for the hot seat. At the MA program in Design Research, Writing, and Criticism at the School of Visual Arts, aka D-Crit, we define design as "anything human-made intended to serve a function." In other words, almost everything is fair game for our graduate students' research—baby monitors, glitter, airports—even invisible or less tangible kinds of design, like algorithms, systems, or experiences.

Any design entity offers a built-in fact-finding mission for a writer: "What is this made of?" "Who made it?" "Who commissioned it?" Possible starting points for research abound. You might suddenly find yourself elbows deep in an archive going through ephemera and sketches, or face-to-face with a subject's inventor for an interview, or dozing on an early morning bus to a dot on a map for site visit. You, the writer, can train the lens of design—this collection of questions about how something works in the world—onto any area of inquiry and use it as a compass to chart a course. You don't know where you'll end up or what you'll discover along the way. But no matter which direction you go, juicy stories are guaranteed.

Design stories pack a one-two punch. Design, which almost always interacts with something else to fulfill its purpose, invites evocative descriptions. When given the spotlight in a publication, design might be illustrated with enticing images or sounds that speak to the senses. But images aren't necessary. A design writing assignment is fertile territory for words that take the reader beyond any illustration, explaining the less visible intricacies and marvels of the everyday. On top of this, every design story has a stealth feature that is gold for a writer: a human element. Design is ultimately the story of the people who imagine, make, and use it. Exploring these rich, personality-laden sub-plots can make design subjects extra compelling for both writers and readers.

But what does it take to make a reader really care about plastic coffee cup lids? Design questions—"What is this made of?"—are deceptively basic. They are, by their nature, context questions, not limited to the subject at hand but invoking the relationship the subject has to its environment. One context question quickly leads to another. When you, the writer, can tap into that constellation of relationships to ask bigger questions—"How did mining this material impact the local community?"— and follow it with meaningful analysis, you've leapt into the realm of criticism. An attentive reader will be hooked, and right there with you, because, by beginning with design, you've been able to answer the most important question of all: "So what?" In other words, why does this matter and why should the reader care.

As someone who primarily works as an editor, I lobby all writers to become design writers. The best writing helps us make sense of the world we live in, and design writing offers an ideal means to this end. It's a mode of writing grounded in research that invites storytelling, and, at its height, connects the dots for the reader in a new way. Design by itself won't save the world, but good design writing has the potential to change the way people see the world.

This volume includes exemplary pieces of writing that demonstrate ways that design writing can work, mostly through showing rather than through telling, although a section of questionnaires, generously answered by contributors, provide some direct insights into the design writer's mind. Many contributions were previously published in magazines and journals. A handful of pieces, however, appear here in print for the first time.

Thanks to its expansive subject, design writing is a big tent. It should be bigger. Too often in business and consumer publications, design stories are relegated to the ghetto, luxurious though it may be, of "lifestyle." My fantasy is to wake up one morning and see that every news, business, and opinion story was written through a design lens. Perhaps in this alternative telling the quandaries of our everyday world could become a little more fathomable, easier to perceive, and even agree on. Design writing speaks directly to our humanity. Like music, it activates both the mind and the senses, operating in a register that is universal and, to many writers and editors—and the readers that follow them around the corner—irresistible.

"A picture is worth (adjust here for inflation) words" is an old chestnut with a lot of truth. But design is already more than words alone. Rather it is the picturing of ideas. Words are not substitutes but complements at times, and often words are design itself. And not just typography on page, screen, or structure, either. They are conjoined as entities that help define one another without which chaos prevails.

DESIGN
NEEDS
WORDS

CHAPTER 1

MY MANIFESTO

BY KARRIE JACOBS

✱

J ust recently, I was sitting at the top of the Red Steps in Times Square being interviewed by a CUNY journalism student for a radio story about public space.

I heard myself telling him that I found sitting there, watching the frenetic activity—the signs, the pedestrians, the cars, the tourists—meditative. It's like sitting and watching the ocean, I said.

The strange thing is that I meant it.

If you're one of my students from SVA's Design Criticism MA, you know the spot. And you will recall that I've asked you to sit there and try to see the scene in front of you as John Ruskin might.

If you've never been one of my students, you might reasonably ask: What does John Ruskin, nineteenth-century art and architecture critic and curmudgeon have to do with twenty-first century Times Square?

Quite a lot, as it happens. Ruskin was concerned with the idea of architectural truth, which to him meant building from stone rather than the technologically chic new material, cast iron. He took the time to codify all the possible deceits that could occur in architecture and to call out, in his words, the "glistening and softly spoken lie."

Here's a sample:

"But the moment that the iron in the least degree takes the place of stone, and acts as by its resistance to crushing, and bears superincumbent weight, or if it acts by its own weight as a counterpoise, and so supersedes the use of pinnacles or buttresses in resisting a lateral thrust, or if, in the form of a rod or girder, it is used to do what wooden beams would have done as well, that instant the building ceases to be—wait for it—"true architecture."

Here's a man whose dedication to the Gothic style and the beauty of carved stone is so great that he sees the industrialization of building techniques, the technological breakthrough of his day—cast iron—as a threat.

John Ruskin found technological change frightening. That makes him one of us.

So, if you try to look at Times Square through his eyes, you might be able to focus on how the canyon of digital images you see in front of you is made. You might begin to notice the shape of the peculiar hole in Manhattan's grid occupied by Times Square. (Hint: it's not a square.)

You might begin to notice the buildings that hold up the signs. You might even come up with your own brand of architectural truth.

What Ruskin does, in his counterintuitive way, is give us a reason to look hard at a place that many of us previously scurried through while averting our eyes, unwilling to be mistaken for a tourist.

But a tourist isn't a bad thing to be, especially if you're an old school tourist, the kind who actually gawks at new sights instead of assessing them for their Instagram potential. You can even be a tourist in your own city and try to see it every time as if you're seeing it for the first time.

Do this: Go to Times Square, climb the Red Steps. Sit very still. Look out. And focus. Do it for five minutes. Do it for ten minutes. Do it for an hour. If you can cultivate the ability to focus there, of all places, you'll find it to be an invaluable tool.

Because Times Square, instead of being an anomaly—a perverse agglomeration of electronic stimulation intended to attract selfie-stick wielding suckers—is actually a microcosm. We live in a world that is as distorted and distracting as Times Square.

Our culture and—in particular—our politics are shot through with attention deficit disorder. We notice and obsess about every little thing for a moment, and instantly forget.

Amusement follows amusement, outrage follows outrage. But then what? We move on to the next thing, trivial or earthshaking. We are living our lives in a virtual Times Square. So learning to focus there, in the real Times Square, is a survival skill. For us as individuals. And maybe even for civilization as a whole.

To focus is to be still or, at least, relatively still. It's about having a point of view, one that is steady, coherent, and identifiable. It is about being alert to what's happening around us and, ideally, to take pleasure in our surroundings.

There are different ways of framing this experience. Ellen Langer, a noted social psychologist known as the Mother of Mindfulness says:

"Mindfulness, for me, is the very simple process of actively noticing new things. When you actively notice new things, that puts you in the present, makes you sensitive to context."

CHAPTER 1

While mindfulness, loosely defined, is a concept that one hears about in yoga class where everyone is striving for some degree of clarity, where everyone is, for ninety minutes or so, separated from their electronic devices, it's another thing to try and apply the concept in the wider world.

But that's what interests me, mindfulness in the wild, in the most inherently mindless environments. It's my own form of meditation. I love to focus deeply in an inhospitable environment, in a place that is antithetical to the idea of mindfulness, that is antithetical to any form of coherent thought.

Of course, Langer's brainchild has taken on a life of its own. While waiting in line in an upstate supermarket, I found myself staring at a magazine on the impulse rack. It was a special issue of *Time* magazine about "the New Mindfulness."

Realizing that mindfulness has become a hot commodity suggests to me that lack of focus is an identifiable crisis. Soon we'll be hearing about it in the same breath as the opioid epidemic. If we're not already.

But it also makes me see that my goals are different than those espoused by the mindfulness crowd. I'm not interested in peace; I'm interested in engagement. If everyone were, as Langer frames it, "sensitive to context," I can say with confidence that we'd be living in a far less troubled world.

About a decade ago, I was working on a book about silence as a man-made thing, something we invented, that doesn't actually exist in nature, and that we've been forced to manufacture to insulate us from a noisy world.

During that time, I spent nearly a week at a Benedictine monastery where I passed my days watching other people pray. I also did a lot of reading there, including the work of a Swiss philosopher named Max Picard. He wrote a book called *The World of Silence* originally published in 1948, in the aftermath of World War II. He argued that the problem wasn't just that the external world has become noisier but that internally, we've lost our connection to silence.

"The individual stands between noise and silence," Picard observed. "He is isolated from noise and isolated from silence."

At the monastery, which was fifteen miles up a dirt road in an astonishingly tranquil New Mexico river valley, the only thing I wasn't isolated from was silence. And for about five days of my weeklong stay, that was a pretty great thing.

What I got out of the experience was a clearer sense that what I wanted was not isolation from noise, but the ability to use it as a foil: to hear through it, or see through it, or think through it.

More recently, I wrote an introduction for a book of photographs by my friend Stanley Greenberg. His methodology is a simple one: he walks around with his eyes open and he notices the things that are right in front of him, things that most of us are too distracted to see. His photos show a New York that could be perceived

To focus is to be still or, at least, relatively still. It's about having a point of view, one that is steady, coherent and identifiable. It is about being alert to what's happening around us and, ideally, to take pleasure in our surroundings.

as more real, more organic: he documents the little sheds that shelter parking lot attendants and the way that the undersides of bridges, epic works of infrastructure, sometimes drop into otherwise unremarkable streetscapes.

While working on the essay for his book, I came around to the notion that Stanley was the photographer I wanted to collaborate with on a project of my own. I invited him to join me on a research field trip, in which I wanted to figure out whether it was possible to walk to La Guardia airport.

As it turns out, it is. And while it's not the normal way for travelers to get there, many of the airport's workers walk there every day.

In walking to La Guardia, following for much of the route, the service road adjacent to the Grand Central Parkway, I began to realize that there is pleasure to be had in walking where you're not really supposed to walk. We weren't trespassing. We were following a route that hadn't been built for us, a route that mostly existed for cars.

For the article that grew out of the walk, I interviewed airport experts, who kept telling me about the ways in which autonomous vehicles would remake the world. What I took from those conversations was that urban places would need to become more predictable, and the meanderings of human beings more restricted, to make an environment suitable for the wholesale operation of Robocars. The picture I had in my head was the "Futurama" exhibit from the 1939 World's Fair.

It dawned on me that walking itself is an act of civil disobedience. It's one of the few things we can do without an algorithm. Walking—assuming you turn off the electronic devices that count your steps and give you directions—takes you offline. It makes you dangerously unpredictable and remarkably free.

It also occurred to me that there is something a lot like mindfulness that I've long practiced. Call it bodyfulness. For me, the origins of bodyfulness coincide with my gradual emergence as a runner, when I transitioned from a treadmill to the streets.

CHAPTER 1

Once I began running the streets of New York I had a superpower, a highly focused way of looking at the city. New York became a movie that unspooled at six miles an hour.

When I travel, one of my primary pleasures and my favorite way of analyzing my surroundings is to run...through the sidewalk tent cities of downtown LA, the greenways of Bentonville, Arkansas, along the river that is the heart of Oslo or along the Lisbon waterfront. My pace is a perfect one at which to absorb the urban landscape, to understand how a city is put together. On foot you learn a tremendous amount about how a city is designed—or not designed—and for whom.

That said, you don't need to be a runner to absorb a city in a bodyful way. You could walk. You could skateboard, or bike, or travel in a wheelchair. The important thing is to take in the world around you in an unmediated, undistracted fashion.

Once you put your smartphone away, you've got choices. You could keep moving. Or you could sit still. You could close your eyes and just listen.

When you're out in nature, you often climb to the top of something, a hill or a mountain, and look out. That kind of looking, an appraisal of the landscape you've traversed ... you can do that in the city, too.

And you don't necessarily have to climb anything higher than the Red Steps.

You could just pause every now and then and look around.

This may sound a little mystical, but that's not the point. I'm not saying you should become an urban monk. Rather, I'm saying that heightened awareness has value. The simple act of knowing where we are—of regarding what's right in front of us, of contemplating our immediate surroundings—is a surprisingly powerful corrective for the state of buzzing preoccupation in which most of us spend our days. In that way, it's a lot like looking at the ocean.

I also believe it makes you a better citizen. From moments of heightened awareness—in which we recognize the extraordinary nature of everyday places, the places we take for granted—can emerge small acts of civic engagement or inspired reconsiderations of the entire man-made environment.

And heightened awareness is where change begins...including political change. Looking at the world intensely, critically, with a focus on what things mean or why they matter, makes you a participant in the culture rather than just a consumer.

Seeing what's right in front of you becomes more difficult with every passing, which is exactly why it has never been more essential.

Copyright © 2019 by Karrie Jacobs. Adapted from a keynote talk given at the MA Design Research, Writing & Criticism Graduate Symposium at the School of Visual Arts, May 2019.

DESIGN NEEDS WORDS

THINKING DESIGN THINKING

BY MARK KINGSLEY

✱

Every endeavor is rife with preconceptions and pretense. Goals, rationales, and hopes exercise their influence upon the bedrock of ideology; where even the most rigorous of practitioners are subject to the deformations of their domains. This is the case with much writing about design.

If one were to map the territories explored by design writing, they would fall into familiar categories: history, biography, critical diatribes, and encomiums. Each of these investigations has its own limitations and prejudices, but they share a general approach to narrative.

The creation of a historical context, as seen over the past couple decades, runs the political risks of inclusion or exclusion, and the categorical risk of imposed narratives. The criteria determining choice of subject is colored by the author's place in time and culture, as well as their tastes. A theme is identified, and a narrative is composed—a narrative which, if the author has a good sense of story, will have a point of tension, or a climactic turning point. Rather than a continuum of events, a stream of moves and countermoves, we end up with what Nietzsche saw as a history consisting of "arbitrary division and dismemberment." Because it is easier to describe and comprehend static slices of time—classical, then medieval— than the flow from classical into medieval.

Each "dismembered" action undergoes numerous small, random fluctuations, which are compounded over time by other actions. Events and influences constantly shift into new patterns, revealing new relationships and revelations— all with a degree of complexity which may appear random at first glance. Contrary to the historical canon of the unfolding of human events, there is no hand of god, no miraculous origin, no miracle. The revelations of the world are the coming together of a complex number of forces. To think otherwise is counter to reality.

But we like a good story. Narratives go down better when the reader can extract some sort of moral or overarching theme. So we end up with genius acts of creativity, or the march of progress; each cycling through variations of villain, victim, or hero. Paul Renner, the designer of the Futura typeface was a victim of the Nazi era: arrest, dismissal, and constant harassment. And Achille Castiglioni, the heroic figure who elevated the most humble of materials—tractor seats, car headlights, fishing poles, etc.—into elegant pieces that helped establish post-war Italian design leadership.

And we also like a bit of sensationalism, if not outright spectacle. Much online design writing—if we can call it that—is either diatribe, hero-worship, or opinion dressed up as thoughtful discourse. The common currency is taste. Taste signaling political alignment. Adherence to taste places one within the fold. Anyone outside is in exile.

Such material fuels the partisans of taste as they argue the merits of one approach over another. Taste offers comfort and location in a constantly changing world. Our taste is our identity; a blanket fort keeping chaos at bay.

But design exists in the world: realpolitik made form. The narrative of the design process follows a general vector. A need or goal is identified; an approach is chosen and applied in order to produce a result, which is then evaluated against any number of indicators: taste, ideology, effect on sales, audience growth, etc. Such a mechanistic, materialist process is an expression of calculative thinking; the product of a worldview of cause, effect, data, and tactics. And calculative thinking is perhaps the greatest belief system of modern humanity, with its pleasures of progress, measured growth, and accomplishment. Meeting such benchmarks closes psychological loops and offers narrative closure. We are free to move on.

Calculative thinking permeates design writing when history becomes a catalog of innovation through creativity. Dominant (often European) tastes and ideologies are reflected and reinforced while often celebrating individual genius. In adhering to this approach, one can easily overlook context, stumble into paradox, and become unable to move beyond descriptive and manipulative actions. Designed objects are seen as the output of a chain of events; a dialectical dance of action/reaction where things interact but remain separate.

Ironically, the lower forms of design writing—encomiums and diatribes—suggest a possible path leading through the object.

The more "serious" forms of history and biography hold the designed object as an operational image. This concept from the German filmmaker Harun Farocki describes images that have a functional purpose: measurement, targeting, or visualization of data. In Farocki's view, they are "images without a social goal, not for edification, not for reflection." The designed object is used to make a point outside the thing-in-itself. It becomes evidence; marking stylistic trends, aesthetic schools, and regional approaches. It indicates economic and social movement. And it is offered as proof of innovation.

But design is the medium of social relationships! We sit around designed tables, on designed chairs, over designed meals, and we interact. Designed objects are both the media and activation of contemplation. Thinking is operational, directed towards something. Contemplation is reflective, and deeper.

So while encomiums and diatribes may be built upon cheap likes and dislikes, their origins begin in the contemplative. Something about the designed object had an effect on the writer that sparked some sort of a connection and moved them to write. At some point, they engaged in an act of contemplation, no matter how embryonic it may have been.

Contemplation allows access to the metaphysical where one reflects upon their relationship to time, space, history, knowledge, and the world. The meaning made through this process collects everything that is or was; we find deeper insights beyond the observations of calculative thinking. We are human beings, not things interacting with other things. And with that comes the ability to sense nothingness and the infinite; revealing the contradictions, paradoxes, tensions, and opportunities which permeate our calculative thinking and the technology that encompasses us.

In 1917 the American modernist poet Wallace Stevens published his first book, *Harmonium*. Contained within was the "Anecdote of the Jar," where the first two stanzas read

I placed a jar in Tennessee,
And round it was, upon a hill.
It made the slovenly wilderness
Surround that hill.
The wilderness rose up to it,
And sprawled around, no longer wild.
The jar was round upon the ground
And tall and of a port in air.

The notion of the wilderness rising up to a jar upon a hill—as opposed to the jar being placed upon the top of a hill—echoes in philosopher Martin Heidegger's essay "Building Dwelling Thinking," where riverbanks become activated as riverbanks by the construction of a bridge crossing the river. The bridge suddenly creates context and gathers the riverbanks into a unique location. In both Stevens and Heidegger, the man-made object reorders the ontology of the total environment.

Designed objects have a similar effect. Their mere existence as intentional products has effects beyond the calculated results behind their creation. Every time we enter an environment, our consciousness reorders the relationships of every object present. We spontaneously raise or lower rankings to reflect our own desires and associations. And since the objects and environments where this reordering takes place are designed, we are now engaging in a different kind of design thinking.

The current state of design thinking—built upon iterative product development—is calculative thinking. There is definitely a need for such an approach. It is how products become more reliable, safer, and better fit for their intended purpose. But there are limits. The things we design do not exist as words, targets, or case studies. They are things-in-themselves, caught up in the needs, goals, rationales, and hopes of calculated thinking.

But through the "thing," we enter into the larger metaphysical concepts of time, space, history, and knowledge. Once we attend to its presence and actions, we gain expanded access to lived human experience and the world. In a sense, we are practicing a higher form of design thinking.

In his essay "Three Academic Pieces," Stevens wrote, "... if we desire to formulate an accurate theory of poetry, we find it necessary to examine the structure of reality, because reality is the central reference for poetry. By way of accomplishing this, suppose we examine one of the significant components of the structure of reality—that is to say, the resemblance between things."

In other words, if one wants to truly know what's happening, ask a poet.

The challenge has never been greater, nor the need more desperate for a deeper, contemplative approach to design writing. There is a poetry to the imagining and creation of a designed object; an individual's existence converted into form. And as we make our way through a time of climate crisis ... as we transition into the digital realm, such a transformation deserves a more reflective consideration beyond the tactical, and beyond the instrumental.

Copyright © 2024 by Mark Kingsley.

DESIGN NEEDS WORDS

ODE TO THE DESIGN EDITOR

BY ZACHARY PETIT

When I joined the editorial staff of *Print* magazine more than a decade ago, there was one part of the job I was terrified to do: Edit Steven Heller.

Now, I had just come from *Writer's Digest* magazine, where I'd been variously tasked with interviewing everyone from beat legend Lawrence Ferlinghetti to best-selling author Anne Rice, and editing the words of some of the most prolific writers on the planet . . . but even they did not have 200+(!) books under their belts, not to mention a daily blog whose surprise contents could range anywhere from 100 words to 5,000.

Heller represented a particularly harrowing assignment, given the sheer number of editors he has worked with over the decades that I'd no doubt be compared to, the utter mountain of words he sits atop, and the fact that, well, he'd been writing for my magazine since I was just a novel notion in my parents' minds. I felt like an imposter on his turf—which is also how I felt when I landed my first writing gigs years earlier, and realized my prose was now at the complete mercy of an omnipotent deity.

In our mind's eye editors are bespectacled, humorless pipe-smoking carps nestled within a gilded Manhattan office, where they ravage words with a callous red pen when not crowning literary royalty (should they deign to do so that day).

And sometimes they are.

But ninety-nine percent of the time, they are not. Generally, they are mere mortals. And the quicker you realize that as a writer, the sooner you'll be on your way. Because when it comes down to it, both writer and editor have the exact same goal: a good story. As a writer, you just have to know the best way to work with an editor to get there.

CHAPTER 1

The challenge, of course, is that there are as many different types of editors as there are writers. A few work with a cudgel, bashing words and sentences and narrative structures into submission on their own, handing you back a draft that bears little resemblance to what you turned in. Others work with a scalpel, carefully excising and moving a few words to a better position elsewhere.

Writing is wildly subjective business—but what you're not often told is that editing is, too. Sure, there are style guides that editors abide by, and in-house stylistic parameters at play, but beyond that every editor has their own approach to the craft. You might think that writing is the truly creative part of the equation, and that editing is more like objective math—but editing has its own alchemy. Any editor can fix a grammar flub or change passive voice to active, but a good one can instinctively feel what's right for a piece of writing; like a sixth sense they can intuitively appraise the rhythm, the structure, what needs to happen next to hold the interest of a reader, what needs to stay, what needs to go. Moreover, every editor is firmly locked into the nuances of their readerships—they know what their audience wants, and that's where they will urge your words to go, be that academic, voice-driven and casual, or any ground in between.

In your career you'll find editors you love ... and editors you despise. That will inevitably inform and shape where you write, and who you write for. One rodeo is generally more than enough to decide if you'd like to hop back on that bull the following week— especially if it delivered a parting shot to the groin as it sent you soaring through the air.

As for how the basic editorial process works, it may seem like it's shrouded in mystery, the purview of that persnickety pipe-puffer, but it's all actually pretty straightforward. Depending on the publication and the type of writing involved, the writer either pitches an idea to an editor and asks her to commission him to write it, or the writer submits a full piece for the editor's review. If things go well, the editor will give the thumbs up. And before too long, it's time for an edit.

There are three essential types of editing that you will encounter in the wild:

The developmental edit. This first type is the most intensive, and thus generally the most intensely wearing on the creative soul. Here the editor is looking at big picture things like structure, what's missing, and overall what works and what does not. Depending on whether the editor's tool of choice is the aforementioned cudgel or the scalpel, they may jump straight to making edits themselves—but more than likely they'll leave comments for you in an email or in track changes of your draft, identifying areas for improvement, what they'd like to see, and more. Then, they kick it back to you for execution. Sometimes you can wrap things up in a single round. Other times, you have to strap the gloves on and go for multiple bouts (with your partner acting as your in-ring hype man to squirt water in your face and keep you motivated if not conscious).

The copy edit. After the developmental edit—or, if your piece is in great shape and doesn't really need one (the ideal scenario for all parties involved!)—comes the copy edit. This is a more drilled-down look at sentence-by-sentence issues. As an editor, I prefer to just fix small things as I come across them (with track changes on, so the writer can see what I've done) rather than ask the writer to, say, add a comma here or cut a word there. (But there are absolutely editors out there who will take the time to ask you to insert an em dash, etc.)

The proofread: This final stage of the process is last call to fix anything that needs fixing. A quick safety net before things go to production to make sure there are no errors in the copy, and everything is good to go.

Like a good doctor, as an editor, my philosophy is do no harm; I want the edits to be so seamless that although I've done everything, the editing is so in sync with the writer's intention and the spirit of their prose that they feel I've done nothing.

And that's probably because, as a writer, I've been burned by overzealous editors with a weedwhacker approach to their craft who would rather leave their mark on a piece of writing than help it sing. So: What do you do if you find yourself in that situation?

First: Allow yourself a few loud expletives (permitting you're in the comfort of your home and not, say, in a PTA meeting when you get the email). Walk the dog (he'll be happy!). Perhaps engage in some minor day drinking or however else you define self-care.

Then, collect yourself, head back to your computer, and draft a calm response articulating your feedback, and what should be changed or addressed. Leave emotion and ego out of it—because edits should never be taken personally. Remember, you and the editor have the same goal: a good story. You've hit a snag. Now your job is to collaborate to achieve that goal. And since we're no longer envisioning our editor on a throne and we're just conversing human to human, the task is that much more possible to achieve.

If the end result leaves you newly balding and bleary-eyed, you've simply learned that you'll never work with that editor again. If it's the opposite, you're on the path to that brilliant symbiosis when editor and writer truly click—and the result, unsurprisingly, is great work that's an utter thrill to create together again and again.

. . . How did Steven Heller and I get on at *Print*?

I've now been editing him for more than a decade, and he asked me to write this chapter. So, hell: He either wanted me to put my veritable pipe down and do some serious self-reflection, or something must be working out OK.

Copyright © 2024 by Zachary Petit.

CHAPTER 1

A WRITING + DESIGN PRACTICE

BY WARREN LEHRER

Two Different Languages

I was a painting and printmaking major in college in the 1970s. On the side, I wrote poetry and short stories. One day I showed a painting teacher a secret stack of drawings that combined abstract marks, shading, letterforms, and words. After leafing through the stack, my teacher shook his head and wagged his finger in my face.

"You're a good student, Warren, but you're barking up the wrong tree here. Words and pictures are two different languages. They operate from different parts of the brain and shouldn't be combined."

I left his office feeling like I'd been given a mission in life. And for better or worse I've been combining writing and visuals ever since.

I went on to get an MFA in graphic design so I could learn the tools and methodologies needed to compose and produce my own books and multimedia projects. Soon after I started teaching, I delved deeper into the origins of writing and design, and eventually, the long, rich history of visual literature. I noticed that historians of literature, art, and design all pointed to cave paintings and ancient pictographic carvings as the origins of their respective fields. They all agreed that most written languages around the world evolved from pictorial systems of representation into phonetic alphabets. That transition marked the split between writing and picture-making and is the very real schism my painting professor was referring to when he warned me against combining words and images. I now understand that graphic designers and practitioners of visual literature are always trying to bring those two modalities back together.

For me, writing and design are inextricably linked. I do occasionally write essays about design and design education, and I'm currently working on a book about visual literature, but the lion's share of my writing/design practice has been as the author/designer of my own solo and collaborative creative projects. That's the work I'm going to focus on here, with an emphasis on my methodologies and evolution within a lifelong quest to marry content and form.

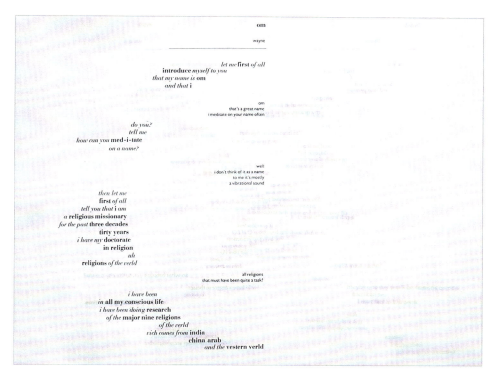

versations. Written & designed by Warren Lehrer. 1980.

The Shape of Conversation

My graduate thesis, versations: a setting for eight conversations, (1980), was a score for a performance and also my first offset-printed book. I called it a "study of human dialogue," and a "celebration of the music and poetics of speech." *Versations* began an obsession with writing prismatic characters and capturing their voices on the page and for the stage, through typography. I set each character in a different type family, and the choreography of each dialogue reflects the interaction between each of the eight duos. On the page above, a religious missionary talks around an unsuspecting subject. I break lines significantly, as in verse, indicating pauses of breath or thought, and I only list the name of each character once at the top of the page. Printed on translucent paper, you see and hear approaching and receding conversations.

versations. 1980. Above, a married couple argues in French, occasionally coming together in laughter.

versations. 1980. They continue arguing while another duo flirt with each other, on the same wavelength.

versations. 1980. The dialogue between two Chinese speakers moves from right to left on the page as the English speakers move from left to right.

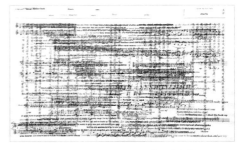

versations. 1980. I orchestrated multiple conversations at the same time, which built up to all eight pairs (sixteen people) talking at once. I was very interested in seeing what that looks like on the page.

Synaptic Gaps and Utterances

i mean you know (1983) continued this approach of book as performance score, but with emphasis on interior thought more than conversation, through seven characters who inhabit the same building over the course of one day. *i mean you know* explores those synaptic gaps and utterances between thoughts and speech that bridge our sometimes-imperfect search for meaning (i mean), and a desire to connect with others (you know).

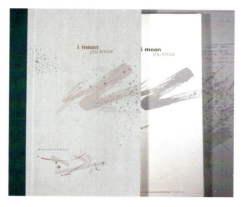

i mean you know. Written & designed by Lehrer. 1983.

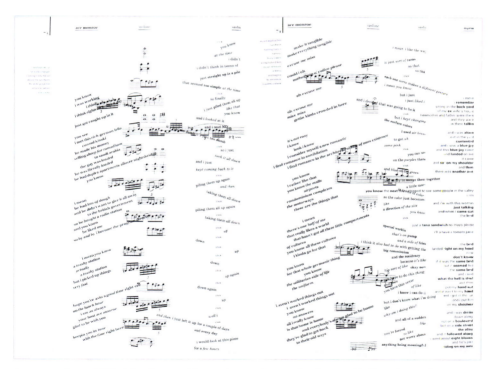

i mean you know. 1983. A 4-column grid superimposed over a 3-column grid allowed me to have as many as 7 voices on a page, thinking and sometimes talking at the same time. Descriptions of the characters' movements and interactions are set in small type within a narrow eighth column on the left side of every page.

CHAPTER 1

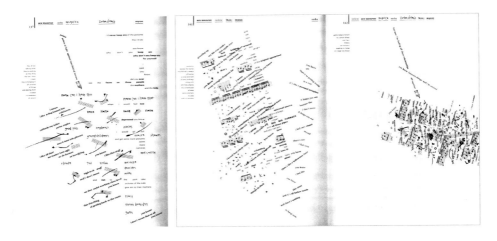

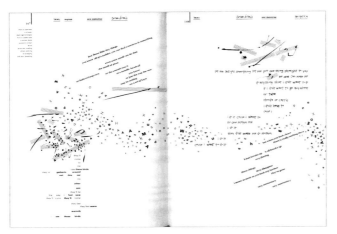

i mean you know. 1983. In the final movement, one of the characters, an artist named Sasha, rebels against me, the male author of this bizarre construction. She orchestrates the movements and speech of the other characters. Columns loosen from their vertical rigidity.

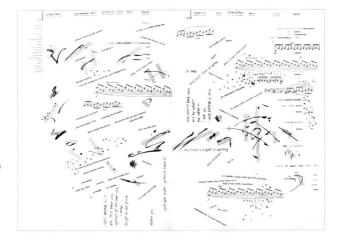

Visual Vernacular

My friend, the poet and journalist Dennis Bernstein, and I were at a McDonald's in Greenwich Village, and we realized it was living theater in there. We decided to write a play together, which would also be a book, set at an American fast food joint. Immediately, I pictured the cover. "Visual vernacular" wasn't in my vocabulary in 1984, but somehow I leaned into a colorful, brash, capitalist American aesthetic, while also continuing my typographic approach to voice, significant lineation, etc.

French Fries. Written by Dennis Bernstein and Warren Lehrer. Designed by Lehrer. 1984.

French Fries. 1984. I set each character, not only in their own typeface, but also color. And the dialogue—about food, money, dreams and aspiration—is illuminated with icons and images that evoke the internal projections of the characters and the repeatable familiarity of the fast food tableau.

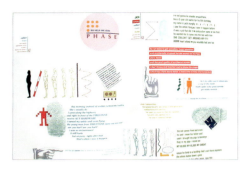

French Fries. 1984. Before the play/book begins, one of the customers is found dead in a pool of blood and ketchup. Each character bears testimony to a different perspective of how and why she died.

French Fries. 1984. Throughout the play, the character Louise Giallanza is researching a book titled *The Potato in America*, which, among other things, will foretell spuds engineered to repel unwanted pests.

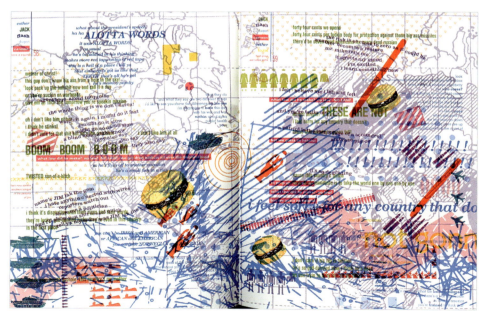

French Fries. 1984. In act six, one hell of a political argument breaks out, reflecting the kinds of intense arguments that took place at the height of the Cold War. Produced pre-Macintosh, all the type was generated by phototypesetting, coding, and a lot of cutting and pasting of words and images onto mechanicals that sometimes had as many as twelve overlays for a single spread.

Book as Cinematic Expression

GRRRHHHH: A Study of Social Patterns is a 464-page animal fantasy fugue based on eight weavings by Sandra Brownlee, with chants and stories by Dennis Bernstein. I scanned Sandra's black and white weavings of "unusual animals" into what we called at the time, a computer paint box, and let the animals reveal themselves to be the lost, forgotten animals of the earth. My approach to this book is cinematic in the way it uses sequences of pictures and words—activated by the turning of pages.

GRRRHHHH: A Study of Social Patterns. Based on weavings by Sandra Brownlee. Chants & stories by Dennis Bernstein. Book by Lehrer. 1987.

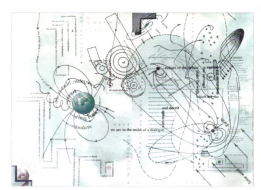

From an 8-page article written and designed by Warren Lehrer and Phil Zimmermann. *Émigré Magazine*. 1989.

True Map of How I Experienced the World

The graphic composition of my work in the 1980s truly reflected the way I experienced the world in my twenties and early thirties. By the '90s, I came to realize that some of my biggest fans—people who collected all my books—hadn't necessarily read them all, cover to cover. As I became more serious about writing, and cared more about the subjects and themes I was portraying, my approach to the visual composition evolved.

Diagramming Character

I had an idea about writing a series of books based on real people who straddle the wobbly line between brilliance and madness. Each book would be proportional to a standing figure, with a photograph of the person from the front on the front cover; from the back on the back; and inside—the guts—first-person monologues, rants, vignettes, and short stories. The first four books in the series formed a quartet of men (1995), which I went around doing readings and performances of.

Mock-ups and Lehrer with the first four books in The Portrait Series, written/designed by Lehrer, 1995.

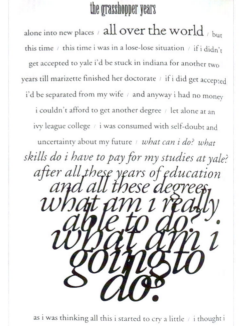

Page details from *Claude: A Narrative Portrait of Claude Debs*, written/designed by Lehrer, 1995.

With so many rich stories, I actually started using a column of text! But I still didn't use traditional punctuation. In the book *Claude: A Narrative Portrait of Claude Debs,* I used slashes to indicate breath or thought pauses. Important memories and epiphanies pierce the walls of text.

Nicky D was a sit-down comedian and stoop philosopher who lived his whole life in the railroad flat he grew up in with his parents and four siblings in Long Island City, Queens. His stories are illuminated by a lifetime of memorabilia that animated his apartment. After the bombing of Pearl Harbor, no branch of the military would take him due to a chronic back condition, so he became a longshoreman loading liberty ships from the Brooklyn Navy Yard.

Claude. 1995. The spread above is from a story Claude tells from his youth, about the last gasps of a dying monkey soaring over a desert landscape.

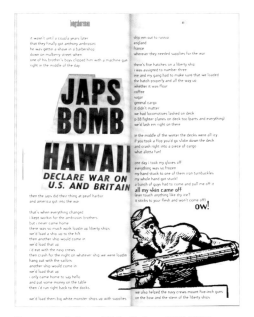

Two spreads from *Nicky D. from LIC.* 1995.

CHAPTER 1

Detail from *Nicky D. from LIC.* 1995. In addition to life stories, Nicky's book depicts a lot of existential questioning. In the detail to the right, he wonders why some people live to a ripe old age and others die young, like "the girl who got killed by that bottle came flying out the window..."

```
think of the odds against a thing like that happening:

the building . . . . . . . .
                    . . . . . . . . the bottle
    the girl . . . . . .
               . . . . . . the grandmother
       the pizza . . . . .
                 . . . . . the ground
         the bottle . .
         . . the grandmother
            the pizza . .
              the bottle
               the girl
                 and
                BING

          right square
        on top of her head
 the whole cranium was cracked up bad
```

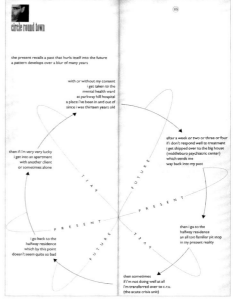

Two spreads from *Charlie: A Narrative Portrait of Charlie Lang.* 1995. Charlie Lang, a dear friend, amazing musician, and brilliant thinker, has also struggled with bipolar disorder for much of his life. On the left-hand spread, Charlie describes being in the eye of an emotional tornado. The spread on the right diagrams a period when he was stuck in a bad cycle, in and out of emergency wards, psychiatric centers, and halfway houses.

Tales of Migration and a New America

Written in collaboration with my wife, the actor/oral historian Judith Sloan, *Crossing the BLVD: Strangers, Neighbors, Aliens in a New America* (2003) documents new immigrants and refugees in our home borough of Queens, NY, the most ethnically diverse locality in the US. Our focus was on people who arrived post-1965 Immigration Act, which forever changed the demographics of the US.

Open the book—you're on the street, Cross SING the BLVD. You see India's Gifted Psychic Reader on top of Queen Toffa's African Weaving and Braiding Salon. Down the block, the Yogi Transmission Shop next to Guyana Gold. At thirteen lanes wide, crossing Queens BLVD can be treacherous, but crossing out of war zones, economic hardships, across borders, oceans, cultural and language divides into the fabric of America is the crossing we were most interested in.

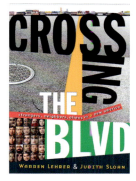

Crossing the BLVD: Strangers, Neighbors, Aliens in a New America, written by Warren Lehrer and Judith Sloan. Design/photography by Lehrer. 2003.

Crossing the BLVD. 2003.

CHAPTER 1

You meet each of 79 people via their photographic portrait, surrounded by their story told in their own words, and reproductions of objects and images they've carried with them from home to home. I continue to cast each person in their own typeface and typographic approach, and list their names once on a page, though I do use traditional punctuation and pack a lot of story on a page, including contextual information in red about the relationship of the US to the person's home country and other information.

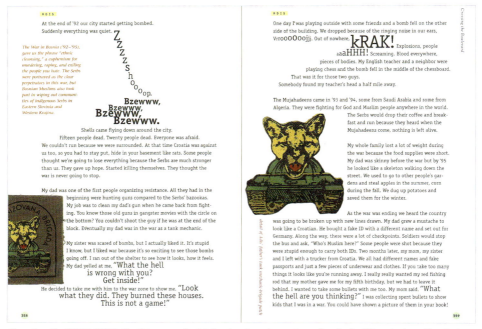

Crossing the BLVD. 2003. On this spread, a high school student whose family fled Bosnia describes being a child of war.

Two spreads from *Crossing the BLVD.* 2003. The last two movements, *Neighborhood Stories* and *Unlikely Bedfellows*, feature people from different parts of the world who share something in common like going to an international high school, belonging to a political club, playing ping-pong or music together.

The *Crossing the BLVD* book sat at the center of a multi-branched project that included public radio documentaries, storytelling workshops, performances, and a traveling exhibition that went to fifteen sites. In addition to photographs, text excerpts, audio stations, and a traveling photo-story booth, I made an animated video titled *Globalization: Preventing the Sameness of the World*, based on Ukrainian-born Eugene Hütz—leader of the gypsy-punk, cabaret band Gogol Bordello—telling us his thoughts on globalization. In the animation, I employ the same kinds of graphic techniques I've used in books, bringing out the voice, ideas, and metaphors of a speaker's text, largely through typography. In this animation, I also played with visual/verbal transformations. In the top rows of these storyboard panels: a keyboard becomes a barcode, which attacks local culture; the word "GLOBALIZATION" rotates on its own axis as a dollar sign takes over . . .

In 2012, Judith and I were commissioned by the Queens Symphony Orchestra to create a symphonic/choral work about the immigrant experience in Queens. Grammy award-winning composer Frank London composed the music. Judith wrote the libretto. I composed expressionistic supertitles that hung above the orchestra and the 150-voice choir. The three of us developing this work collaboratively—from its inception—had a lot to do with its power and effectiveness.

Storyboard panels from the animated video *Globalization: Preventing the Sameness of the World*.

CHAPTER 1

1001 Voices: Symphony for a New America, 2017 Performance, Queens Symphony Orchestra.

In 2016, the Sorensen Center for International Peace and Justice at CUNY Law School commissioned me and Judith to create a response to Donald Trump's "Muslim ban." The resulting 17-window installation, *Anthem for a New America*, is a poetic defense of "sanctuary cities" like New York. Through the fusion of poetry, typography, photography, and color, it re-envisions Emma Lazarus's "The New Colossus" (written in 1883 for the Statue of Liberty) for our time.

I love finding ways of presenting poetry in public places and creating conversations within communities.

From 2015 to 2019, my Community Design class at SUNY Purchase worked on a large-scale "Visual Poetry in Vacant Storefronts" project in downtown White Plains, New York, in collaboration with their Business Improvement District. The class's visualizations of Judith's site-specific poems were produced as large-scale vinyl prints, lenticulars, animations, and projections. In those five years, we transformed hundreds of storefront windows. The project was credited with helping revitalize the downtown and lowering the vacancy rate from 23 percent to single digits, prior to Covid.

Anthem for a New America, 17-window installation at CUNY Law School.

DESIGN NEEDS WORDS

"Visual Poetry in Vacant Storefronts" Project, Courtney Brown/Lehrer's Community Design class. Most people think of White Plains as a suburb of NYC and don't realize that nearly as many people commute from NYC to work in White Plains. In this lenticular setting of Judith's poem "Reverse Commute," designed by Courtney Brown in the first year of the project, pedestrians experience the poem differently depending on the direction they're walking.

Illuminated Novel

After working on the Portrait Series and *Crossing the BLVD*, representing very real people and their stories, I felt a need to work on a project that left more room for invention and getting at the truth through the interior dimensions of characters. In my illuminated novel, *A Life in Books: The Rise and Fall of Bleu Mobley* (2013), I ended up not only inventing a character—who whispers his story into a microcassette recorder over the course of one

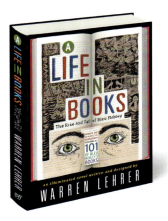

A Life in Books: The Rise and Fall of Bleu Mobley. Written & designed by Lehrer. 2013.

CHAPTER 1

sleepless night from his prison cell—I also invented his entire body of work (or so it seems), encompassing over 101 books, their cover designs, excerpts that read like short stories, catalog copy, and the characters and themes in his life that influenced the characters and themes in his work.

Writing Bleu's narrative and book excerpts and designing the book covers and the various (faux) artifacts was a fluid, iterative process. Writing influenced design. Design influenced writing. I call *A Life in Books* an "illuminated novel" because Bleu's books (covers, catalog copy, excerpts) illuminate the life story, and vice versa. The visual components don't illustrate the text. They are an integral part of the storytelling.

In chapter one, Bleu recalls his introduction to printing in the letterpress shop of the Joan of Arc Jr. High in Queens, New York, where he composes his first books.

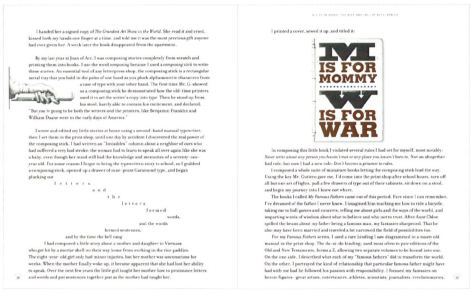

A Life in Books. 2013.

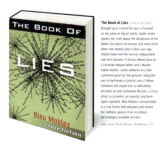  

A Life in Books. 2013.

After returning to New York from a two-year stint as a war reporter, Bleu writes experimental novels, like: *The Switch*, about a day on earth when everyone is switched with their number one enemy; *Narcissistic Planet Disorder*, about a planet that thought it was the center of the universe; *The Book of Lies*, inspired by his best friend who turned out to be a pathological liar. Bleu became a little famous for writing a one-sentence, 365-page novel that takes place inside the mind of a man painting a red barn red.

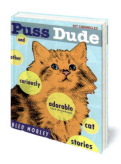 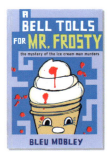  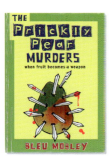

A Life in Books. 2013.

When Bleu's daughter is stricken with a potentially deadly blood disease—which requires the best medical care in the world including treatments his health insurance won't cover—he hires writing assistants who help him come out with five to eight books a year. His first murder mystery, *A Damn Good Plot,* is followed by *One Good Plot Deserves Another*, followed by *Plotsville*. He forays into pet lit, culinary murder mysteries, and other hybrid-genres like a children's pop-up book on the history of capital punishment.

CHAPTER 1

Under the self-help pseudonym Dr. Sky Jacobs, he comes out with a slacker's guide to not accomplishing your full potential, followed up with books that help Bleu grapple with his own sense of loss, crisis of purpose, and hard-to-figure-out conflicts.

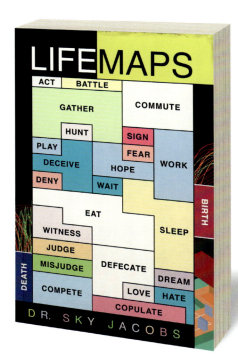

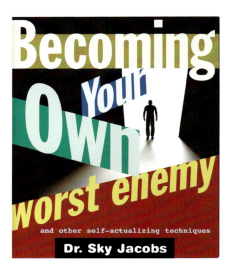

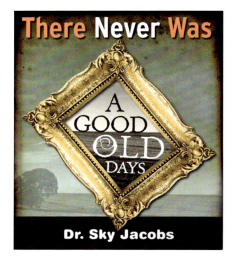

A Life in Books. 2013.

DESIGN NEEDS WORDS

Towards the end of the novel, Bleu sees that books aren't as central to people's lives as they once were, so he starts making coloring books with pictures of war atrocities; rolls of toilet paper poems; book toys for books that drive, chugalug, and fly; book clothes and accessories; and a line of illuminated book lamps "that light up a table and give you a warm literary feeling."

A Life in Books has multiple offshoots including a retrospective exhibit of Bleu Mobley's life's work, and I just completed fleshing out one of the 101 sub-books into its own full-length novel, *TRACE: A Surveilled Novel*, which I aim to have published in 2025.

CHAPTER 1

Memoir in Visual Poetry

In the last several years I've balanced writing and designing my own long-form prose works with collaborative poetry projects. The first of those, *Five Oceans in a Teaspoon* (2019), is a large collection of short visual poems written by Dennis Bernstein, visualized by me. I looked through thousands of Dennis's short poems written over 45 years, selected 225 of them, and structured a book into eight movements that reads like a memoir in visual poems. I let

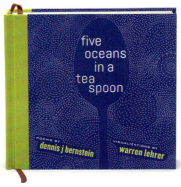

Five Oceans in a Teaspoon. Poems by Bernstein. Visualizations by Lehrer. 2019.

the texts lead the way to typographic compositions that give form to the interior, emotional, and metaphorical underpinnings of the poems. At their best, the resulting compositions leave room for readers to become active participants in the navigation, discovery, and experience of each poem. For instance: in the very first poem in

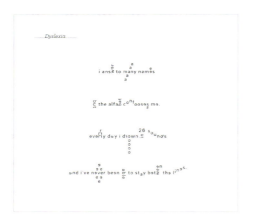

"Dyslexia," *Five Oceans in a Teaspoon.* 2019.

Spread from On the Streets, Under Lock'n Key movement, *Five Oceans in a Teaspoon.* 2019.

Spread from Lake Childhood movement, *Five Oceans in a Teaspoon.* 2019.

Spread from Tracings movement, *Five Oceans in a Teaspoon.* 2019.

the book, "Dyslexia," letters multiply, extend, cascade, rotate, and struggle to form words and meaning, evoking Dennis's experience from an early age. I made animations of select poems from Five Oceans, bringing Dennis's words to life in different ways with the help of time, pacing, and original soundtracks by composer, multi-instrumentalist Andrew Griffin.

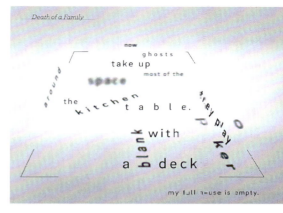

Animation still from "Death of a Family," based on a poem in the final movement of *Five Oceans in a Teaspoon*. 2019.

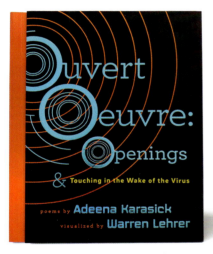

Ouvert Oeuvre: Openings. Poems by Adeena Karasick. Visualization by Lehrer. 2023.

Visualizing Re-Opening After a Global Pandemic

Ouvert Oeuvre: Openings (2023) is a collaboration with poet, cultural critic Adeena Karasick, made up of two long poems about re-opening after a global pandemic. The title poem is an intralingual exploration of different kinds of openings. Following the lead of this propulsive, sonic poem—words grow in size, swell and recede. The spaces between left and right pages and the many parentheses and brackets Adeena used in the poem came to represent inside/outside, walls/barriers that can stop you or be overcome. The poem is also very alliterative, so I alliterated too, visually, by accentuating certain letters, like the o's. Sometimes the o's split and multiply like COVID-19 cells. The second poem is about navigating touch in the wake of the virus, so the setting is more tactile and textured. Adeena uses many slashes in that poem, so the slash came to represent obstacles that sometimes form a maze that words and readers need to navigate. The book comes with a Q-R code that links to a recording of Adeena performing both poems with musical accompaniment by Frank London. In live events, Adeena performs as I project the text in real-time.

CHAPTER 1

Spread from title poem, *Ouvert Oeuvre: Openings.* 2023.

Ouvert Oeuvre. Spread from "Touching in the Wake of the Virus." 2023.

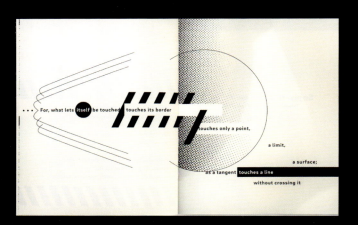

Adeena Karasick performs *Ouvert Oeuvre: Openings.*

DESIGN NEEDS WORDS

The Geometry of Loss

Former *New York Times* reporter turned poet/small press publisher Rick Black sent me the draft of a book about finding a way to deal with the bottomless pain of losing a loved one. The text came to me with only a few words on a page and a license from Rick to breathe another kind of life into them. *Letter Box: The Geometry of Loss*, due out in 2025, will function both as a work of art and as a talisman for people dealing with loss.

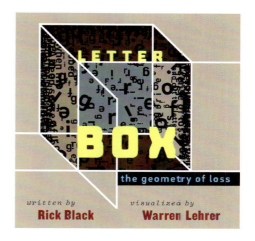

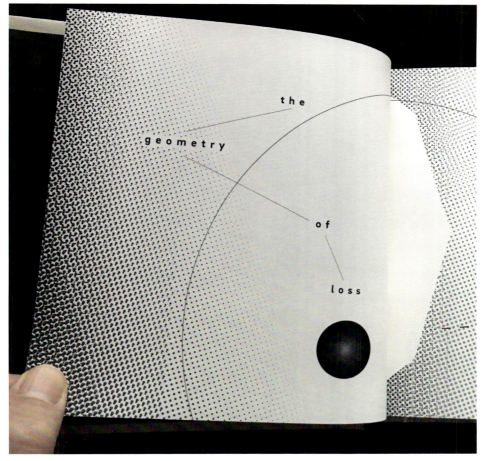

LETTER BOX: The Geometry of Loss. Written by Rick Black. Visualization by Lehrer. 2025.

CHAPTER 1

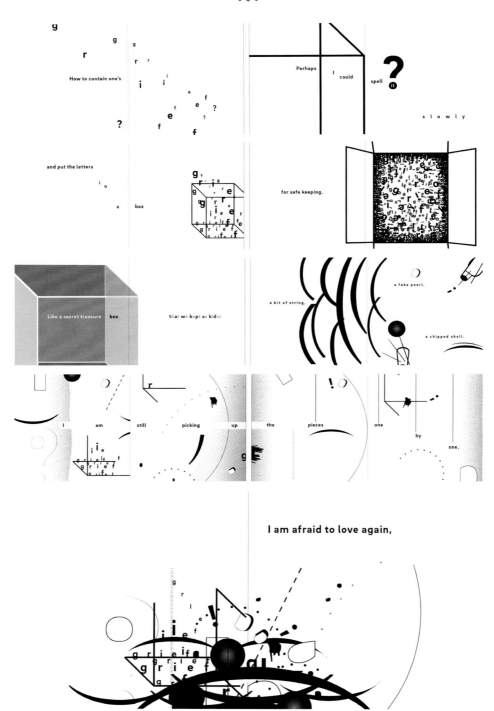

Select pages from *LETTER BOX: The Geometry of Loss*. 2025.

Designing Empathy

Most recently, I wrote *Riveted in the Word* based on the true story of a writer's hard-fought battle to regain language after a devastating stroke. I decided to design and publish it as a multimedia electronic book (2024) as a way of situating the reader inside the mind of my protagonist as she recalls her journey with Broca's aphasia. The interface toggles between columns of text that you read at your own pace and animated sections that evoke gaps between perceptions (thoughts, memories, desires) and the words needed to communicate. The story about overcoming seemingly insurmountable obstacles is told with kinetic typography and an original soundtrack by Andrew Griffin.

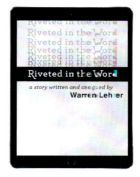

Riveted in the Word. Electronic book by Lehrer. 2024.

My journey as a writer/designer began with an intense interest in formal, visual, and musical structures that attempted to give form to the shape of thought and speech. Over the past four decades, the emphasis of my practice evolved more and more toward telling undertold stories, creating empathy through primary-source research, and carefully crafted writing and design. Some design writers and literary critics still describe my work as "experimental." While I continue to take chances, improvise, and explore the spaces between story and picture, page and screen, books and performance, old and emerging technologies—I wouldn't call it an experiment. I'd call it a practice, a craft, a body of work that fuses writing and design and connects to a long lineage of visual literature, which I'm glad to say is alive and thriving today in many manifestations around the world, and represents one of numerous paths young designers can learn more about and possibly pursue.

A few screen shots from *Riveted in the Word.* 2024.

Copyright © 2024 by Warren Lehrer.

CHAPTER 1

GOOD DESIGN AT ITS WORST

BY VERONIQUE VIENNE

Design can make things look good, but the result isn't always a pretty picture.

Good Design doesn't mean well designed. Good Design is a timeless entity like Beauty and Elegance. Striving for it can drive you crazy. It can also get you into a lot of trouble.

Take Gutenberg for example. His bibles were well designed, but they weren't good design. They were handsome indeed, but they were not useful. When he invented printing, Gutenberg didn't set out to solve a problem that would benefit humanity, even though, in the end, it did. His goal had been much more prosaic. All he wanted was to find a way to reproduce mechanically documents that took months to copy manually. His business was the counterfeiting of manuscripts. His printing press was nothing but a complicated copying machine.

Gutenberg's printed bibles, it turned out, had one fatal flaw—they were flawless. The lines were perfectly even, and there were no ink smudges or spelling mistakes. They looked too good to be true—with some people suspecting that they could only be the work of the Devil. As such, they didn't sell well. Gutenberg couldn't pay his creditors and lost his business to one of his investors, who, in turn, struggled to make ends meet.

It's often the case with innovations. It takes time before their creative potential is understood and exploited. Gutenberg had invented printing, but he cannot be credited for inventing literacy. That honor goes to Claude Garamond, a Parisian punch-cutter who, inspired by Venetian printer Aldus Manutius, realized that the main function of the printing press wasn't to reproduce old manuscripts but to publish new ones.

Garamond invented Good Design.
Unlike Gutenberg, he understood that striving for perfection was counter-productive. Noticing that it was easier to read uneven letters than uniform ones, he designed an idiosyncratic alphabet with distinctive peculiarities. His lower-case letterforms were deliberately playful. He contrasted a spirited "e" with a bottom-heavy "a". His "f" was overgrown while his "t" was stunted. Whether in upper or lower case, no two serifs were alike: slanted, scooped or rounded they seemed to have a life of their own. Yet, when formed into words, the Garamond letters sparkled like crystal beads strung together on a silk thread.

Unwittingly, Garamond had stumbled upon the idea of legibility—a characteristic of Good Design. Whereas Gutenberg's goal had been to preserve information in its original form for an elite group of scribes and scholars, Garamond's idea had been to share information with the general public—a large audience for whom the ability to read contributed to making sense of the world.

. . . as it was on the facade of the Bauhaus Dessau building— Bayer's letterings looked really good. But evil has been known to masquerade as good.

Few type designers have been able to match Garamond's feat. Today there is no shortage of fonts that fail the Good Design test by being overdesigned. Austrian-born polymath Herbert Bayer is a most celebrated example of someone who did it right but got it all wrong. Steeped in Bauhaus rhetoric, he believed that typographical embellishments were distracting additions that interfered with the legibility of a text. He designed a "mono" sans serif alphabet that was a mixture of majuscule and minuscule letterforms. The result is Universal, a compelling set of syncopated typographical signals quite pleasing to the eye. But, until recently, no foundry published this oddly distinctive font because it was hard to read.

However, when used large—as it was on the facade of the Bauhaus Dessau build-ing—Bayer's letterings looked really good. But evil has been known to masquerade as good.

Today, Universal lives in infamy as the typeface of a malicious inscription on the gates of the Buchenwald concentration camp. Joseph Goebbels, Hitler's chief propagandist, a linguist with a doctorate in philology, had picked the idiomatic slogan Jedem das Seine (to each his own) as a motto for the camp to warn incom-ing inmates that each one of them would get his or her due. Cut out of metal and painted in bright red, the spiteful inscription stood out while prisoners were taken into custody as slave workers, or were processed and killed immediately upon arrival.

The sign had been designed by Franz Ehrlich, a former Bauhaus student who was detained at Buchenwald as a suspected communist. Why did he select Universal, no one knows. The Schutzstaffels who ran the camp probably didn't know either. Chances are they did not pick up on the sick humor of their sign maker's typographical choice. Was Ehrlich trying to be defiant, or, on the contrary, was he trying to ingratiate himself with his captors? Was he a collaborator or a victim? Or both? Only one thing is certain: the Nazis must have appreciated his contribution because they kept him busy (and alive) all through the war with various design projects around the camp.

How one selects a typeface is not always meaningful, but somehow, even if it's arbitrary, it will end up looking deliberate. The things that are designed are always assumed to be intentional. There will always be the suspicion of a bias. To assess whether a design solution is good or merely adequate one needs to study its context. In the case of Ehrlich's sign, the list of factors to consider includes the use of modern design by twentieth-century totalitarian regimes, Herbert Bayer's ambiguous relationship with the Nazi ideology, and the banality of evil as defined by Hannah Arendt.

Looming large over these issues is the way good looking design is used to whitewash bad intentions.

Context is the invisible part of a design solution that gives it its gravitas: what was going on politically at the time; who's paying for what; where do the raw materials come from; which means of production were available; was slave labor involved; and so on. Also important is information that's either omitted or deleted. Critical design elements to consider are pictures without captions, quotes without attributions, sources unnamed, titles misspelled, photo credits missing, controversies undisclosed, and timelines jumbled up.

Case in point, Edward Steichen's beloved 1955 landmark exhibition The Family of Man, sponsored by MoMA, then called the Museum of Modern Art. It was one of the most successful, anti-Communist propaganda operations of the Cold War, touring the world for eight years, in thirty-seven countries on six continents. It featured the work of 273 photographers from sixty-eight countries—an impressive parade of emotionally charged argentic tableaux. However, none of the show's 503 black-and-white photographs were identified with a caption. The images were supposed to speak for themselves. The only information available was the barely visible names of the photographers and the locations where the pictures were taken. On walls, random quotes by the likes of Plato, Montaigne, or William Blake gave visitors the impression that some great minds were involved.

According to most commentators in the press at the time, the exhibition, also available in a book form, was Good Design at its best—a brilliant photo installation celebrating the universality of the human experience. Today, a number of critics disagree. They contend that The Family of Man was, in fact, a classic example of the way imperialistic ideologies can masquerade as humanistic endeavors. Indeed, had Edward Steichen insisted that each photograph be identified with a small but accurate caption, he would have shown the kind of consideration for other people's culture one expects from champions of democracy.

But he didn't. Was it a small design flaw, or, on the contrary, a deliberate design statement—an arrogant gesture on the part of one of the most prestigious American cultural institutions?

We now know that MoMA, indeed, was actively engaged in the Cold War, and that, as such, it was responsible for the concept of Good Design acquiring a political dimension. It is no secret that the museum, in cahoots with the CIA, promoted the cause of Capitalism by insinuating that modernism and consumerism shared similar goals. The architect of this campaign was Edgar Kaufmann Jr., whose father owned the Kaufmann department store in Pittsburgh. The scion of a wealthy merchant family, Kaufmann Jr. was MoMA's director of Industrial Design. Between 1950 and 1955, he curated a series of Good Design shows for which he orchestrated three exhibitions a year, each displaying as many as 400 consumer products—from designer furniture to minimalist housewares—presented in retail fashion on shelves, tables, and countertops—all bearing a Good Design stamp of approval and . . . a price tag.

A price tag? Imagine going to a museum to see a Rembrandt show and discovering that each masterpiece on display has a price tag that reflects how much it would fetch if sold at an auction!

For Edgar Kaufmann Jr., Good Design was a commodity.

One thing we tend to forget is that midcentury modernism had to be sold to the public as a valuable attribute. In post-WWII America, average consumers were suspicious of novelties. They tolerated modern appliances in their kitchen but preferred Queen Anne furniture elsewhere in the house. Truth be told, the man of the street never understood what design was all about. Raymond Loewy who earned fame by applying futuristic-looking forms on everything from locomotives to soap bars, avoided the term "design," using "streamlined" instead. To this day, a lot of people believe that design is a style, not a discipline. When, in 1973, IBM president Thomas J. Watson Jr. declared that "good design is good business," there was a widespread sigh of relief. He got everyone onboard with a formula that is probably the most cynical admission that, in the corporate world, "good" design is first and foremost a profitable practice.

Indeed, for some reasons, the dictatorial corporate culture at IBM sets off people's fantasies, with an equal number of admirers and detractors. For the formers, the strict rules make IBM one of the most dynamic and creative work environments.

However, in his case, "good" design turned out to be an invaluable form of deception as well. The rebranding of IBM, as implemented after WWII, is an example of Good Design at Its Worst.

In the mid 1950s, Tom Watson decided it was time to modernize the image of the huge conglomerate that his father, Thomas John Watson Sr., had built. Officially, he had been motivated by his admiration for the way Adriano Olivetti, his very successful Italian competitor, was using design to project an image of creativity. In 1954, Olivetti had opened a showroom on Fifth Avenue in Manhattan, a few blocks from the IBM headquarters at 590 Madison Avenue. There, Olivetti typewriters and calculators were presented as desirable consumer products rather than staid business machines. Some were displayed on slender pedestals on the sidewalk, where anyone could approach them, touch them, and test them, without the intimidating presence of salesmen.

In the context of the Cold War, the race to dominate the electronics market was a political issue. Tom Watson understood that he couldn't afford to lag behind. His patriotic duty required he match Olivetti's progressive image. He had to catch up, but he didn't know how to turn things around.

He asked Eliot Noyes, a glider pilot he had befriended in the US Army Air Corps during WWII, to oversee this project. By then, Noyes was a well-established architect and industrial designer who had worked for the Museum of Modern Art in New York. A White Anglo-Saxon Protestant from Boston, he was a Harvard man with impeccable pedigree and a large network of socially prominent friends in the art world.

Most urgently, and most expediently, Noyes needed to modernize the company's graphic language and infuse it with some levity. He recruited graphic designer Paul Rand to help him. Rand, who had made a name for himself in advertising, was not from the same social class as Noyes, but he was a sincere and dedicated modernist, one of the rare American designers who embraced the values of the Land of Opportunity—yet was familiar with European design and Bauhaus aesthetics.

The two men were a study in contrast, with Noyes cast in the role of the enlightened mediator while Rand played the part of the uncompromising artist. Both talented, and both outsiders to the IBM culture, Rand and Noyes were able to implement innovative design solutions. One of their first, and most visible accomplishments was the transformation of the original, heavy-handed IBM monogram into a versatile and playful design element.

However, getting the approval of IBM upper management had been a delicate operation. At first, Rand's avant-garde design proposals were not well received. It took years of progressive adjustments, but eventually Rand and Noyes were ready to propose a truly innovative design solution—a striped version of the existing IBM monogram, one that they felt would transform it into a powerful trademark.

Imagine the scene: calmly, yet adamantly, as was his habit, Paul Rand began to explain that linking together the three letters of the logo with thin white stripes would suggest something legal and serious, like the parallel scan lines on bank checks or official deeds. But, as the story goes, no one in the audience seemed convinced. The half dozen executives attending the meeting remained stoned-faced as Rand carried on, extoling the advantages of the 8-bar logo versus the 13-bar logo. To no avail. The resistance in the room remained palpable.

Rand was at his wits' end when someone at long last spoke up, explaining that the reason he didn't like the design was the fact that it reminded him of a prison outfit. Suddenly everyone agreed that the logo looked like it was behind bars. That's when Noyes cut in. Before Rand had time to protest, he took over the meeting. He knew what to say. He talked about the stripes on the American flag, the scan lines on a computer screen, the horizontal rules on spiral notebooks.

Soon order was restored. The trademark with lines running across was validated. Whenever Eliot Noyes spoke, everyone listened.

But Rand wasn't listening. He was doodling. In his notebook, he drew inmates wearing prison outfits; a convict saluting the IBM logo; a dog on a leash wearing a striped jacket. Something about the remark had sparked his imagination. Instead of being insulted by the unflattering comments, they got him thinking. IBMers wore uniforms, like prisoners. At IBM, a rigid corporate dress code was mandatory. All employees showed up for work wearing a button-down white shirt, a dark suit, a navy-blue tie, and wing-tipped shoes. Maybe, unwittingly, Rand suspected, the striped logo had hit a nerve and released some uneasiness buried in the secret recesses of the corporate culture.

Indeed, for some reasons, the dictatorial corporate culture at IBM sets off people's fantasies, with an equal number of admirers and detractors. For the formers, the strict rules make IBM one of the most dynamic and creative work environments. For the latter, the tyrannical atmosphere turns employees into

CHAPTER 1

No one was ever supposed to find out that IBM, this progressive company, had invented a most deadly weapon—the punch card technology that enabled the Nazis to round up Jews before and during WWII.

zombies. This dystopian vision was the setup of the famous 1984 Apple commercial broadcast during the Super Bowl. The action took place in what looked like a nightmarish penal institution in which countless inmates were forced to march around under the watchful eye of Big Brother—a direct reference to Thomas John Watson Sr., the authoritarian figure who ran IBM from 1914 to 1956.

Unlike most employees who had to abide by the rules in order to survive at IBM, Paul Rand and Eliot Noyes enjoyed a special status. Neither had signed exclusive employment contracts, keeping their distance from internal power struggles and office politics. As a friend of the boss, Noyes was respected by upper management while Rand, considered an artist, was allowed to voice his opinions. Grudgingly, people had to admit that their work added to the company's prestige, even though few understood the role of design, or appreciated its impact on business decisions. However, in the world at large, IBM had become synonymous with Good Design. On top of Rand's work, the various contributions of Charles and Ray Eames were simply dazzling.

When Noyes died prematurely in 1977, Rand soldiered on, working on collaterals, letterheads, packaging, brochures, annual reports, and posters, never letting the graphic system he had invented become stale, always on the lookout for that one quirky graphic touch that made all the difference. In 1981, he came up with his now famous rebus Eye-Bee-M poster, deemed too disruptive and banned by upper management. By 1991, he chose not to renew his freelance arrangement with IBM— but his legacy lived on. Once contentious, his striped logo is today prominently displayed on the facades of more than 175 buildings worldwide, from Ahmedabad, India, to Warsaw, Poland.

Only after Rand's death in 1996 did the dark side of IBM begin to transpire. Less than five years after Rand passed away, American historian Edwin Black published IBM and the Holocaust, an investigation of the prominent role of the corporate giant in the Final Solution. Had Paul Rand known about his client's involvement with the Nazi party, he would have resigned on the spot—and corporate design as we know it would never have become the acclaimed discipline it is today.

Born Peretz Rosenbaum, Paul Rand had changed his name to avoid the kind of discrimination he would have encountered as a Jew. But with Eliot Noyes vouching for him, he never was the direct target of anti-Semitism. He probably thought that he had landed in a safe place. Design was his religion. Modernism was his faith. Visual language was his creed.

He would never have guessed that he had been hired by one of the worst offenders to the Jewish cause.

To put it bluntly, Rand's job had been to create a graphic environment that drew attention away from the company's criminal activities during WWII. His visual communication program had been in fact a cover-up operation, an attempt to conceal the most damning evidence of wrongdoing. No one was ever supposed to find out that IBM, this progressive company, had invented a most deadly weapon— the punch card technology that enabled the Nazis to round up Jews before and during WWII. In every death camp, IBM tabulators had been installed to keep track of inmates, their ancestry, their vital statistics, and their whereabouts. IBM consultants had been dispatched to camps regularly to service and clean the machines. After the US declared war to Germany, IBM had used its European subsidiaries to keep operations rolling.

But back then no one was talking.

What did anyone know?

Did Thomas John Watson Sr. know that during the Holocaust the US government restricted the number of Jews who could immigrate to the United States to escape the pogroms?

Did Tom Watson know that his father, who had coined the slogan "World Peace Through World Trade," was using his European IBM affiliates to do business with the enemy?

Did Eliot Noyes know that the numbers tattooed on the arms of death camps inmates were IBM numbers?

Did IBM upper management know that their employer had contributed to sending five million people marching to their death?

But now we all know. Books, articles, essays have been written about IBM's role in the Final Solution. What's next? Documentaries, TV series, feature films?

Let Good Design be the last victim.

Copyright © 2023 by Veronique Vienne.

CHAPTER 1

IF YOU ARE WRITING AN ESSAY OR A THESIS

BY CHAPPELL ELLISON

If you are writing an essay or a thesis

Don't start by researching.

Start by writing.

How else will you know what you're looking for?

If you are writing an essay or a thesis

And it's about an object

Acquire that object if you can.

See what it's like to touch it

And live with it.

Witness how others react to it.

See if you can break it or make it better.

See if it changes your mind.

If you are writing an essay or a thesis

Ask someone else what they think about the topic.

Ask your mother, your spouse, a cousin.

DESIGN NEEDS WORDS

Ask a postal worker, an electrician, a hair stylist.

Ask a stranger.

Ask someone whose first language isn't the same as yours.

Truly listen to them.

Listen until you hear the story they have to tell.

If you are writing an essay or a thesis

Don't build it with the bones of a dead person's theories.

Instead, let that person be a ghost that sometimes haunts the spaces between your sentences.

If you are writing an essay or a thesis

Start by writing the last paragraph.

You might find that it becomes your first.

Eventually you might find that in writing

There is no first or last.

If you are writing an essay or a thesis

Let go of the idea that you need to say everything.

Choose one window through which to view your topic.

Make it your window.

Hang drapes and pull up a chair.

Don't worry about the window to your right or the other one to your left.

Those windows are for other writers.

If you are writing an essay or a thesis

Don't think of it as an essay or a thesis.

Think of it as a really engaging conversation.

One you might have with a friend

Until you look at the clock and can't believe how late it is.

If you are writing an essay or a thesis

CHAPTER 1

Remember that you have read and written thousands of words before this day.

And that you will read and write thousands more words after this day.

Today is another day you get to spend with words.

If you are writing an essay or a thesis

Make discovery of the new your goal.

Not reheating the frozen goods of the past.

Make as much of your meal from scratch as you can.

This is healthy for you

And it tastes much better in the end.

If you are writing an essay or thesis

Know that you do not have to act on every idea.

Some ideas are meant to be leaves

Floating by on the surface of a river.

Just let them go.

If the idea is truly important to you

It will float by again.

If you are writing an essay or a thesis

Do not feel disheartened

When you discover others have written about the same topic.

Remember, they are looking through their window

And you are looking through yours.

No one else's window has your drapes.

Or thickness of pane.

Write from your window

As no one else can.

Copyright © 2016 by Chappell Ellison. Published on Medium.com, April 18, 2016.

DESIGN NEEDS WORDS

THE FINE ART OF LOVING AND LIKING: HOW TO SURVIVE THE EMOJI ECONOMY

BY SARAH BOXER

Question marks used to be my thing. I loved how they looked on the page, their open-endedness, their curiosity, their insinuation. I loved how much 'tude, hiding as pure questing innocence, you could pack into a single sentence ending with one. I was so addicted to them that certain editors put me on a question mark diet, limiting me to, say, ten question marks per two-thousand-word essay. I don't remember the exact limit, but I do remember straining against it. Just one more question, please?

I've moved on. Now I'm into exclamation points! So much healthier! While question marks are, by sense and by shape, sneaky and snaky, exclamation marks are effectively one-eared rabbits jumping up and down. They're cute! They're excited! And because they're excited, they generate excitement! When I used to binge on question marks, I'd sprinkle them through a text. Casual-like. La-di-da. When I binge on exclamation points, I pack them all together at the end of a sentence or a fragment! The more the merrier!! The more you use, the higher you go!!!

CHAPTER 1

. . . Or rather the higher your reader goes. With exclamation points, I'm thinking about my dear readers. Most of my exclamation points are in emails, especially thank-you emails. A period at the end of a sentence, even at the end of a really nice compliment or a heartfelt thank you, just doesn't cut it anymore. It's almost rude. You might as well not write anything nice at all. As the Guardian columnist Rhiannon Lucy Cosslett tweeted years ago, "Older people—do you realize that ending a sentence with a full stop comes across as sort of abrupt and unfriendly to younger people in an email/chat? Genuinely curious" (no period).

The question is, how many exclamation points should you add for peak friendliness? One makes things nice, but still can seem stingy. What are you saving them for? It's not like you get a limited number in a lifetime. Why not add another exclamation point! And another!! Make your reader happy!!! OMG!!!! So happy!!!!!

With punctuation inflation, periods get bumped up to exclamation points, and single exclamation points get bumped up to two or three or four. And ALL CAPS? Don't EVEN get me started!!! It's NOT just for CRAZY people anymore!

And this brings me to the fine science of Loving and Liking with emojis. Emojis are effectively pictorial punctuation, and there too you can feel the inflation. Let me say off the bat that with social media I'm most secure on Instagram, where you have only two clicking options, Loving or Leaving without clicking at all. I also feel fine on YouTube, where it's Thumbs Up or Thumbs Down. What worries me is Facebook, where your options run from Liking, to Loving, to Caring, to Laughing, to Crying, to Being Shocked, and Being Angry. So many ways to go wrong!

Sure, it's easy to dish out Love when it's your only option, but when you must choose among seven emojis, it gets dicey. Therefore, on Facebook, I spend an embarrassing amount of time thinking about the economy of emojis—what they mean, how they're used, who uses which emojis and why, and what effects they have on me and on others.

My anxiety makes me nostalgic for the day when punctuation was the only way to inflect my writing. In honor of that day, I've tried to translate the Facebook reaction emojis into their rough equivalents in punctuation. The Like emoji (Thumbs Up) is effectively a period. The Love emoji (Heart), which copies the "I Heart NYC" created by Milton Glaser, is an exclamation mark. The Shock emoji, a yellow face with big black eyes, high eyebrows, and a wide-open black oval mouth, is a question mark and an exclamation mark together. (Is it any surprise that it's my favorite?!)

But certain reaction emoji's can't be boiled down to punctuation. The Laugh emoji, a big open-mouthed, red-mouthed laugh, with the eyes reduced by mirth to angle-bracket eyes, like this > < , is the equivalent of LOL!!! Or LMAO!!! The Crying emoji—that yellow face looking up then down with a blue tear rolling down one side of the face, then the other—is so specifically expressive that it has, I believe, no punctuation equivalent. And the Anger emoji, a red face shaking with disbelief, well, it's close to Charlie Brown's AAUGH but not quite!!!

I've thought a lot about how various emojis make me feel when I'm on the receiving end. When I see that someone has Liked something of mine, I think, hmm, okay. It's like a period at the end of the sentence. It's a B. It's okay, it's really okay. But when I see that Heart emoji, signifying Love, it sends me. I feel squishier about those who Love than those who Like. It's petty but there it is. My least favorite emoji to receive is the Care emoji, the little yellow thing hugging a heart. Whose heart is that yellow face hugging anyway? Its own heart or someone else's? Does it mean "I feel sorry for you"? Or "I pity you"? Or does it mean "I want you (and others) to see me caring for you"?

My feelings about the emojis I receive in turn condition how I react to other people on Facebook. My first thought is, if I'm going to send someone some emoji rather than nothing at all, why not Love? Love's the best! Why be a tightwad? On second thought, it's not really stinginess that makes me economize on the Loves. What if I were to get into the habit of Loving everything. Wouldn't that lower the value of my Love?

Come to think of it, I secretly admire people who tend to Like rather than Love. Maybe they're too busy to find other emojis. Maybe they've got higher standards. Maybe they worry that they'll be caught giving Love to some and only Like to others. Quite honestly, Love isn't always the right emoji. Should you really be giving Loves to those who hand out only Likes? And what about giving Love to a stranger? No matter how taken you are with what someone you don't know has said, or done, or posted, isn't it going overboard to send them Love? I know I've done it before, but it's weird.

By contrast, the Shock emoji is, I feel, nice for friends and strangers alike. In fact, it's one of my favorites to give and to get. It shows that you've been moved, but it doesn't have the emotional baggage of Love and it doesn't have the coolness of Like.

I wonder if anyone else goes through these contortions, if anyone else has noticed what the hyper-inflated language of emojis does to one's sense of oneself and others. Is it at all possible to have a pure reaction that takes place in a public sphere? If someone is stingy with you, can you be generous with them? If someone is generous with you, can you be honest with them? I really don't know the answer to any of these, but I am pretty sure that I have gone way past my quota of question marks.

Copyright © 2023 by Sarah Boxer.

CHAPTER 1

PARIS CLICHÉS

BY KEN CARBONE

April in Paris and Other French Clichés

When does a visual cliché become an enduring symbol? Every day. They often have a negative connotation and can be painfully banal. However, contemporary graphic design is rife with clichés whether it be a "heart" symbolizing love, an "apple" meaning education or a bitmapped "hour glass" signaling the passage of time. Or how about "little bird" communicating a short chirp of a message in 140 characters. Get the picture? Clichés are part of every graphic designer's conceptual toolbox and no one is immured from their magnetic appeal.

Cliché is a French word and nowhere do they seem more obvious (ubiquitous) than in Paris. I just spent five days in the "City of Light" and they're everywhere. A man in a beret, a poodle on a leash, an artist at an easel. Next to New York, Paris is like my second home. Every visit one of its many clichés warms my heart.

(Other examples: *The Thinker*, Eiffel tower, *The Kiss*—even Rodin criticized it as being "kitsch"—French bread, crepes, French fries.)

The evolution of a visual cliché often has noble beginnings in art. A masterpiece or monument seen as groundbreaking can be so beloved and celebrated that it then is overused, becomes obvious, and finally triggers disdain. In the worst case it can be used as a cultural stereotype. But like a "phoenix" (another cliché) it is resurrected as a form of universal communication and that's why we use them. These clichés are a deep-rooted part of our cultural lexicon and when used in graphic design, become immediately understood nonverbal language.

Here are a few examples:

DESIGN NEEDS WORDS

◆ ▶ ◆

Rodin's *The Thinker*　　　　　　　French bread (baguette)

Eiffel Tower: For decades this was the tallest structure on the planet.

Copyright © 2024 by Ken Carbone.

Designing messages is about creating words into soothing or jarring patterns and rhythms. Words need support on the page. This comes through the typeface that is selected—its style, size, and weight, as well as its emphasis either on page or screen. Sing-song prose demands a similar tone of typesetting. The two are inextricably wed and when it works the chemistry is extraordinary.

WORDS NEED DESIGN

CHAPTER 2

WRITING FOR THE EAR

BY JULIE LASKY

There is a form of writing called "writing for the ear," designed for words that are meant to be read aloud, say, in speeches, on the radio, or in podcasts.

It is based on the belief that reading and listening are different modes of reception and that words should be tailored differently to the roving eye and the inert ear. Eyes, by their nature, take in written text in fits and jumps, moving up and down the page, or returning to earlier pages, when meaning has not fully penetrated the mind.

Ears, by contrast, are portals into which we can control entry (they can be blocked) or volume (they can be muffled), but not the conscious, selective screening of information. If our minds wander as we listen to something read aloud, we can recapture what we missed only if it is recorded. If we are bored and want the story to move on, we must grit our teeth and wait for it to unfold.

Because of these auditory constraints and the linearity of time, people who write for the ear are advised to use short, simple sentences that mimic common speech. Leave the flowery adverbs and subordinate clauses to writing for the eye, they are told.

But what is missed in this division between sense organs and their inputs is that many of us hear language even when we stare at a page or screen. A sentence that is indigestible when spoken runs a good chance of not being palatable when read.

Which means that we should always write for the ear, even when no one is listening.

I learned this in an odd way—by working as an editor at a graphic design magazine in the late 1980s and early 1990s. At that time, design was steeped in the postmodern movement, which was fueled by the revolution in desktop computing technology, and it was often not pretty.

Once graphic designers got their hands on software that allowed them to manipulate type, they went crazy. Often, their layered typographic experiments were aesthetically groundbreaking works of art, but just as frequently—I would go so far as to say almost always—they were nightmares of blasted legibility.

Poster headlines and publication display type would be letterspaced to such a width that the eye had to inhale and leap like a hurdler to traverse the echo-y distances within single words. Lowercase and uppercase were indiscriminately mingled, so that characters that shouted and characters that whispered were joined in a single cacophonous collective.

Because of these auditory constraints and the linearity of time, people who write for the ear are advised to use short, simple sentences that mimic common speech. Leave the flowery adverbs and subordinate clauses to writing for the eye, they are told.

Designers frequently defended these experiments by stating that their aim was to stoke curiosity—to draw readers closer to the page or poster by extending what the designer optimistically imagined was an irresistible compulsion to decipher it. Zuzana Licko, the Czech-born co-founder of the California-based design magazine *Émigré*, which made gorgeous, groundbreaking demonstrations of computer-manipulated type in that era, defended the legibility, or lack thereof, of her experiments by stating, "People read best what they read most." Which is to say that you can't completely efface literary appeal even if something is very, very hard to read, just as you can't discourage people who are determined to scale Mount Everest simply by subjecting them to altitude sickness and frostbite.

It was these intrepid designers who taught me how noisy non-spoken language could be, and their lessons persisted even when postmodernism went belly up and texts calmed down and got easier to read. I began to understand why so many great musicians (Joni Mitchell, David Byrne, Kim Gordon) had started as visual artists, and why so many designers were musical to their bones.

CHAPTER 2

Art Chantry, for example, a designer associated with Seattle's post-punk independent music scene to the extent that the *Seattle Times* anointed him the "godfather of grunge," translated soundwaves into degraded type and explosive color. He did this so deftly that his posters and record covers looked like they spontaneously erupted, even as they communicated every detail you wanted to know about a band or performance.

It is no accident that Art Chantry was—and remains—a mesmerizing writer and talker. Consciously or unconsciously, he understands that the ear is hardwired to the eye. We don't just see what we hear, conjuring visions to illustrate words. We hear what we see, sensorily entering the texts that lie before us, or backing away if they don't hook our attention.

Possibly because I'm a writer, I often think in full sentences. I compose things in my head. Words rattle around in there like music. Sometimes I hit on a groove before I'm conscious of the words it will carry. I don't believe I'm alone in that. My husband is also a writer, and sometimes he just stands there with a funny look on his face.

"I'm working on a story," he explains.

Copyright © 2024 by Julie Lasky.

WORDS NEED DESIGN

WRITING ON THE WALL

BY ANGELINA LIPPERT

✱

To write about design, be it a tea towel or a teapot, a pavilion, or a poster, requires the author to approach the object as an art historian, a general historian, and a pop culture historian. Design straddles all of those worlds, often equally, and placing it within all of those contexts is essential to understanding how that object functions—what it tells us about the creator and the society that would use it.

Writing about design for a museum exhibition is one of the most challenging forms of expression within design writing. Your audience will be naturally quite broad, from school groups to scholars to foreign tourists—which means that your text needs to be approachable and engaging, with numerous points of entry and understanding so that no one reader feels alienated. The worst sin a museum curator can commit is writing solely for their peers—it's easy to express ideas in a vacuum, but if only someone with a PhD can understand what you've written, what's the point? Museums are there at the service of the public, and while the text should be critical and rigorously researched, it is also, at its core, info-tainment— voluntary learning people engage with out of personal desire to understand. Don't lose that good will by making your text so complicated that everyone gets confused or frustrated and stops reading. At the same time, do not talk down to your audience. Curatorial pretension is rampant, and we all know how smart you are. Your job is to make every possible reader feel welcome.

There is also the issue of limited attention spans. Plenty of studies have indicated that the average museum visitor spends five to thirty seconds on a given piece. Roughly about half of your audience will glance at the wall text. If that text fails to draw them in instantly, that number gets much smaller very fast. While a bit unconventional, I often suggest that individual wall labels be written as bullet points, with no more than four for any given object. This choice is actually great for both the author and the viewer. Without the need for fully developed paragraphs that move fluidly through ideas, bullet points allow the writer to hit disparate concepts quickly and succinctly—essentially, all the coolest things anyone need know about a given object ticked out on a greatest hits list. For the reader, bullet points are an easy sorting mechanism for the eye, an extension of a social media feed where you can stop at a word or phrase that feels relevant to you. If the first bullet is about the materiality of the object but you're more of a standard history person, you can skip to the bullet about World War II. At Poster House (where I am Chief Curator), it is the one aspect of our museum curation that gets complimented on time and time again. Think of it as designing the text to be peak functional—which is probably the goal of many of the design objects you're writing about.

As far as what content to consider when writing about design, it is important to look at the object from all facets of its use and purpose. Unlike a fine art painting that is often the result of an artist's personal expression, design objects are the byproduct of an artist fulfilling a brief. Measuring the success of that brief is part of writing about design. For example, let's look at this poster by Jean Dupas from 1928, advertising Arnold Constable: First and foremost, what is being promoted? Arnold Constable was a department store in New York City, similar to what Lord and Taylor used to be (so we know it's catering to a middle- to upper-middle-class clientele). As this poster was printed during the Roaring Twenties, the central figure in a fashionable 1920s dress feels appropriate and youthful, but what are the other figures doing? When considered in relation to the accompanying text about "mode" (a word essentially meaning "current fashion"), we can interpret the leftmost figure as being representative of the "mode of yesterday," while the rightmost figure stands in for "the mode of tomorrow." But whereas the yesterday figure is clearly based on historic fashion, how should we interpret Dupas's 1928 idea of what future fashion would look like? Why would he have seen that particular type of minimalist gown as representative of the future? What about that weird hat? And what do the symbols around these figures—the flowers, the strange lawn sculpture, the doves—mean? Finally, is the artist tapping into larger art historical trends or ideas when creating his design? I am often reminded of Fernand Léger's female forms when looking at Dupas, as well as some elements of the work of Giorgio de Chirico. Why would Dupas have been influenced by those two artists?

As far as what content to consider when writing about design, it is important to look at the object from all facets of its use and purpose.

Once you've dissected the actual signs and symbols within the poster, consider the unseen elements of the poster as a historic document. Jean Dupas was one of the most prominent designers of the Art Deco period, but he was based in France. Why, then, would he have created a poster for an American department store? Does the printing information indicate where the piece was physically printed? And does that printing information provide clues as to how and where it was distributed? In this case, the poster was printed in France, which makes choosing a French artist more sensible. But why would Arnold Constable want to have its poster printed in France and pay to have piles of heavy paper shipped across the Atlantic? Was it because lithographic printing quality was higher in France than in the United States at the time, and the company wanted to spare no expense? Was it perhaps because Dupas was a very prominent fashion illustrator, and having someone that notable outweighed the cost of shipping? Was it because not all the posters went to the United States, but maybe went to the United Kingdom and elsewhere in Europe for distribution in an effort to attract tourists who would be coming to New York? Dupas created numerous posters for London Transport, so his reach was already outside of France. These are just some of the investigative questions you should be asking as you dive deeper into what a given object is telling you about a particular time and place—and in many cases, not all of these questions will have clear answers, but it's still very important to think about them as they will lead to a domino effect of hows and whys about design.

After you've firmly situated the object within its historic context, both as an expression of popular culture as well as a reflection of general mass history of the time, you should then begin analyzing its function and success as a piece of design. Does this object solve the problem the designer was given? In this case, does the poster accurately reflect the brief of selling upscale women's ready-to-wear garments? What do all of these combined elements tell us about the visual literacy and symbolic shorthand of the time? I often say that if a poster does not express itself clearly in under a second, it's failed. Would this poster have been able to grab and maintain your attention on the street when surrounded by dozens of similar advertisements? Is the message obvious to the average viewer? How does it compare to other posters for similar companies from the same period, both locally and internationally?

CHAPTER 2

While I certainly do not answer all of these questions in every wall label I create, many of them serve as guiding points in exhibition text construction. Below is the wall label I created for this poster in the 2023 exhibition *Art Deco: Commercializing the Avant-Garde*.

Arnold Constable, 1928
Jean Dupas (1882–1964)
Poster House Permanent Collection

Located in downtown Manhattan, Arnold Constable was at one point the most luxurious department store in New York. Here, French artist Jean Dupas positions the institution as the tastemaker in fashion for the past, the present, and the future.

Created the year before the Wall Street crash, this poster represents the height of American Jazz Age glamour and excess.

Dupas was one of the most prolific and notable painters and illustrators of the Art Deco period, not only providing numerous fashion plates for publications like *Vogue*, but also designing part of the interior of the SS *Normandie*, for a time the largest and fastest passenger ship ever built. Dupas's version of Art Deco combined the weight of Fernand Léger's Cubist figures with elements of Giorgio de Chirico's Surrealist landscapes—an Italian-French hybrid that reflects his formal artistic education in both countries.

Note that I start by explaining what the poster is advertising. The most basic information most people will want to know about an object is what does it do (or, in the case of a poster, what is it trying to get the viewer to do). I then couch the design of the poster within the cultural context of the period—in this case, a reflection of 1920s luxury before the Wall Street crash. Next, I explain why this particular artist was chosen for the project and how it fits within the rest of his oeuvre before finally relating it to a broader art historical context. There is enough diversity in the type of information that most readers will find a topic they are curious about, and that will likely serve as a reason for them to keep reading about other aspects of the object that may not have been natural entry points for them, and which they would not have noticed were it not for the bullet-point format. No matter what, keep it brief and keep it interesting. The biggest compliment is when something you've written inspires someone to want to learn more.

Copyright © 2024 by Angelina Lippert.

CHAPTER 2

CLUTTER
IS
GOOD FOR YOU

BY ROB WALKER

✱

Several years before she died, my mother began sending me things—ostensibly significant objects. These included expected items like jewelry and photographs and also puzzling ones. For example, one afternoon I opened a package containing a carefully wrapped eight-inch-tall ceramic leprechaun that I don't recall ever having seen. (My family has no connection to Ireland.) Not long after, she announced that she wanted to send along her collection of bird figurines, in which I had never expressed any special interest.

Clearly this was no longer about handing down heirlooms. It was about getting rid of objects—basically, a form of decluttering. I had to put a stop to it, and not just because these objects didn't actually mean anything to me. Much more important: They did mean something to her. In fact, what I most enjoyed about her accumulation of bird figurines and ceramics and sand dollars from Texas beaches was her enjoyment of these things. Her unselfconscious confidence about what she liked was one of her most admirable traits.

So I persuaded her not only to keep her figurines but also to let herself continue to appreciate their presence. Because ultimately my mother's urge to purge struck me as illuminating something misguided about our general relationship to material culture. In short: What we often dismiss as "clutter"—all those nonessential, often oddball objects that a third-party observer might write off as needless junk—can actually be good for us.

The villainization of clutter has perhaps been most insistently pushed by the "tidying up" guru Marie Kondo. Its latest iteration pairs a yearning to neaten up pandemic cocoons—crowded with stuff thanks to a couple of years of online shopping as a monotony-fighting tactic—with a trendy take on minimalism that equates the blank-space aesthetic with mindful sophistication. But the underlying vibe is a suspiciously familiar one. Yet again, minimalist scolds insist that we should repent of our materialist ways: Things, they are forever lecturing, just aren't that important.

It seems hard to disagree. Yet it's also hard to square that pronouncement with, to pick a recent example, the frenzy of attention around the auction of Joan Didion's personal effects—which in addition to books and artworks included a box of loose buttons, a bunch of seashells and pebbles, a "miscellaneous group of eyewear," and other items that one observer bluntly described as "junk," and that even the auction house called "ephemera." The highbrow musing around this focused almost exclusively on the high prices fetched ($10,000 for the collection of specs, $27,000 for a single pair of Celine sunglasses) or the possible motives of those who paid for them. But what we might reflect on instead is the fact that she kept this stuff in the first place. Nobody demanded to know why Didion didn't declutter—whether, say, all those paperweights (there were at least five) truly "sparked joy."

There is, it turns out, a counter to the decluttering imperative—inevitably given the unattractive label "cluttercore"—that frankly celebrates the human relationship to stuff. Search YouTube and you'll find video tours of (mostly young) people's extensive and colorful collections of stuffed toys, figurines, gewgaws, and knickknacks. TikTok clips tagged #cluttercore, sharing what the home-design site Apartment Therapy described as "organized, nostalgic chaos," have more than 80 million views.

As one cluttercore advocate argued to *Architectural Digest*, social media has fostered aesthetics that tend toward the neutral, the acceptable, the blandly conformingly tasteful: an endless series of unobjectionable tidy backdrops "devoid of personal style." Cluttercore, in contrast, wholly depends on idiosyncratic personality and rarefied interests, and thus "celebrates radical individuality." In an era when imitation is everywhere, *Architectural Digest* asserted, so-called clutter represents something that "can't be duplicated."

Admittedly, some iterations of cluttercore verge on a candy-colored version of straight-up hoarding, and obviously I am not defending mindless accumulation any more than a craft cocktail aficionado would defend binge drinking. But the point about individuality not only rings true; it hints at the reasons the instinct to appreciate clutter is correct, natural, and frequently underrated.

The anti-clutter nags conflate two distinct forms of materialism. In behavioral psychology terms, "terminal materialism" refers to acquiring and valuing an object purely for its intrinsic properties—like a fancy new iPhone (that will inevitably

CHAPTER 2

"We found that things are cherished not because of the material comfort they provide," they wrote, "but for the information they convey about the owner and his or her ties to others." Moreover: "We began to notice that people who denied meanings to objects also lacked any close network of human relationships."

become obsolete). The worthless-looking junk we hang on to often exemplifies instrumental materialism, valued for its connection to another person, a place, a time in our lives, a meaningful affiliation. These can take obvious forms—a wedding ring, a crucifix. But they can also be as eccentric and inscrutable as an abundance of paperweights or a ceramic leprechaun.

The objects one keeps close at hand "create permanence in the intimate life of a person," Mihaly Csikszentmihalyi, the psychologist who became known for the concept of "flow," and the sociologist Eugene Rochberg-Halton wrote years ago in The Meaning of Things, an early, seminal dive into the psychology of materialism, "and therefore that are most involved in making up his or her identity."

Their conclusions were based on surveying 82 families about a total of 1,694 meaningful domestic objects. "We found that things are cherished not because of the material comfort they provide," they wrote, "but for the information they convey about the owner and his or her ties to others." Moreover: "We began to notice that people who denied meanings to objects also lacked any close network of human relationships."

That is not, of course, to suggest that minimalists are inhuman or that true connection depends on material totems. But these personal links between meaning and objects certainly challenge the familiar critique that material attachment is a function of hollow status signaling. Describing cluttercore as something for "those who have loads of items that each hold their own story," Apartment Therapy added the crucial point that this means "things they love, no matter how wacky, minuscule, or unimportant it may seem to someone on the outside." We might imagine an audience, however intimate, for the stories our clutter tells. But really, these are stories we're telling ourselves.

And that's fine—or more than fine. Because the objects you already own are much more likely to be interwoven with the people and experiences that give life meaning. That's why your weird old clutter is probably more important than whatever It-object innovation you might acquire next. (Often, I suspect, the "decluttering" minimalist directive is actually a stealthy terminal-materialist argument that you need to clear out yesterday's trendy, influencer-hyped joy-flops . . . so you can make room for tomorrow's.)

More to the point, as I argued to my mother, nobody else will ever enjoy your clutter quite the way you do. For nearly a decade, I've taught an annual workshop on writing about objects for the design research department of New York's School of Visual Arts. Scores of participants from around the world have invariably chosen subject-objects that most of us might dismiss as clutter—a coffee mug, a lighter, a poodle-shaped stick pin—and yet the tales they tell about them are deeply meaningful and serve as a helpful way for the students to introduce themselves.

More recently, I worked with the author and editor Joshua Glenn to explore his interest in a material culture category that doesn't get much attention but offers a different take on decluttering: the meaning of objects we used to own. Specifically, we asked various writers and artists to tell us about the things they had lost—misplaced, broken, had stolen, thrown out, given away. A few even described willfully getting rid of stuff—a pair of walking shoes, a piece of macramé art, a Dodge Dart—only to long to see it again, or at least to lament the loss of the time it represented. In almost every scenario, nothing clarifies the instrumental value of an object more thoroughly than its definitive disappearance.

I'm sure you can think of a personal example: an object that's gone missing from your life that you'd love to have back, or at least see again. But I wonder—would you have known, when this thing went AWOL, that you'd miss it? If my mother had shipped her bird figurine collection off to me, would she have glanced wistfully at the empty spots on the shelves where they were displayed?

I can only speculate. But the lesson I've taken is: Be careful what you purge. Today's decluttering victim is tomorrow's lost object, and lost objects are forever. That's why I'm keeping my embarrassing ceramic leprechaun. I'm learning to appreciate it. It holds a connection for me—to my mother and to all her best intentions and instincts—that I never want to lose.

Copyright © 2024 by Rob Walker. Published in *The New York Times*, January 2024.

CHAPTER 2

PORTFOLIO

BY RICK GRIFFITH

> When you get it—and teach from that place—others will too.

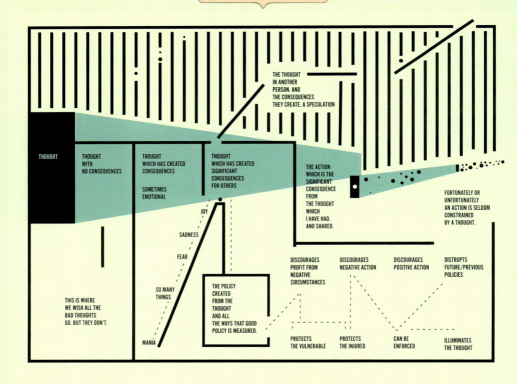

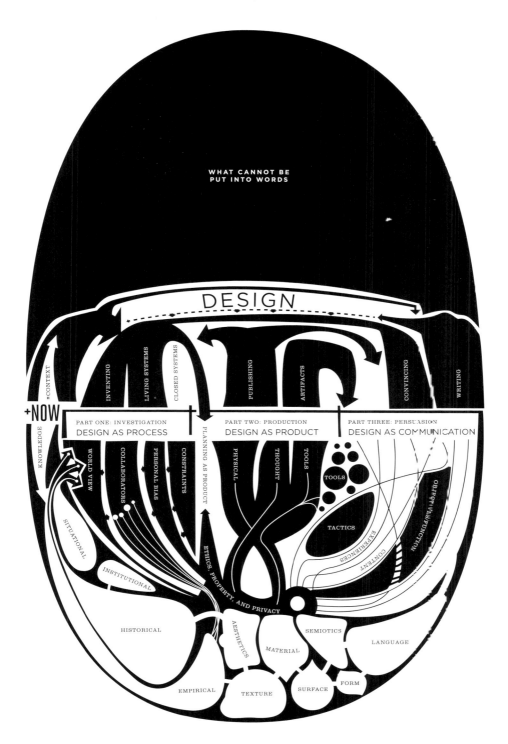

CHAPTER 2

An open system might specifically have an adaptive sensor which closes or opens an aperture for flow and quantity.

An open system might have a general effect rather than a specific contained effect, which in-turn allow for outcomes to be more spontaneous and human accessible.

A closed system might create a material only useful to itself.

A living system metabolizes something.

In other words, there is a fuel.

A closed system might be understood as having less contact with external variables, even though NONE would be very difficult.

A living system might have the characteristic of exchange or interdependency.

A closed system may have a flow door which may only open one way.

SYSTEM AWARENESS
PART ONE

VISUALIZATION: RICK GRIFFITH/MATTER LTD.

CHARACTERISTICS OF SYSTEMS

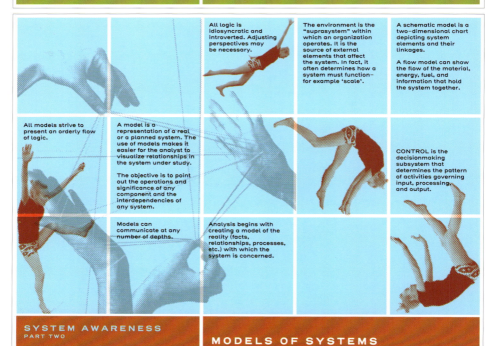

All logic is idiosyncratic and introverted. Adjusting perspectives may be necessary.

The environment is the "suprasystem" within which an organization operates. It is the source of external elements that affect the system. In fact, it often determines how a system must function— for example 'scale'.

A schematic model is a two-dimensional chart depicting system elements and their linkages.

A flow model can show the flow of the material, energy, fuel, and information that hold the system together.

All models strive to present an orderly flow of logic.

A model is a representation of a real or a planned system. The use of models makes it easier for the analyst to visualize relationships in the system under study.

The objective is to point out the operations and significance of any component and the interdependencies of any system.

CONTROL is the decisionmaking subsystem that determines the pattern of activities governing input, processing, and output.

Models can communicate at any number of depths.

Analysis begins with creating a model of the reality (facts, relationships, processes, etc.) with which the system is concerned.

SYSTEM AWARENESS
PART TWO

VISUALIZATION: RICK GRIFFITH/MATTER LTD.

MODELS OF SYSTEMS

WORDS NEED DESIGN

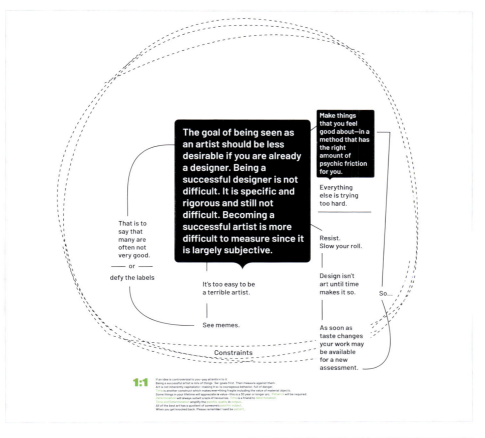

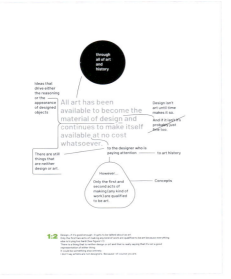

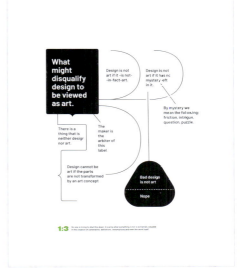

73

CHAPTER 2

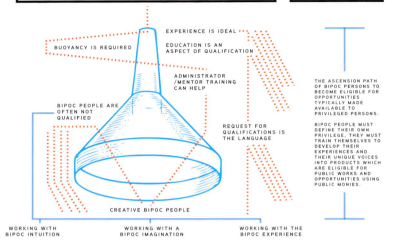

OPPORTUNITY IS WHY

THE OPPORTUNITY IS PERPETUALLY STATIONARY EVEN THOUGH IT IS A PRODUCT TO BE BUILT FROM THE IMAGINATIONS OF CREATIVE PEOPLE.

EVEN THOUGH SYSTEMS REQUIRE MORE EQUITY THE ELIGIBILITY MODEL DOES NOT SHIFT FOR FEAR OF CREATING MORE WORK FOR THE JURORS AND ADMINISTRATORS NEW SYSTEMS WHOSE REACH WILL NOT BE UNDERSTOOD WITHOUT DEEP AND THOROUGH INVESTIGATION

EXPERIENCE IS IDEAL
BUOYANCY IS REQUIRED
EDUCATION IS AN ASPECT OF QUALIFICATION
ADMINISTRATOR /MENTOR TRAINING CAN HELP
BIPOC PEOPLE ARE OFTEN NOT QUALIFIED
REQUEST FOR QUALIFICATIONS IS THE LANGUAGE

CREATIVE BIPOC PEOPLE

WORKING WITH BIPOC INTUITION
WORKING WITH A BIPOC IMAGINATION
WORKING WITH THE BIPOC EXPERIENCE

THE ASCENSION PATH OF BIPOC PERSONS TO BECOME ELIGIBLE FOR OPPORTUNITIES TYPICALLY MADE AVAILABLE TO PRIVILEGED PERSONS.

BIPOC PEOPLE MUST DEFINE THEIR OWN PRIVILEGE, THEY MUST TRAIN THEMSELVES TO DEVELOP THEIR EXPERIENCES AND THEIR UNIQUE VOICES INTO PRODUCTS WHICH ARE ELIGIBLE FOR PUBLIC WORKS AND OPPORTUNITIES USING PUBLIC MONIES.

BIPOC INTUITION, IMAGINATION, AND EXPERIENCE

DEVELOPING BIPOC IMAGINATIONS
BIPOC RUN, BIPOC SERVING
SHARED TOOLS, SHARED EXPERIENCE, SAFE SPACE

PRELIMINARY BUDGET ↓

36K RENT
5K UTILITIES
9K RENOVATIONS
4K CURRICULUM DEVELOPMENT
8K TOOLS
2K INSURANCE

68K ONE YEAR LONG EXPERIMENT
-18K RENT INCOME
50K NET COST (YEAR 1)
5-6 RESIDENCIES PER COHORT
2-3 CYCLES PER YEAR
SUBSEQUENT YEARS ~30K
4TERLY EXHIBIT/PUBLISHING CYCLE
@$300 PER MONTH EA.

There are opportunities, though it is more accurate to say that the opening which grants BIPOC people access to these opportunities defies gravity and is very narrow. So the handful of BIPOC people who are buoyant (able to thrive in mostly White spaces) and fast (prepared) can compete with every other competitor.

If the 'historically exclusive' eligibility conditions do not change then it becomes the responsibility of White people and arts administrators to make BIPOC people more eligible. This is done through training (& mentorship)—to become compatible with these opportunities and policies which STILL lack equity. Which in turn creates—for BIPOC persons—the requirement for gratitude, obedience (in the same systems which lack equity) and silence (less criticisms of the systems which they endure), which becomes the cost of receiving a competitive advantage.

BIPOC persons realizing their full artistic potential is ideal. Eligibility shifting to meet creative BIPOC people where their tools and strengths already exist goes a long way to help creative BIPOC people and their imaginations feel valuable and eligible for any opportunity.

If BIPOC people have been historically denied access to the means of production then the imaginations of BIPOC people will have to suffice as a qualifying instrument. But this must now be rectified. We (BIPOC Persons) will train BIPOC persons to bring their whole selves to the opportunities, in making monuments and objects.

WORDS NEED DESIGN

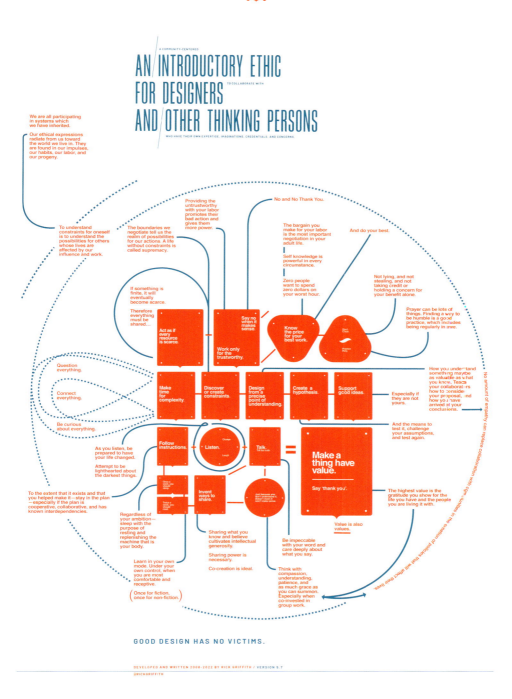

Copyright © 2022–2024 by Rick Griffith.

Questions demand answers. Design writers and interviewers once left designers to create their work, not to hawk it to a client—that's why middlemen were invented. But today, the designer has as much to say, if not more, than a mere salesman. Although some Q and As are little more than hype, many are handled artfully and bring out hidden decisions and motivations that reveal rationales that the interviewee has never plumbed before.

THE INTERVIEW

FACE TO FACE
SCREEN TO SCREEN

CHAPTER 3

THE ART OF THE INTERVIEW IN 10 SHORT LESSONS

BY ADAM HARRISON LEVY

On Being an Interviewer

Interviewing can be an act of empathy, or it can be an act of skepticism. It can be evocative, or it can be provocative. Or it can be both.

Interviewing is a performance. But it's an inverse performance because you aren't the center of attention, your interviewee is. It's your job to create an atmosphere that is conducive to revelation, a place where truth can be spoken. But you aren't speaking the lines. You're speaking the lines that prompt the lines.

To be an interviewer is to be part litigator, part therapist, and part scholar. You are a walking paradox: asking questions while listening to the answers, probing while responding, being forceful while staying flexible, and being willing to improvise while sticking to the script.

Effective interviewing is anything but formulaic. It's the balance between structure and improvisation, agenda and tangent, emotion and fact, that makes interviewing such a compelling form of inquiry.

1. On Questions

What makes for a good question? That is a question that someone recently asked me. For one panicked moment, I was stumped. But then I realized that being stumped was part of the answer. A good question zings through the air, creates a pause, and demands a considered, hopefully authentic reply. A rambling question usually leads to a rambling reply. It's hard to answer clearly when you don't know what is being asked. In the business world, it is stated bluntly: "Crisp your ask." More poetically, ee cummings wrote: "Always the beautiful answer who asks a more beautiful question."

2. On Not Listening

One of the biggest interviewing mistakes is the most obvious: not listening. You're thinking about your next question. You're wondering if you should have asked the previous one. You're worried that you're running out of time. You are running out of time. You're anxious that the interviewee thinks you're stupid. The interviewee is stupid. If you're not listening carefully, you can't ask your next question skillfully.

You might have your questions typed out on a piece of paper, noted on your device, or even memorized, but if you're not listening closely, you'll miss the pause that suggests doubt, the self-aware smile, the statement that contains a contradiction, or the intake of breath that reveals the impact of memory.

3. On Anxiety

Anxiety is as much a part of interviewing as breathing. Or it should be. Anxiety will drive you to research your subject thoroughly. It will also force you to think about your questions beforehand, arrive on time, and double-check your recording device.

But most importantly, anxiety will force you to pay attention to the words that are being spoken as well as watch for non-verbal clues. Anxiety, if you can befriend it, will keep you in the moment.

If you get an attack of the butterflies, remember what the great American journalist, Edward R. Murrow, once said: the only difference between the pros and the novices is that the pros have trained the butterflies to fly in formation.

4. On Interrupting

I have an elderly aunt who lives inside my head. Let's call her Edith. If an interviewee is going on a tangent my first instinct is to interrupt. But Edith chides me: it's not nice to cut someone off, she says. It's important to hear someone out, she whispers. Edith makes an important point. It's our job to give interviewees the space to make their criticism, articulate their ideas, or tell their stories as fully as they can.

On the other hand, Edith is way too polite.

Interviews are often about power. One of the most effective power moves anyone can make (most often by men) is to unleash a monologue that renders you, the interviewer, moot. PR people call this messaging, other people call it bullying.

When faced with a verbal onslaught, I practice conversational jujitsu. I wait for the initial wave of talk to roar past while making notes—mental or written—on aspects of their answer that will need clarification for shorter, more usable quotes. When the interviewee starts to slow down, I redirect with follow-up questions:

"That was fascinating. What I thought I heard you say was …"

"That was an impressive explanation, but I believe you overlooked …"

"Can you clarify the point you just made about …"

I find this technique of not immediately interrupting the least likely to lead to antagonism (unless that is what you want). The interviewee feels that they have said their piece. Now is the moment to move in quickly with your questions and get your quote.

5. On the Sweet Spot

There is a settling-in point, ten to fifteen minutes into an interview, when you've taken the measure of the interviewee, and the interviewee has taken the measure of you. Group your most important questions here. This is the sweet spot.

How do you know when you're in the sweet spot? The back and forth has become fluid and there are minimal hesitations or false starts. The attention of the interviewee is engaged. You're engaged. It feels like you are having a conversation.

You know you're in the sweetest of the sweet spot when your interviewee is answering your questions before you've even asked them. This is your opportunity to listen as closely as you can to evoke the answers that you need while spontaneously posing questions that you didn't even know you wanted to ask.

The sweet spot is finite: this flow state can last ten minutes but usually not more than twenty. Don't let it slip away.

6. On Silence

An effective technique to draw information out of a reluctant interviewee is, counter-intuitively, to stop asking questions. Most people talk more freely when they realize you are asking less. Worried that they are boring you they will try to keep your attention by filling up the silence with talk.

Robert Caro, one of America's greatest biographers, uses a notebook during his interviews. While waiting for his subject to continue speaking during a pause, and hopefully divulge some crucial information, Caro jots SU (for Shut Up) in his notebook to remind himself not to talk. His notebooks, he says, are full of "SUs."

7. On Ego

One of the most critical things to learn about interviewing is how to get out of the way. What I mean by that is cultivating the ability to stop trying to prove yourself. That's not to say that you shouldn't put your intelligence and your research into play, but it means not putting yourself first. Of course, you want to show you've done your homework, but there is no need to flaunt it. Your job is to ask questions that evoke answers.

Drawing attention to the depth of your research can be counterproductive. You don't want your interviewees to think that you're showing off: they might clam up. Why should they share their insights if you already seem to know so much?

8. On Not Knowing

You've done your research—read all the books, watched the videos, and prepared your questions. You've rehearsed, chosen your clothes, eaten properly, and turned up on time.

Even with your diligent prep there inevitably comes a moment during the interview when your mind goes blank. Empty. Nada. And you think: it's curtains. I'm a failure. I'll never work again.

But life is a fine teacher. Fearing that you've lost everything can be the right place to be: a place of not knowing. Now you can't hide behind your research. Your overprepared mind has abandoned you. As a result, you have to be fiercely attuned to the moment.

From this place of uncertainty, you're forced to be authentic. Since you've temporarily forgotten everything, all you have left are your spontaneous questions. As a teacher of mine once said, "Not knowing is deepest."

9. On the Inner Landscape

At its best, an interview is a journey into the landscape of another person. Sometimes it's a quick incursion in search of a short quote. Sometimes it's a longer exploration to help explain a design trend, an architectural practice, or a rebranding.

But there are deeper journeys as well, often for longer profile pieces. You might ask your interviewee to talk about their childhood memories, their struggles in graduate school, or the first years of their practice. The factual ground can lead to emotional ground: the public narrative giving way to the private story, the mask slowly dissolving to reveal a more authentic, perhaps more vulnerable, person underneath.

10. On Ending

My favorite last question, which has prompted some surprising answers, is one of the simplest: Is there anything else you would like to add?

Copyright © 2024 by Adam Harrison Levy.

CHAPTER 3

MARK MOTHERSBAUGH

★ INTERVIEW BY STEVEN HELLER ★

Mark Mothersbaugh is the co-founder, composer, lead singer, and keyboardist of DEVO, the eclectic New Wave band whose 1980 song "Whip It" was a top 20 single. A polymath and experimenter, Mothersbaugh creates music for television (including the long-running *Rugrats* series and *Pee-Wee's Playhouse*), assorted films, and video games through his production company Mutato Muzika. As a solo musician, Mothersbaugh also produced four studio albums: *Muzik for Insomniaks*, *Muzik for the Gallery*, *Joyeux Mutato,* and *The Most Powerful Healing Muzik in the Entire World*.

His long-awaited new book, *Apotropaic Beatnik Graffiti* (Blank Industries) is a hypnotically hyper-visual collection of neo-Dada stream-of-conscious visual poetry, representing one human's observations of "life on a sliding planet." I had to look up the word *apotropaic*—and you should now do the same.

Q. *It makes sense that a founder of DEVO would create such a beautifully bizarre book, but what does APOTROPAIC BEATNIK GRAFFITI mean to you? And how is the reader meant to interpret it?*

I started drawing, writing, and making collages on postcard-sized pieces of paper in the late '60s, and by the time the early '70s rolled around, I had come to realize they represented one spud's observations of life on planet Earth. They included everything from ideas for lyrics and sketches of dreams to questions regarding humans being the one species out of touch with nature. My obsession with these cards led to me creating a sort of intellectual repository of my work when I found this specific type of red archival album I still use to this day to keep my cards. At present, I have collected about 700 of these books, each containing 100 pieces of artwork. The central image of each of these cards is a photo of a plaster eye I had purchased in a botanica in downtown Los Angeles, between 1977 and 1979 ... I really don't remember the exact date, but I was impressed that the eye was intended to ward off evil ... its job was to protect someone from such schadenfreude, jealousy, maledicta, and evil-doers of all shapes and sizes. I repurposed the image into my artwork, adding stream-of-conscious writings and drawings, and creating my own take on apotropaic imagery. Inspired by the Beats, which had a significant influence on my early artwork and DEVO, and graffiti, which evolved as a vehicle for anyone to express their pure, unfiltered, honest thoughts, I created *Apotropaic Beatnik Graffiti*. The book isn't your average black-and-white print book. There are over 500 full-color images and about 40 pages of text with a flexi disc of a song I made using phrases derived from this book. There's no specific way to interpret this book other than being encouraged to go with your instinct. If you feel inclined to tear out a page that speaks to you and hang it above your bed or front door, by all means, go for it! The book can also be used like a Gideon's Bible or an oracle deck, where one can flip to any page and live out the key wisdom presented to them that day.

Q. *You refer to the book as interactive, which includes the reader is involved with destruction, construction, and reconstruction. How do you imagine the outcome of this?*

As I said, the "reader" is encouraged to rip out a page and place it under their car seat for protection or above their bed for good dreams. I hope to one day fill the bedside tables of all hotel rooms with copies of *Apotropaic Beatnik Graffiti*.

Q. *How does the book represent the activities of the serendipitous mail art movement?*

It doesn't really represent the mail art movement. Actually, once I realized I needed to keep these cards, I stopped mailing them out to people, and every time I finished another hundred cards, I would put them in an archival binder that I would purchase from a local post stamp collectors' shop. That was fifty-five years ago, and now there are approximately 700 of these red archival binders, representing close to 70,000 drawings and writings in my personal library.

CHAPTER 3

Q. *You have built a nonlinear book around a consistent and static image—an eye. Why the eye?*

Okay, this book draws from only five books in the 700 total I've been talking about, and they are atypical in the adherence to a central eye image on each card.

I was actually working on another much larger book than this, when these images caught my eye, so to speak.

Eyesight has always been an important concept to me since a young age. I was legally blind up until age eight when I received my first pair of prescription eyeglasses that forever changed the way I looked at the world. With this new superpower, I had the option of seeing the world as I had known it, blurry moving blobs of light and color, and this new-to-me perspective that was like seeing the world through a fish-eye lens or doorknob. That's how the size of the postcard became my preferred size for artwork, as that size was the only thing that didn't become curved and distorted from my glasses. In 2020, I became an early covid patient, and refused to believe it wasn't something "I was gonna just kick on my own." However, I landed in the hospital, luckily making it through, but suffering from an accidental eye injury along the way. Since then, eyesight has taken on a whole new layer of significance to me, as I can only now see out of one eye.

Q. *The eye does not seem mechanical but the book, despite what's going on around the edges of the meticulously positioned, fixed eye, leads this reader to wonder what is your intention? As I read it I feel I am being observed by an all-knowing presence—is this valid?*

No. It's merely a collection of thoughts and ideas from one human's perspective of the world around him. And, maybe. Maybe some of the eyes are reaching out to you in an attempt to protect you from the evil that floats around you ...?

Q. *You state that this is the compilation of many books you've made. Are you still making these?*

Yes. I draw on cardstock at some time during the day, pretty much every day. Sometimes I wake up in the middle of the night realizing I hadn't drawn on a card that day, and finish off a few more, making it easier to fall back asleep.

THE INTERVIEW

CHRISTOPHER LONG

★ INTERVIEW BY STEVEN HELLER ★

Q. *I had worked a long time researching Lucian Bernhard's life and work, and failed to uncover as much information as you have in what you refer to as a brief book? Where does the majority of this rich discovery come from?*

By the time I began writing this book in 2021, the trail had grown very cold. All of Bernhard's children had died, and I was forced to rely almost exclusively on printed sources. I simply followed the trail from one printed source to the next, looking very carefully for clues in each piece. Because many sources are now digitized, I also searched his name in a very large number of finding aids.

Q. *You note, and as I already knew, Bernhard had concocted some of the facts and lord knows how many—of his life, and his sons kept some of those myths going—for instance, one of his names was Emil Kahn— how did you separate the wheat from the chaff in your research?*

To be honest, Bernhard, as I wrote in the book, was a sort of serial fabulist. I discovered very quickly that I could not rely on anything he said or wrote. Instead, I used two strategies: one was to rely on pieces published at the time and to try as much as possible to confirm every fact. The second strategy, though, is a historian's trick—I simply asked myself if the story I was uncovering made any sense, and I looked for contradictions or assertions that seemed unlikely. It helps that I have worked extensively on German and American modernism in this period, so I knew when something did not smell right, so to speak.

CHAPTER 3

Q. *Without the benefit of talking to his sons (who worked with him when they finally arrived in New York from Germany) and daughter, Ruth Bernhard, the well-known photographer, how did you ferret out the material that you needed to tell his story?*

It was certainly a challenge not to have people I could interview. It is also a problem that the German newspapers, unlike those in Austria, have not been fully digitized. I simply and very doggedly read through every likely source. The primary published sources told the story. To the extent that it was possible, I also relied on archival sources, but that is hit or miss since so many were destroyed in World War II.

Q. *What are the original—and sometimes shocking—revelations that you made during the course of your research?*

The most surprising discovery for me had to do with the famed Priester poster. Nothing Bernhard had said about its genesis turned out, on closer inspection, to be true. What most shocked me was that it was the product of a long design process, lasting perhaps a decade. It is still a work of absolute genius, but not in the way that Bernhard wanted us to believe.

Q. *I was one of those who wanted, and did, take the stories at face value. Bernhard's work took a different turn when he came to live in New York. Do you believe that the American period of mundane poster work was because he no longer had German plakat style to play off against, and American advertising just beat him down?*

Bernhard was ever the realist. He did what he needed to do in New York to survive, and for him that meant adopting a far more "American" style. But I also think that he recognized that the time for the German Sachplakat had passed, and that he needed to evolve and change with the times. I do not think he ever believed that he had sacrificed something. He just kept moving on.

Q. *He designed over 50 typefaces between his German and U.S. work, what should be remembered most about Lucian Bernhard?*

It is difficult if not impossible to summarize the accomplishments of someone as prolific as Bernhard, but if I had to put it in a single sentence, I would say simply this: He was one of a tiny handful of figures who invented modern graphic design.

THE INTERVIEW

DEBORAH SUSSMAN
1984: AN INVASION OF BUTTERFLIES

★ INTERVIEW BY ALISSA WALKER ★

Alissa Walker launched the online platform Torched.la in 2024 with a goal of training "a critical eye on the civic investments and policy decisions that Los Angeles is making in preparation for its megaevent-hosting era, including the 2026 World Cup, the 2027 Super Bowl, and most notably, the 2028 Summer Olympic and Paralympic Games." One of the first pieces Walker posted on Torched was a 2014 interview Walker had with designer Deborah Sussman that delves into Sussman's role on the design team for the 1984 LA Olympics with architects Jon Jerde (JERDE) and Paul Prezja, who was her husband and partner at SP&Co.

When legendary designer, fashion icon, lover of LA, and my friend Deborah Sussman passed away in 2014, I had a month-old voicemail message from her saved on my phone. I'd known Deborah for over a decade and had covered her inspiring work many times over the years. And the last story I had written about her was an as-told-to about designing the 1984 Olympics published in *Los Angeles* magazine's '80s issue that summer. This had prompted her voicemail, where she praised the story—then offered a ten-minute design critique of the publication. "Alissa. Deborah Sussman. Fantastic story. Just a few thoughts about this magazine . . ."

As soon as I heard Deborah died, I decided I would publish the entire interview on my old blog, not only because she tells some fabulous behind-the-scenes stories about 1984, but also because the whole conversation reveals so much about Deborah, her lens on the world, and the very particular way she went about her work. As I was typing it all in—this was before the days of AI transcription tools—I could feel her personality leaping off the screen.

I spent several hours at the West LA home she shared with her husband and design partner Paul Prejza, which was filled with colorful trinkets gathered from around the world (and Eames loungers, of course). She insisted on pouring us tall flutes of cava at four in the afternoon.

"It's much better than champagne," she said as she set the bottle on the counter, definitively.

I took a sip and held up the flute to the light. She was right. The bubbles were tinier and sparklier than any effervescent drink I'd ever had. How had I never noticed this? Of course Deborah had.

For those of us who were lucky enough to know her work—and her blue fur boas and her Rudi Gernreich dresses—you can see that it is that same attention to detail which drove all her creative decisions, from her adamant insistence to use LA-specific flowers for the athletes' bouquets during the Olympics, to always selecting the perfect shade of hot pink.

When I wrote a story for *The New York Times* about the opening of her retrospective, "Deborah Sussman Loves Los Angeles, " one thing she said still resonates with me:

"Isn't this something?" Sussman remarked, her turquoise-lined eyes glittering behind purple-framed eyeglasses. "All my life, I was a hard worker, and I would add that much of the time, I loved what I was working on."

I hope one day I can stand in a room looking back at my life like that and think the very same thing. I think she would really enjoy me sharing some of these never-before-heard tales about one of the things she loved working on the most.

Q. *I did record a little bit of when we did the event at the gallery, so I do have a few things that you were saying that night, which was fun.*

DS: You know, all of us who were part of putting it together, we were all drunk. I think it was mainly because Barbara [Bestor] invited us to Musso's and we were all having martinis, and there were some people there that didn't really drink who were at our table. The rest of us got smashed.

Q. *That's how it should be. You were celebrating! So, I'm going to take you back to like five different moments we can use to tell this story, and the first one is when you received the call, when you found out that you were being tapped to work on this project.*

Well, it started not with a bang but a whimper, because we had thought that we were appropriate to work on the Olympics. However, before that all happened, they had told us—I don't know how much detail to go into—that it was all given to John Follis and Robert Miles Runyan. Robert Miles Runyan did the "Stars in Motion," and then they were going to give all of the environmental graphics to John Follis, who was older than me and he'd been a mentor mainly in terms of how you do environmental graphics, and what are the steps, and what's the fee and constraints. He was a mentor that way, and he had a name as a designer, and he was part of the then-old boys club, of which I was not.

Q. *And how old were you at the time?*

Well, I was born in '31 and we're talking about '82, '83, so I was 51-ish. And then along came Jon Jerde. Jon was a great strategist, and we started with the best client in the world, Harry Usher. He was an entertainment lawyer; he was charismatic, handsome, intuitive, risk taking, charming, and Jon had met Harry Usher and talked about the impossibility of building anything and the absurdity of trying to build a stadium or anything with just a couple of years and no money.

And Harry went along with Jon's concept. That was to take existing facilities and adapt them for the needs of the Olympics, so where you wanted big structures, the idea was use ordinary building scaffolding, and where there were intimate transactions with cashiers and tickets and so forth, that could be done in tents rather than in solid buildings. And so it was making use of the constraints in a very brilliant way.

And so Jon's office was working on ideas like for—I think in the beginning it might have been, well, I'll have to remember the sequence, but anyway the idea of using bar mitzvah tents and tweaking them, and the building scaffolding, and chain link fences, fencing, because everybody was all freaked about safety.

So there were all these more or less disregarded materials used for other purposes that were temporary, and the Olympics is a temporary event. So Jon came up with the strategy—it wasn't even adaptive reuse; it was using materials that were meant for one purpose for another purpose, so Harry loved the idea.

While that was happening I had been told, of course we probably called this guy, Dan Stuart, and he said well, thanks for your call but we've given everything to John Follis and Robert Miles Runyan. Well, that combo didn't sit well with Harry Usher. Jon was looking at it in a more or less logical somewhat conventional way. Jon had met us, and me, and he'd already started to talk to us about—or maybe we were already working on Horton Plaza—so we finally got an assignment, and the first assignment was only to do the signing plan for the UCLA Village on the field, so the athletes shouldn't get lost. And Jon said to me, don't even think about that. You dream, dream, see the big picture, and I did.

Somehow I saw in my head the sky and the ground sprinkled like confetti—sprinkled with all magical stuff that shimmered and that expressed joy, excitement, you know, expressed the goals of the Olympics. I have this thing in my head, and it came out. First of all, everybody was crying for a color palette, we need a color palette, and John Follis had already started a color palette, but it was very sort of academic and it certainly didn't have magenta and those crazy colors. He just thought there should be bright colors in the foreground, I think it was, and Mediterranean colors in the background.

Well, when I involve myself with color it's conceptual. I'm very intuitive, however, but when it comes to color, I'm also very conceptual. I don't just choose colors I like. I choose colors that are appropriate for the program at hand. So I went to the paper drawers—this is so long ago, can you imagine? I'm talking about early '83. Nobody used computers. We had paper drawers and we cut up paper, my favorite activity, cut up paper, and I had a mania for collage which was nourished in my years with Ray [Eames] and with Sandro Girard. And so I pulled these colored papers out of the drawer and they turned out to be the very colors that we used.

Q. *And you said they were papers you'd collected?*

Well, mostly those papers were solid-colored papers, but I also have a paper collection of rarer papers, but that's how we did color. So I pulled out these colors and I began to play with them, and they were the colors I had observed in celebration and areas of celebration along the Pacific Rim—Mexico, Japan, India, and little bit further away, China—the colors, basically, of the Hispanic communities that impact Los Angeles, and the Asian community.

We have a vast collection of photographs of Mexico, India, Japan—that's just FYI. Once, when the Olympics were over, we were invited to a conference in Mexico and we went to Mexico and Paul took pictures of fields of flowers, magenta mainly, that were in the Olympic colors, after we had done. So, had I never been at the Eames Office, had I never known Alexander Girard, known as Sandro, I don't know what I would have done, but nobody else in the world ever would either.

While it was going on, there was [Richard] Koshalek and the head of CalArts. Koshalek was at MOCA and—it'll come to me—and Koshalek came around while we were working and he said it's going to get the world's applause, and it did. But he said that while we were working in this big warehouse.

THE INTERVIEW

Q. *That's right. Tell me how you worked, when you had the team assembled.*

Well, Robert Fitzpatrick is the name of the head of CalArts who came along and said, he saw what we were designing, and he said, I want something of that on every one of my forty-eight, whatever it was, arts venues, so we did that, too.

So in the beginning, the committee was on the UCLA campus, and then it moved to this building where SCI-Arc used to be. Anyway, they wanted us designers to come and work in their headquarters and Jon said no, we have to have our own space. We have to be free. So they rented a warehouse on 6th Street near downtown. No, it was on 8th Street.

Q. *So, on the other side of 110 from downtown?*

I think it may have been just this side of it. But it was this big space, and I've got lots of stories about that, but I don't want to tell anything that's going to be bad for somebody. So what we had was sawhorses, and it was all temporary, like the Olympics. And Jon rightly strategized for all the Olympic design activity to have them under that one roof. And it was fantastic, because I could walk around, I mean there was a whole group of graphic designers and architects and industrial designers. And we at the peak numbered 150, but in the beginning it was just a few of us rattling around. And then we hired more and more people, and nobody had a budget, nobody knew how much it was going to cost, but we got paid.

So, that's what happened, and we gradually, I mean I have pictures of me pointing at some presentation board, you know, so people came and worked there. It was in the open, so that the leaders could see what people were doing. And everybody had goodwill. We were working just like an athletic team. The goal was further, higher, faster, and that's how we felt. And our group grew and grew, and it finally got organized into teams of people that would make sure that the stuff that was built and in rolls and everything came to 8th Street and went out to the right venue on the right truck.

Designers were doing this, not just designing, and that was one of the things that was so extraordinary and so fascinating, that people kind of—there were leaders of different components of what needed to be done, and there were people doing it, and we were all living under the same roof.

Q. *And just the fact that everything was manufactured here, everything was being produced, it was all local.*

Well, it was. At one point the committee said we've got all our sponsors lined up now. That was Peter Ueberroth's outreach program, and money is no object. But by then it was so late in the game, and almost every supplier west of the Mississippi was working on the LA Olympics.

I'll tell you another funny thing. When we were in 8th Street, maybe there was a conference room area, maybe not, but we put up this huge, huge piece of photo paper, floor to ceiling, and it was going to be the outline and the schedule and the spreadsheet for everything. Well, we got as far as the first week, and then nobody ever filled it out. Nobody knew what to write. We just did, we did it, and we made it, and we got paid. Could that ever happen now? I doubt it. I don't know, maybe.

Q. *What was one of the moments where you were challenged, and I'm sure there were many, but when you were kind of maybe scared that it wasn't going to be pulled off, or the drama moment.*

There were mistakes. I did a boo-boo. But before I forget, I just wanted to mention to you, and I don't know if this should be on the record or off. This should be off the record.

[She tells me something off the record.]

Sometimes you get so passionate about every aspect of what you're doing, at least I do, I get so emotionally involved and I want everything to be just right, and exactly just right, and things are coming along very well. So, there was a design that was supposed to be attached to the walkway to a bridge, above the walkway at the UCLA campus that separated the field from the village and the buildings on the left. It was the major walkway and there was this bridge, and the bridge had chain link fence on it. And so designers were making this beautiful mural that would have to be sewn or held together out of the different colors of nylon. And it was such a beautiful design.

So I went there. It was going up. It was in the evening, and the colors looked glorious, but all the pieces of nylon, the edges were crooked and sagging and I made them take it down. And I was saying to one of my lieutenants; let's just make it out of board so it'll be straight. And the awesome shots of it, unfinished in the nylon, like stained glass, glorious colors coming through, and I made them take it down. Isn't that awful? Awful, but that's in the fever, I was having a kind of fever.

THE INTERVIEW

Q. *Were you actually out there going to every site and looking at things?*

No, there were too many sites too simultaneous, so we had teams going to different sites. And Paul and I and Jon decided that the sites that were the most feasible for us to affect, and will be the most seen, were the ones that made our core group's attention, like the stages at UCLA Village and USC and the USC Village in UCLA, and the swimming venue.

And everybody was great. Everybody was great, except there's always somebody, one or two people, you give them thirteen or fourteen colors and that's not enough, they have to get some more colors of their own. That happened very briefly and not very seriously.

Q. *So as you're getting closer to the time and you have so much less time than Olympics now, like it's crazy how much more time they get to do things.*

Oh, they did before, too. Other countries had like ten years.

Q. *So why was the time so limited for LA? They didn't have the money?*

Maybe Paul remembers. I think it's partly because it wasn't going to be handled by the feds. It wasn't getting any government money, so that means all the money had to be raised, but the work had to be done while the money was being raised, and that's why everything was on the cheap, on the cheap, on the cheap, and at the end they said you can spend any money you want, and it was too late.

Q. *Did you ever get to take advantage of that part of it, maybe for the opening ceremonies?*

The opening ceremonies, oh, the ceremonies is a story all by itself, and it's not very pretty. David Wolper was in charge of ceremonies, and he did everything he could to ignore what we were doing. We had this design guide, and it had all the approved colors on it, and even though there was a red and blue, it had next to it approve colors, disapprove relationship. The disapprove relationship was red, white, and blue, but David Wolper did everything he could to make the ceremonies red, white, and blue with that Sam the Eagle and this fake rocket, and it couldn't have been more corny and more different from everything else in the Olympics.

CHAPTER 3

Q. *But were you behind when everybody held up those—*

No. That's a classic staging trick. We were not involved in that, and I don't even remember whether David made the colors red, white, and blue. There's a picture of us all looking at the coliseum in the *Design Quarterly*.

Q. *Okay, so there was that tension I guess between the red, white, and blue.*

Well, that is the only instance that I can remember. Sam the Eagle was a fait accompli long before we were hired.

Q. *Do you remember a moment where opening ceremonies happens? whatever, did you remember a moment where you could sit back and actually enjoy it enjoy what you had done?*

It was hard, because everything I saw, if only it could be this, or if only we had had another one of those over there. But it was pretty exciting. I mean, it was almost like I was in a dream.

Q. *Well, it was your dream. Were you seeing your dream coming true everywhere you looked?*

Yeah.

Q. *The confetti especially. There were a few moments I feel like where I saw videos, the confetti or something, or it just felt like confetti itself was sprinkled across the city. That's very much the way it looked.*

Well, Jon invented this phrase, "An invasion of butterflies." And he also invented "festive federalism," because we had inherited the story motion. If the story motion was in use, like on a moving vehicle or on a fast-moving screen, it blurred. But if you took the idea of the stripes and then you did playful things with them, you did other things with them in the different colors and not in red, white, and blue that became a language that Jon Jerde called festive federalism, and he said that about what I was up to.

THE INTERVIEW

Q. *What was your favorite small detail that maybe people didn't notice, that only you would notice?*

I'll tell you about two things. One was that there are people who work for the Olympic committee that get involved with the Olympics hoping and thinking and experiencing that it got them a lot of money and they got some notice. So there are these Olympic committee groupies that travel around, and sometimes we saw their picture in the paper, claiming that they did what we did. We never even met them. But we did meet one of them, and this guy was English, I believe, unless he was German.

And we came up with the idea that the winners would all get appropriate local, exotic flowers, including birds of paradise and other southern California or California kind of florae. And this guy said, you must be crazy. Athletes get roses, and that's what we want them to have. We? He. So we went ahead with our plan and there are all these pictures of the athletes with exotic flowers and birds of paradise, looking great. We have pictures. *Sports Illustrated* mentioned the flowers.

Q. *That's awesome. That's the kind of detail I like! You knew it was part of your style guide, you knew that would exactly fit particularly, and somebody wouldn't understand that who didn't have that same level of finesse.*

That triggered another memory that I wanted to tell you. One day, working down at 8th Street, I was sketching. I sketched; we didn't have computers, it was all done by hand, paste up, and so there was a picture of the hurdles and athletes jumping over them, and part of our mission was to identify everything that we possibly could as part of the LA 84. So I'm sketching on the hurdles, and I'm sketching that LA 84. It fit in that Corbu stencil type on the hurdle.

And Harry Usher came walking by and looked at what I had done, and he said, this is going to be very useful to us. And one of the reasons why it's so useful and so ubiquitous is that it didn't have those lines in it that the "Stars in Motion" had. It was very bold, very direct; it said LA 84, and that LA 84 became the name and everything it could be applied to, it was.

Q. *So that actually became the name of everything.*

That little sketch, this big. I had another story, too. When we began to work on the village and then everybody began to say, well what are the colors, what are the colors, there was a young man in our office of Asian descent, and he was very talented, and he said you're not going to use those colors for the Olympics. He said the Olympics are pure, they're like religion. They should be white. Well, his desire was lost in the avalanche of color.

Q. *But there was a lot of white, it felt like.*

Well, here's another story—I mean, I can go on for the next two weeks with stories. I don't think I will, though.

Q. *There was a brightness, that everything didn't have a lot of—*

Well, for example, if you're not sure what colors things are going to eventually need to be you can start off with a blank canvas, white. So one day, in the middle of all this, the committee hired this construction company to help make sure that everything got built, and so we dealt with this guy who in my memory is eight feet tall but he wasn't quite that tall, Big Ed. And Big Ed came over to me and he said, we're going to have chain link over every venue, it's a security thing, and so we need to know how many miles in each color you want, and we need it by the end of today.

So, you know, make use of the constraints. I just said make it all white and we'll put the color on it, and that's what happened. That decision to make it all white was something born out of the constraints of designing for the Olympics with almost no money and hardly any time. But then, we have many examples of graphics and color on the chain link fence, on the white material, because you could put anything on white, and you could leave white. So that's part of that story.

Q. *How long was it from the beginning to the end, the actual games themselves?*

The games were from sometime in July to sometime in August. I don't have it in my head right now but it's amply recorded, and I also have here the two volumes they make, about such a volume, that the LA Olympics Committee had to provide. Every Olympics has to have a record, and the record is of every venue and how many square meters and who won, and all those records and records and records.

THE INTERVIEW

Q. *Did you find, because things had to be up for a long time, were things getting stolen, were they getting vandalized?*

Here's a story. In many of the venues there was landscaping, a lot of landscaping, and so what was that landscaping going to look like and what was it going to be? So the landscape architects determined what flowers and plants would survive, and then we got involved with them and then all the plantings were grown offsite and then installed in the Olympic colors in the Olympic designs.

So, some naysayers said look, forget your dream. It's all going to be trampled and destroyed on the first day. Well, by the last day nothing had been trampled, and nothing had been destroyed. And I think the moral of that story is you do something really good for people and they will respect that. Now, that's not always the case, but it was the case in the Olympics. And we have photographs of the plantings in use and not being destroyed.

Q. *A lot of people said things like that, like it gave a sense of pride that LA hadn't seen before. Could you feel that when it was happening?*

Yeah.

Q. *Were people saying things to each other? What was the word on the street? I know people were worried about the traffic—*

All my cultural friends went to Europe or wherever, and all the culture of Europe and of Asia was right here.

Q. *So people left town because they were so scared?*

A lot of people left town. Was the previous one in Munich? I can't remember now. But everybody got lost. It was a disaster. So everybody knew that in the beginning, and that's where John Follis came in because he was well known for signs. The biggest challenge was going to be signing and people getting lost. Well, nobody got lost. It was easy, you know, we did the banners, there was David Meckel who fought with the DOT and the MTA and all of those things to get them to allow us to even have a little piece of the Olympics on some of these signs on the freeway.

Q. *So people definitely felt like it was their civic pride swelling during this time?*

Yes, I think so.

Q. *And a lot of people said that it made the city feel smaller, it made it feel—*

Accessible.

Q. *Accessible, yeah, I mean were you sad that it was temporary and that these things had to go away?*

Yes. Well, the Coliseum is a good example. When we were doing the Coliseum, the Coliseum commission, in all its wisdom, so distrusted the Olympics Committee that when the committee found the money to at least paint the coliseum and do a few other things they made the committee guarantee that they would bring it back to its pre-Olympics condition. And then when they saw what we had done, the Coliseum wanted to keep it but it was too late, it wasn't built to last.

You know that a number of the people who worked on the Olympics are no longer with us. Jon is barely with us, from what I understand, barely, and he hasn't been communicative for quite a while. And there are still people around who claim they did what they didn't do. You know, they were part of it.

Q. *We know that LA is going to be bidding for 2024.*

Do we know that for sure?

Q. *The guy that was at your event came up to me and gave me his card and said that he was the person from whatever, and then I also got an email from someone else saying that they're definitely doing it in '24, I think.*

When did you get these?

Q. *One guy reached out to me after I wrote an article, probably a few months ago, right after your show went up, and then the guy at your thing was like, yeah, we're bidding, it's happening.*

At which thing?

THE INTERVIEW

Q. *At your event. I can give you their names.*

I have the name of somebody, the guy who brought me up to say hello to Eric Garcetti. But at the same time, there's another thing going on and that's the LA World's Fair, and I keep getting emails about committees meeting and yada-yada, and between a World's Fair, which is basically a thing of the past, and Olympics which is a thing of forever, the Olympics is the way to go. Well, I would certainly be happy to meet with them and talk with them and so on.

Q. *Give them some ideas.*

Yeah, well, I think Eric Garcetti is just great. We are lucky. You can print that.

Q. *What's your reaction when you see other Olympic games now when you have watched the millions of Summer Olympics since these went up?*

First of all, my mind was blown with Beijing. You could never do that here. That level of discipline and conformity among that many people, it was just fantastic. With London, it's a weird story because they ended up using my Olympic LA 84 palette, and there are pictures of the London Olympics with a lot of magenta and a lot of aqua. And I thought, oh, so this is a picture of LA, and it wasn't, it was London 2012. And I tried and other people tried to get into a dialogue about why they used the LA colors and it never really happened. But I would never have used those colors to represent London. I can't give you the answer of what I would have used right now, but they wouldn't have been Pacific Rim, southern California colors.

Q. *I remember when they revealed it, and it's so funny now because I remember writing about the London stuff so long ago and when it happened it didn't feel that radical at all. But I think it was a lot of shock value, I think a lot of what they were trying to do was surprise people and not really make it much about London, just get a lot of attention.*

I thought the ceremonies were just enchanting, you know, queen and all those—I thought the ceremonies were absolutely just right on, because with the memory of the mass discipline of Beijing, the fact that they made it so quirky, and English humor was just the right way to go, is what I felt, and not make it pretentiously monumental.

CHAPTER 3

Q. *What did you feel the personality that was being put forth from LA was? Because you've mentioned two really interesting things about those, what was the kind of global opinion of what LA was putting out in '84? How were we perceived back then?*

That's a good question.

Q. *Do you think the Olympics changed that?*

Oh, I think the Olympics definitely contributed to put LA on a map that it didn't used to be on, that there is a flavor here. There's a flavor of Paris, pardon me, but for comparing Paris is my favorite city in the world, but LA was just big and white and movie stars and not serious, and I think it made LA more substantial in the eyes of the world. I never said that before.

Q. *I mean, it was a tough time. There are things that are bad that happened before, obviously, a lot of things had been changing, but it was kind of this thing of optimism we could hold to us. What about television, since it was broadcast so widely? Were you considering that?*

Oh, yes. One of the things that Jon pointed out, and one of the things that ABC—there are millions of people who are going to see this on TV, so it was very consciously designed so that it could be seen on TV. And I remember there were people that worked with ABC camera people and producers to make sure that the camera was pointed at the things—not just at the sports but got the rest of it. And so I think there were people who were saying it was the first time that it was designed to be seen on TV around the globe, and I'm not the expert on that.

Q. *I think that's true, I think it was the first time they had sold the rights to broadcast it and made money off of it, and so it was this amazing media deal and it was exclusive to ABC and all that stuff. So it was kind of the beginning of a media partnership that defines everything we do. And I think that's true, I think for the first time it was this package produced show?*

Of course it was on television, and the Olympics had been on television before and you could watch it at home, but this was the first time that it was this very polished package that you would tune into and it really made it part of your evening programming, or whatever time of day you were watching.

THE INTERVIEW

I think for a place to have mastered that, the fact that it was LA was pretty great because hopefully we'd be good at that since we produce so many things here that you're supposed to watch, so it's good that we mastered that one.

It's interesting also to compare some of the ideas that we had for television with Putin's games, because they took, the designers took patterns from classic—I don't know if it's all Ukrainian—graphics and fabrics and all of that, and I thought when you looked at each one of those compositions it was really beautiful, but the way they used them was kind of spotty.

The athletes had these vests that were cut on the diagonal, so you saw very little of the pattern. And whereas in our venues the entire screen, the entire field of play was ringed with a continuous design, whereas in Sochi, they were clumped. And I felt that had they been more continuous they would have been more effective and less complicated, because if you have a complex design in a complex shape they're fighting each other, so there, my Russian friends.

Q. *I think the Olympics that had been just before were the Moscow ones, talking about geopolitics, so remember we had boycotted them and then they had boycotted us. Was any of that weighing upon you, or did you feel like it wasn't—*

One of the reasons why Harry Usher was so interested and excited about bringing the design to the forefront was that the games themselves were going to be less exciting because of the Russians not being here. So to him, what our effort was, was also in response to the fact that they weren't here. I don't think we would have designed it any differently had they been, but that gave him a heightened interest in the design.

Copyright © 2024 by Alissa Walker. As published in torched.la, April 15, 2024.

CHAPTER 3

LAUREN CANTOR
A PINCH OF ARTIFICIAL, A DOLLOP OF INTELLIGENCE

⋆ INTERVIEW BY STEVEN HELLER ⋆

AI has triggered joy and fear, fascination and wariness, love and hate. It underpins the future of just about everything we will do, won't do, will make, won't make, as well as our fundamental beliefs as artists, filmmakers, musicians, designers, and educators.

Lauren Cantor, a polymath, multidisciplinary strategist with a focus on venture-based design, is an accomplished management executive who changed careers and graduated from the School of Visual Arts MFA Design program in order to follow her passions after working on Wall Street for close to twenty years. She now runs her own design consulting firm, Field & Edge, is a founding partner for an AI-driven consulting collective, NextAccess, and teaches design entrepreneurship.

Cantor's venture Verses Over Variables—which I consider the best online/email digest of AI innovation, education and elucidation—launched in June 2024, driven by what she describes as a trio of realizations: "the wealth of AI insights I wanted to share, my passion for writing about AI, and a desire to illuminate AI's transformative potential in productivity and creativity."

THE INTERVIEW

Q. How did your intense interest in AI develop? And what triggered the newsletter?

It was the fall of 2022, and Dall-E and Midjourney had just been released to the public. I was teaching at ArtCenter College of Design and SVA at the time, and I've always made it a point to stay ahead of my students when it comes to new tools. Once I started playing around with these AI platforms, I was completely hooked. It was like falling down the most fascinating rabbit hole you could imagine.

The real turning point came when ChatGPT was released. That's when I realized we were on the cusp of something truly transformative. Last summer, I co-taught a course on using AI for branding design. Watching students harness these tools to amplify their creativity was nothing short of mind-blowing.

As for the newsletter, the genesis is quite interesting. During the pandemic, I had started a newsletter about pop culture, tech, and business—primarily as a personal, intellectual exercise. I found a small but engaged audience.

The real catalyst came during my 25th business school reunion at Wharton last spring. Conversations about my newsletter and my teaching led to two unexpected outcomes: a daily WhatsApp chat with classmates where we dive deep into AI technicalities, and the formation of NextAccess, an AI consultancy with 12 of my former classmates. I transitioned to Verses Over Variables in June 2024.

Q. What are your general sources and how do you weed out the useful from the junk?

My approach to curating AI information is deeply rooted in my background as a Wall Street trader. In that world, sifting through news was crucial; company earnings, regulatory changes, elections, economic announcements, even weather reports could impact your trading position. This experience honed my ability to quickly identify relevant and impactful information across various domains.

While I've developed an AI program for headline searches, I still prefer a hands-on approach. I rely heavily on trusted newsletters and tech websites. This method allows me to maintain a holistic view of the AI landscape balancing technical developments with broader implications.

It's a combination of using cutting-edge tools and good old-fashioned critical thinking. In the world of AI, where developments happen at breakneck speed, it's crucial to have a discerning eye and a solid foundation of knowledge to separate the signal from the noise.

CHAPTER 3

Q. *What triggered your pivot to education . . . or has it always been there?*

The truth is, education has always been a passion of mine, dating back to my college years when I served as a TA for executive education science labs. After graduation, despite my degree in astrophysics and a minor in mathematics, I faced discouragement when trying to enter the teaching profession. I was told outright that "girls don't teach math or science"—a statement that seems almost unbelievable now, but was all too real then.

Throughout my career, I've always played the role of a "translator," making complex concepts accessible across various fields. I did this with my research and presentations on Wall Street, my seminars with Strategyzer, and my personal consulting work.

The pandemic provided an unexpected opportunity to reignite my teaching career through online platforms (especially at SVA). This experience reaffirmed my love for making business concepts accessible, leading me to expand my teaching engagements. I found that I really enjoyed making business accessible, so I reached out to ArtCenter.

What I've discovered is that teaching, particularly in the realm of emerging technologies like AI, allows me to combine all aspects of my background—the analytical rigor from my science days, the fast-paced decision-making from Wall Street, and the strategic thinking from my business ventures. It's incredibly fulfilling to be able to bridge these worlds for my students.

Q. *What is the goal of your AI explorations?*

At its core, my exploration of AI is driven by an insatiable curiosity and a commitment to lifelong learning. If I could be a professional student forever, I absolutely would. Currently, I'm taking a class on AI agents and developing automated tools, constantly pushing the boundaries of what's possible for me with AI.

But it goes beyond personal interest. Through NextAccess, the AI consultancy I co-founded, I'm working to help businesses navigate the complex landscape of AI, identifying opportunities for innovation and efficiency.

On a day-to-day level, I use AI constantly. It enhances my productivity, sharpens my thinking, and allows me to create things I never could have on my own. It's like having a tireless collaborator that's always ready to brainstorm or tackle complex problems.

Ultimately, my goal is to be a bridge between the technical aspects of AI and its practical, real-world applications—whether that is through writing or teaching or consulting. I want to demystify AI, to show people its potential for boosting productivity and creativity in tangible ways. There's so much fear-mongering about AI, but I see incredible possibilities for human-AI collaboration, and I want to help others see and seize those opportunities.

Q. *How do you believe AI will change design education and, ultimately, practice?*

AI is not just changing design education, it's revolutionizing it. It's becoming an indispensable part of the curriculum because, frankly, students need to master these tools to stay competitive in their future careers. The old adage, "AI won't take your job, but someone who knows how to use AI will," rings truer every day in the design world.

Education itself is evolving rapidly. We're moving away from traditional lecture formats towards more project-based, collaborative approaches. AI tools allow us to create immersive learning experiences that were simply not possible before. For instance, I can now use AI to generate a virtual negotiation partner for my students or create complex funding scenario simulations for startup workshops.

In professional practice, AI is becoming an invaluable tool for ideation, rapid prototyping, and even project management. It's not about replacing human creativity, but augmenting it. Designers who can effectively leverage AI will have a significant advantage in the job market.

The challenge for educators is to stay ahead of this curve, to teach not just the tools themselves, but the critical thinking skills needed to use them effectively. We need to prepare students for a world where AI is a collaborator, not just a tool.

Q. *There has been debate whether to call it a "tool" or something with more weight. How do you feel?*

I view AI as a tool, but an extraordinarily powerful one. It's comparable to how the calculator or the internet transformed various fields. AI eliminates much of the grunt work, allowing professionals to focus on higher-level thinking and creativity.

That said, it's a tool that requires skill and judgment to use effectively. I often describe it as having a tireless intern—it can do a lot of the heavy lifting, but you still need to guide it and verify its work. The real magic happens when human creativity and AI capabilities are combined thoughtfully.

Calling it "just a tool" might understate its transformative potential, but elevating it to something more than a tool risks obscuring the crucial role of human insight and creativity in its application. The debate itself is fascinating because it reflects our evolving relationship with technology and our attempts to understand its place in our work and lives.

Q. *Can AI become its own "artform," or is that off the table?*

I believe AI is already emerging as its own form of artistic expression, particularly in the realm of graphic art. The big issue, of course, is how the models are trained when it comes to copyright. But I think the new models, or at least the way responsible artists are prompting them, are moving away from directly referencing other artists' work.

It's reminiscent of how painters initially reacted to photography, or how traditional artists viewed digital art. What constitutes the artist's palette in the age of AI? Personally, I find that AI tools like Midjourney give me a creative freedom I've never experienced before. As someone with a math-oriented brain, I've always found it challenging to break rules or draw outside the lines in traditional artforms. AI tools provide a new medium for expression that isn't constrained by my technical drawing skills.

That said, I've worked hard to understand the techniques and the ethical considerations of using these tools. It's about finding that balance between leveraging AI as a creative medium and respecting the work of other artists. As this field evolves, I think we'll see entirely new genres of art emerge that are uniquely enabled by AI, just as we saw with the advent of digital art tools.

Q. *Where do you think you will take AI . . . or where will it take you?*

That's the million-dollar question, isn't it? I'm committed to continuing my journey as both a student and an educator in this field. I hope to expand my teaching to reach a broader audience, helping more people understand how AI can enhance their daily lives and professional practices.

On the consulting side, I'm excited about the work we're doing with NextAccess. We're helping businesses navigate the AI landscape, identifying opportunities for innovation and efficiency. I see tremendous potential for AI to solve real-world problems, and I want to be part of that solution.

Personally, I'm always pushing myself to learn more. Whether it's diving deeper into the technical aspects of AI or exploring its philosophical implications, I find this field endlessly fascinating.

THE INTERVIEW

Ultimately, I think AI will take us to places we can hardly imagine right now. My role, as I see it, is to help people navigate this new landscape—to see the opportunities, understand the challenges, and use AI as a force for positive change. It's an exhilarating time to be in this field, and I can't wait to see where it takes us next.

Copyright © 2024 by Steven Heller. Published in "The Daily Heller," www.printmag.com, August 23, 2024.

CHAPTER 3

HOW TO USE QUOTES

BY ADAM HARRISON LEVY

At its best, a quote communicates what I like to call the "grain of the voice"; it gives your nonfiction essay a texture that otherwise would be missing. What do I mean by texture? It can be your subject's distinctive word usage, the way he or she articulates an idea, or it can relay a piece of factual information that you, the writer, wouldn't otherwise know. A quote can be used as validation or as amplification. It can be damning or it can be uplifting. Deployed in various ways and for a multiplicity of purposes, the quote is one of the most powerful tools that a writer has at his or her disposal. The following are some of the most effective ways to use quotes:

As a Window onto Reality

Let's say you have spent your lede, the first three or four lines of your opening paragraph, summarizing what your essay will be about and perhaps introducing one or more of your cast of characters (if it's a profile). You have established the facts and laid the foundation for what will come later in the essay. But your text still lacks validation, the proof of original reporting: in other words, the grain of the voice.

A quote is a window of reality that punctuates the wall of your text. One of the most effective placements of this first quote is in the last line of your initial paragraph. You've built your establishing foundation brick by brick and then, just before you close out the paragraph and move on to your next thought, you provide a burst of light, the cadence of a quote, the zing of reality.

Mica in the Sand

The best quotes sparkle in your paragraphs like mica in the sand. Chosen with care, they shimmer with meaning. If you have a long passage in your transcript that contains important information, but would be too long to quote in full, choose the defining words, at most two sentences, that crystallize the core of what is essential in the words of your interviewee. This is commonly called the "pull quote." It's usually the most attention-grabbing or best articulated part of the passage. When writing a long essay, or making a podcast or documentary video, you will probably have transcripts of your interviews (whether generated by AI or you typed it out from the recording). It's useful to read through the transcript marking those phrases that initially jump out at you (your first instincts are usually the best). Once you find those, carefully read the surrounding text. You'll want to summarize the meaning in your own words with the intention of setting up your sparking quote to the greatest effect. You are providing the context that makes your quote shimmer.

The Witness

This is one of the most crucial uses of a quote. If you have interviewed someone who has experienced an event that you could have never seen, a quote from her or him will give credence to your story in a manner that is authentic and verifiable (it's your job to fact check) and will give your essay an immediacy that is unbeatable. A witness to a tragedy (a shooting, a bombing, a horrific accident) comes immediately to mind, of course. But also witnesses to history that you, the writer, could never have experienced. This is the timbre and substance of a first-person account. If used correctly, it has unassailable gravitas. I interviewed the man who, on August the 6th, 1945, handed President Truman the telegram that reported that the US had successfully dropped a nuclear bomb on Hiroshima. There is no way that any description of that moment could match George Elsey's words.

On the Shoulders of Your Ancestors

Quotes can validate your writing in a way that can be both effective and power-ful. Well chosen, a quote of a secondary source can lend your essay intellectual grandeur. It says: I have drawn my own hypothesis, analysis, or conclusions about this subject (be it a typographic form, a cantilevered building, or the evolution of car design) and here is a previous writer who legitimizes my ideas. You might want to call in the big guns of the last one hundred years: Susan Sontag or Roland Barthes or Walter Benjamin. This use of a quote can work as validation but also as amplification, but use it wisely. You don't want to sound pretentious, or that you are copping out by using someone else's thoughts as a means to drive your essay. Having said that, quoting a well-respected critic is a deft way to weave their insights into your text and suggest that you are building on a lineage of thinkers. In other words, you are standing on the shoulders of your ancestors.

How Long Is Long Enough?

There is no hard and fast rule about how long a quote should be. I like to keep them on the short side, one or two lines at the most. That's for two reasons. First, I'm a bit of an egoist when it comes to directing the flow of my writing, and conceding more than two consecutive lines I feel is giving away too much power. There are provisos of course: the primary reason for using a quote on the long side is if it's too difficult to edit without de-contextualizing the meaning. This is an ethical question and up to each individual writer. What do you feel is the morally correct edit? If you cut too much, are you willfully opening the door to a misreading? The second reason is aesthetic. This has to do with the musicality of your writing. Does the quote influence your tempo in either a positive way (it carries your rhythm forward) or is it a tripping stone that breaks the flow of your composition? Speaking personally, if I'm reading someone else's text and I see a long "block quote" coming up (i.e., an indented quotation) and it looks like it's more than two lines, I tense up like I'm about to get a dose of unpleasant medicine. I don't think that's a reaction you want. Try to keep it short.

Sometimes the Beautiful Quote

Sometimes you just can't muster the wit, the words, or the vocabulary to articulate an idea as well as your interviewee does, even if what they are talking about is not directly relevant to your argument. This is aesthetic cheating I know. Although I write with the classic dictum "kill your darlings" in my head, sometimes I think it's okay to let the darlings bloom and grow, especially if you have interviewed someone who is particularly articulate. This can communicate character more directly than any description you can write. As an editor once said to me, "try for just one delight" per essay, meaning one aesthetically pleasing turn of phrase that will add beauty to even the most pragmatic text.

An Emotional Truth

This overlaps with The Witness but has some distinct qualities. You might be writing about an event, or crafting a scene, which sets off an internal emotion that you, the writer, could never plumb with the same authentic individuality as the subject of your piece. Gore Vidal, the master of the mid-twentieth-century essay, wrote a reflective piece about the playwright Tennessee Williams called "Some Memories of the Glorious Bird." They are having lunch with Williams's mother, Miss Edwina, the real-life model for Amanda in Williams's classic play *The Glass Menagerie*. They are all eating shrimp. Miss Edwina asks her son why he is making funny noises in his throat while he is eating. Vidal quotes Williams's retort. "Because, Mother, when you destroy someone's life you must expect certain nervous disabilities."

THE INTERVIEW

The pathos and humor of that line is extraordinary, and it would be downright negligent for a writer not to quote it; it encapsulates the damage of a mother and son relationship with a raw emotional truth that Vidal could not have captured in any other way.

Signing Off

This is a case-by-case, essay-to-essay, article-to-article call. Generally speaking, the concluding paragraph is an opportunity to draw your themes together and recapitulate your argument. A tried-and-true method of ending your essay is to loop back to your lede but to give it a new twist in light of the journey you have just taken your reader on. Studies of memory, first undertaken in the 1880s, have proven that memory works by what is called the Serial Position Effect: that memory is influenced by the order in which information is presented in a sequence. The optimal place for information retention is at the start of the sequence (your lede) and at the end (what I like to call the sign off). It's in the middle of the story that gets hazy. The Recency Effect is what kicks in at the end of the essay: the readers' short-term memory holds onto the most recently learned information because it takes a relatively small amount of mental processing power as compared to what has been crammed into long term memory. In media slang this is "the take-away"—the powerfully memorable conclusion that you want your reader to take home with them. It's usually preferable that you have the last word: you are demonstrating your hard won "take" on the subject at hand. Or you might conclude that you can't conclude, which is a valid conclusion. However, there are instances when you may want to give it away and let someone else do the work of the final sign off for you, especially if your quote is unexpectedly humorous or evocative or ties into themes of your essay. Sometimes a quote can make more use of the Recency Effect and with greater impact and unexpected surprise than you could ever muster. So I'm going to sign off with a quote that I can't beat: Porky the Pig's "That's All Folks."

Copyright © 2024 by Adam Harrison Levy.

There are two kinds of critical, discursive, scholarly, and personality design writing for whichever the genre: short and long. The short form can be on major or minor themes, only requisite is that the finished text comes in at 900 words or (much) less. Some may argue that it is easier to write short than go long. Others may say that the short-form author is too lazy to write longer. Others say that long and short are two sides of the same coin. Value is not determined by size, only by content.

SHORT
FORM

CHAPTER 4

THE REAL BAMBI

BY STEVEN HELLER

✱

Let's consider Bambi. Yes, the bittersweet tale of a young doe downed by a hunter in that ages-old battle between cagey humans with weapons and innocent animals with instinct.

If social media had done nothing else of virtue over the past few years, it has been that Instagram Stories, Twitter, Facebook Reels, etc., have collectively given the animal kingdom a chance to star in countless cute videos (I have yet to find what is the equivalent on the dark web). Forget about invasive species, these cutesy videos speak to the joy of animals in their natural habitats—be it farm to forest—scampering and beguiling and otherwise showing sides of the domestic and wild kingdoms that we rarely see or cannot see enough of (how many of you are currently panda-obsessed?).

But back to Bambi.

According to a recent review by Piers Torday in the *London Spectator* of *The Original Bambi: The Story of a Life in the Forest* by Austrian author Felix Salten, Walt Disney had agreed to purchase the rights of this 1923 allegorical bestseller along with the license to alter it (for $1,000), not unlike other famously Disney retrofitted menacing yarns by the likes of the Brothers Grimm, et al.

"Walt is reputed to have suggested myriad unhelpful plot additions to the simple story. 'Suppose we have Bambi step on an ant hill,'" writes Torday, "he offered at one script meeting, 'and then cut away to see all the damage he's done to the ant civilization?'" Was Walt a fan of genetic engineering or did he have another hidden agenda with his metaphors?

SHORT FORM

•◆•

The Disney writers knew where to draw the line and changed the story considerably. Piers Torday writes, "The resulting 1942 forest fantasia, which leaps in swooning bounds from one extravagantly colored and orchestrated natural history lesson to another, was nominated for three Oscars, and by 2005 had grossed $102 million."

Salten, a Jew living in Austria who exiled with his wife to Switzerland, "never saw a penny of the Disney movie's global success" and died alone, forgotten. As it turned out, Bambi, along with Salten's one other novel, was among many books banned in 1935 by the Nazis, who considered it Jewish propaganda.

A surprising dark translation by the American scholar Jack Zipes illustrated in black and white by Alenka Sottler (published by Princeton University Press, 2022) underscores the fact that Bambi (who identified as a male deer) was never intended for children, although it was a coming-of-age story. With the exception of Bambi none of the original characters are present in the Disney version. Neither version is an evocation of violence—indeed the opposite is true—but the Disney "classic" was toned down a few notches.

Zipes makes it clear in his introduction to this new translation, Salten was a hunter but also became an animal rights advocate: "He was a man who hoped to overcome his own contradictions through literature, who believed that 'only when people truly understood how the animals suffered persecution from hunting in the forest could they create peace among themselves.'"

"It's quite evident," wrote Zipes, "that the shooting and the treatment of the animals are an allegory of the situation Jews found themselves in at that time." The Disney version implied hunting animals is wrong; authored after the Great War and before the rise of Nazidom, Salten's original may have been predicting that hunting humans is the next step.

Copyright © 2022 by Steven Heller.

CHAPTER 4

SPOT ADS

BY STEVEN HELLER

✳

I t was the X (formerly Twitter) of the nineteenth century, or was it? Rather than 140 characters, spot advertisements (like telegrams) were priced according to the number of words used. Often the shorter the ad the more bang for the buck, as long as one was able to read the small "agate" type. Late nineteenth-century newspapers, like this 1893 edition of *The San Francisco Examiner*, were typically typeset—and designed—to allow for as much news as could fit on a column or page, and to allow as many adverts as the word-packed page could hold.

The ads may not be poetry or poetic typography, but they are relics of a period shortly before the advent of advertising agents and long before newspaper designers walked the earth. These raw, hand typeset spots were both a popular and ubiquitous method of advertising everything from "Fall and winter bonnets, ribbons, flowers, plumes &c." to "Improved Ambrotypes" (early kind of photograph), to "Sea otter, land otter and beaver skins." As tweets of the day, they could not afford verbose copy or decorative flourishes. Some ads included the occasional, excruciatingly tiny spot engraving. Yet amazingly, the small space had quite a hard punch. Eyes moved to the rhythm of the page.

The general late nineteenth-century newspaper reader was conditioned to see (and read) the small type, but also to have their eyes widened by the large headlines and subheads. They understood that bold type signaled something special, so take notice or that all caps was an announcement not to be missed. Type foundries knew they needed to make fonts that would capture attention while fit within the proscribed fields of the paper measurements. And the advertiser understood the value of targeting certain words or phrases—the birth of the word- or sound-bite.

It was all quite primitive and chaotic. When analyzed today, the hodgepodge made from dozens of discordant typefaces, the unwieldy settings—some justified and others asymmetric as though fighting each other for a place on the page—suggests anarchy. Yet this un-designed composition is reined in by the confines of the page. There is a curious balance, the sum of many parts that made a sublime whole.

Copyright © 2010 by Steven Heller.

CHAPTER 4

CAN POSTERS HELP?

BY STEVEN HELLER

This is a loaded question and a vexing title. I am going to try to answer it. Posters have since the nineteenth century served many different social, political, and commercial functions. If you consider social messaging to include politics and health care, among other human rights and services, then the answer to the question must be addressed in two parts. Posters are tools of commerce and society—sometimes the two intersect but not always. To the former is the answer: Yes! Posters continue to have a vital place in the consuming culture. They advertise everything from food and fashion to cars and computers—in fact, everything we consume can be introduced for the first time to the public, who as a rule are delighted to see the constantly changing posters on walls, hoardings, and billboards. These commercial posters inform and entertain on themes as broad as art shows, musical concerts, television programs, lifestyle products, and so on. The latter requires a more ambiguous answer.

Posters can also, just as importantly, advocate, protest, caution, and educate a viewer or audience on such topics as glory or horror of war, the serenity and virtues of peace, the dangers of climate change, the necessity of safe space, the norms of community, the gift of hope, and the value of events that bring individuals together.

SHORT FORM

Taken as a whole and assuming the design and content of the posters in question meet certain qualifications—grab attention, elicit response, challenge perception, and infiltrate the mind of the receiver—then and only then can posters help augment reality. In short, they do help in a variety of mnemonic ways.

Not all posters function at the same level of useful intensity. Self-indulgent design can be a liability. Over-stylized imagery can dilute a message. Yet legibility and readability (two different attributes; sometimes the former means the latter is inescapable). Posters for social (including among other issues, gender and sexuality), political (including issues rights, law and freedom in general) and any personal concerns (whatever they may be at any given time and place) can be accomplished as quick as the creative (or polemic) mind can conceive them, produced and distributed in large numbers through a specific locale or countries around the world.

The golden age of the poster has long been considered the pioneering turn of the century, then the modern mid-twentieth century, then the psychedelic sixties, and so on through the decades, in Europe, the U.S., and Asia. Today is another golden age. It is the digital golden age. Can posters help? They will help issues, causes and most important they help people be aware of the world in its present state.

Copyright © 2015 by Steven Heller.

CHAPTER 4

THE EVIL EYE OF ENVY

BY MOLLY HEINTZ

I f you buy a piece of jewelry in Greece, you may later discover a strange blue-and-black bead in the box, nestled against your gold bracelet or necklace. You should *not* return the bead or throw it away. This miniscule glass orb is for you, and your life may depend on it.

The Evil Eye, that ancient curse delivered via menacing glare, is intended to bring harm or even death to another human being. A special edition of this curse, the Evil Eye of Envy, goes beyond general bad vibes and acts as a kind of cosmic comeuppance. Any good fortune publicly displayed in the form of a new house, healthy children, or diamond earrings makes a prime target for Envy, who is always on standby to ruin the year of one of Fortuna's favorites.

The Greeks have long believed that the best protection against the potent Evil Eye of Envy is its own image. Personal amulets intended to be apotropaic—able to turn away evil—often bore elaborate scenes of threatening animals like ferocious lions and pointy-beaked cranes attacking a giant eye. Over the years, this iconography was streamlined and reduced to the simple image of the Eye itself, always in blue. (In the Mediterranean region, the rare blue-eyed person may be an unwitting carrier of Evil Eye powers.)

My own Evil Eye bead sits in the coin section of my wallet and monitors the daily cycles of my personal wheel of fortune, where dollar bills come in and out, credit cards approach their limits, and taxi receipts accumulate in direct proportion to delusions of grandeur. About a third the size of a marble, the Eye is at once present and discreet. I received it from a superstitious friend around the time my son was born, and I've carried it with me ever since, as a form of free, otherworldly insurance.

If I downsize my gear for a weekend afternoon and transfer some essentials to a smaller coin purse, the Eye comes along, too. I cannot prove it's functioning, but even on tough days, when I glimpse its bright blue flash or touch its smooth surface while digging for an elusive dime, I think, "Who knows how bad it could have gotten without the Eye?"

Copyright © 2017 by Molly Heintz. Published in *HiLoBrow: Talismanic Objects,* June 8, 2017.

CHAPTER 4

THE CARCAÇA

BY FREDERICO DUARTE

✹

The "O Design Nosso de Cada Dia" [Our Daily Design] feature ran from June 5 to September 25, 2011 in Pública, the Sunday magazine of Público, Portugal's daily newspaper of record. "The Carcaça" was the last of seventeen articles published over that summer.

A carcaça is made of water, flour, yeast, and salt. But this piece of bread does not reach our hands, or our mouths, as a simple amalgam of raw materials: it reaches us in a certain way and with a certain form. Before it even becomes what it is, a carcaça only comes into being after the salt has been extracted, the wheat milled, the water piped, and the yeast packaged. These are just some of the countless processes, systems, and devices that underpin not only the production, distribution, and sale of products such as bread, but our entire life in society. All of them are the result, in one way or another, of a design process.

The carcaça was conceived and designed by a Portuguese person. Who in this case, as in so many other examples, is not even a designer by profession.

Vítor Moreira is a chemical engineer by training but has long been known as the "Bread Pope," a title that recognizes the importance of this octogenarian to the bakery trade and industry in Portugal.

He was already working for the Fábrica Portuguesa dos Fermentos Holandeses (the Dutch Yeasts Portuguese Manufacture) when, in the 1950s, to compensate for the increase in the price of grain—which, according to him, meant that "a kilo of bread would cost less than a kilo of flour"—and to limit imports, Salazar's government authorized a reduction in the weight, but not the price, of bread.

To improve the profitability of each bakery given the tiny margins allowed by law, Moreira took the papo-seco, "a Lisbon bread," and made two simple, yet important changes to it. First, he removed the two pointed ends, the popular "maminhas" (boobies). Then, he made a slash along its length.

Due to the "finishing" of its edges, a papo-seco needed to be made with two hands. Them gone, a carcaça was produced with one hand only: just take a small portion of dough, roll, rest, and score.

This meant that instead of an average of 40 papo-secos, a "reasonable baker," as Moreira recalls, could make "up to 70 carcaças per minute."

The name "carcaça" evokes "a type of bread already made in a large format," so large the slash was made with the forearm. This slash also had, both in the old and the new carcaça, a function: by increasing the surface area exposed to heat, it intensified the expansion of the dough and, consequently, the volume of each piece of bread. In other words, "more bread" for less weight.

In the following years, the courses and demonstrations promoted by Fermentos Holandeses for bakers across the country were responsible for spreading Moreira's design, making it the everyday bread of many Portuguese bakeries.

At the same time, the gradual inclusion of machines in the manufacturing process—such as the leaven and delay conveyor belts or rolling tables he designed—industrialized the process that through the gestures Moreira introduced became more "machine like." This increased the scale, efficiency, productivity, and yield of bread-making. And much like other manufacturing processes in which design, or design thinking, intervenes to save resources and increase gains, also this had as one of its main goals the reduction of manpower: to make more bread with fewer jobs.

Nevertheless, Moreira himself assumes that still today "our bread-making is artisanal," or semi-industrial: although it's made with machines, bread is not made without people. And the making of bread is only a part of the process, and of the designs, that take its four raw materials to our table.

It was not to take this feature's title, "Our Daily Design," literally that we chose the carcaça as the last of its subjects. Rather, it was to reaffirm that just like bread, design is neither an adjective, nor an addition, or an exception to our daily life. And that, just like bakers, designers respond to our needs and most basic desires, reflecting in their activity the technological, social, cultural, and political contexts in which we live. Almost always discreetly. And every single day.

Copyright © 2011 by Frederico Duarte.

History is storytelling, myth making, and reflection. Writing design history has become a viable discipline, having grown during the past five decades from very few to many writers and researchers. In turn, more readers take pride in learning the legacies, myths, and forecasts of the design arts. Research is integral to the practice. The writer must be aware of what has been and what will be by virtue of their own discoveries and commentaries. History should never be pedantic but it must reveal, engage, and demand forethought in creating an arc and cadence that the reader will gladly follow.

WRITING HISTORY NOW

CHAPTER 5

TYPOGRAPHY CRACKED THE VOICES OF SILENCE

BY STEVEN HELLER

✳

"Typography cracked the voices of silence," Marshall McLuhan famously wrote, in *The Gutenberg Galaxy: The Making of Typographic Man* (1962). Typography also injected words with expression, emotion, and, let's not forget, dimension. Yet when Gutenberg's typography began filling the void, McLuhan further argued, "the human voice closed down. People began to read silently and passively . . . Architecture and sculpture dried up too. In literature only people from backward oral areas had any nuance to inject into the language."

Come on, professor M! Can typography really be to blame? Through a multitude of styles and variations, typography contributed more to communications than any discovery, with perhaps the notable exception of those storied prehistoric cave paintings at Lascaux, La Marche, and Cave of Niaux. Typography may have impinged briefly on oral narrative traditions yet the extraordinary accessibility to printed words increased other widespread forms of storytelling.

Dimensional typefaces made all kinds of stories even more visible. These typefaces were not designed for solitary reading or quiet contemplation. They are loud and bold. And if you capture the eye, the mind will follow. Noisy letters were made to demonstratively impact consciousness through exaggerated scale, shape, and ornament.

"It was the nineteenth-century printer who was first confronted with this demand on his skill," wrote Canadian typographer Carl Dair in *Design with Type* (1952). "He turned to strong display and decoration as a means of attracting attention to the message. Highly decorative types and ornaments were cut to meet the demand for something new and different; printers competed among themselves to see how many different type faces could be jammed into the setting of a single message; type founders cut large wood type, hoping that sheer size would over-power the reader; compositors outdid themselves in bending and twisting their rules and type lines, only to produce a typographic wreckage."

An orgy of decoration produced a plethora of shadow typefaces. Designers and craftspersons used wood, metal, and even glass to create typography for selling products and, as Dair explained, "the results found a ready sale among the newly rich merchants and members of the industrial class," who expected to make their businesses visible to the general public. Shadows were more than mere graphic tricks, they were signposts of consumption.

The genesis of shadowed letters is not entirely in the shadows. They can be seen in liturgical manuscripts (albeit in very elaborately decorated forms). They make rare appearances in late eighteenth-century merchants signs, as well. But come the early nineteenth century, shadows begin to profoundly emerge as hand drawn iter-ations of both classical and newly invented type styles. Introduced as metal type-faces as early as 1815, the typefounders Vincent Figgins, William Thorowgood, and Blake Garnett popularized many of the most lasting. But the shadow's widespread use for printing developed later in the nineteenth century, when it was essential for burgeoning businesses to compete with posters and bills increasing in the multitudes. And signs and adverts on urban and rural buildings employed shad-owed lettering for visibility.

Many shadowed types began as fat faces with typically thin stems and hair serifs that often proved difficult to print faithfully on conventional presses. Consequentially, type founders compensated by adding dimensional devices to the more troublesome cuts—and were pleased with the surprising illusionary results.

"It is as if the designers were absorbed in enjoying the ingenuity of their own invention," wrote type historian Nicolete Gray in her book *19th Century Ornamented Typed Faces* (University of California Press, 1977). Commercial job printers quickly adopted dimensional faces since whatever the size they seemed to jump off the printed page.

With the surge in popularity among printers and their clients, foundries issued generous selections of styles and sizes—some were rather awkward concoctions while others were curiously elegant. Even the literary giant Honoré de Balzac, the proprietor of his own Parisian type foundry, issued a lavish specimen catalog that

Shadow faces are typographic trompes l'oeil, facsimiles of real three-dimensional architectural letters and inscriptions, which are dramatized owing to the numerous ways in which natural or artificial light falls upon them.

included a varied assortment of *Lettres Egyptiennes Ombrées*—heavy slab serif types with linear dimensional shading. Shadowed wood type, which came in extra-large sizes, was also in demand during the late nineteenth century, designed for outdoor use, to seize the eye of the frantic passersby. Shadows—custom drawn or as types—were indeed perfect as newspaper and magazine mastheads, product labels, signs of all kinds and posters galore.

Toying with viewers' perceptions is the job these letters perform so well. From their inception, shadowed letters challenged limits of cognition. Whether framed by a subtle tint or bold silhouette, in color or black and white, a shadow adds dimensional bulk, enabling words to rise monumentally and voluminously from otherwise flat surfaces. Shadow faces are typographic trompes l'oeil, facsimiles of real three-dimensional architectural letters and inscriptions, which are dramatized owing to the numerous ways in which natural or artificial light falls upon them. Light increases or decreases the tactility and depth of the shadow as the sun rises and sets, altering both shapes and proportions. This sculptural essence adds immensely not only to the letters' visibility, but also to their allure.

Commercial sign painters mimicked these sculpted letterforms in hand-painted facsimiles that were routinely rendered on glass, wood, canvas, enameled metal, or whatever acceptable surface. Although shadowed typefaces are frequently found on small printed pages and posters, the finest—indeed most colorful—examples appeared on late nineteenth and early-to-mid twentieth-century store windows and glass or enamel merchant's signs—all of which were created by hand with uncommon precision. Before the explosion of neon in the early twentieth century, and even afterward, shadowed letters substituted as virtual illumination. Depending on the intensity of the artificial light source, hue of the silhouette, and color of the background on which they sat, the letters were often radiant. Years of hard-earned skill were needed to make these shadows work because when ineptly handled the letter could look unpleasantly grotesque.

Shadowed typefaces exemplify the nineteenth-century gilded age aesthetic. But shadows have never become entirely passe. A well-composed stack of luminescent shadowed letters on a poster can still be as aesthetically satisfying as any beautifully designed piece of furniture. Like hemlines, shadows increased or decreased in size depending on fashion's vicissitudes. During the early twentieth century, typographic or branding styles did not fluctuate quickly as they do today. So merchants were not as quick to replace their signs, trademarks, or publicity on a whim. Shadow type was, therefore, more integrated into the overall vernacular of commercial art. And as graphic styles evolved from Victorian to Art Nouveau to Art Deco, shadows evolved as well. Only during the Bauhaus and later Swiss typographic periods of the 1920s through 1940s were drop-shadows considered to be decorative indulgences.

The specimens and examples collected here date from the turn-of-the century throughout the 1930s (signaling a streamline ethos), with some from the 1940s (expressing a noir sensibility). Shadowed types from the 1950s were nothing particularly new, essentially copies of earlier designs. Yet in the 1960s, with revivals of Victorian, Art Nouveau, and Deco and the transfiguration of vintage typography into psychedelic youth codes, shadow letters returned in full flower. Today, they are just another lettering and typographic option in the designer's tool kit. Yet for us this type of typography truly casts a long and exciting shadow.

Marshall McLuhan, *The Gutenberg Galaxy: The Making of Typographic Man*.
Essay Copyright © 2023 by Steven Heller.

CHAPTER 5

PLAYING TO TYPE

BY VIRGINIA POSTREL

Given its subject, Michael Bierut's *Seventy-nine Short Essays on Design*, published in 2007 by Princeton Architectural Press, is remarkably plain. It has no pictures. It isn't oversized. It doesn't even have a dust jacket.

Yet the book is a graphic extravaganza. Each of the 79 essays is set in a different typeface, ranging in age from Bembo, designed in 1495, to Flama, created in 2006. This profusion of typefaces would have been inconceivable when Bierut, 50, was starting out as a graphic designer.

"I'm not sure in 1982 I could have come up with 79 different text fonts," he says.

Nowadays, even nonprofessionals take an abundance of typefaces for granted. My computer includes about 100 English-language fonts, many of them families encompassing multiple weights—Baskerville in bold, bold italic, italic, regular, semibold, and semibold italic, for instance—and all available instantly. Basic cultural literacy now demands at least a passing familiarity with typefaces: witness a November episode of *Jeopardy* that featured the category "Knowledge of Fonts," with correct responses including "What is Helvetica?" and "What is Bodoni?" A thoroughly entertaining (really) documentary called *Helvetica*, tracing the rise and fall and rise of the 20th century's most ubiquitous typeface, played to sold-out crowds on the film-festival circuit last year.

The profusion of fonts is one more product of the digital revolution. Beginning in the mid-1980s and accelerating in the 1990s, type design weathered the sort of radical, technology-driven transformation that other creative industries, including music, publishing, and movies, now face. Old business models and intermediaries disappeared seemingly overnight. Software replaced industrial processes. Tangible products—metal, film, computer disks—dissolved into bits and bytes sold over the internet. Prices plummeted. Consumers started buying directly. From their kitchen tables, independent designers could undertake experiments that had once required bet-the-company investments.

"Having an idea for a typeface used to be like having an idea for a new-model car," says Bierut. Now the distance between idea and execution, designer and user, has contracted.

Though still a tiny number—maybe a couple hundred worldwide—more people than ever are making a living designing type. Many others, mostly graphic designers, have turned type design into a profitable sideline. And more people than ever are buying fonts. Tens of thousands of fonts already exist, and more are created every day. The question is why.

For designers, the rigidity of an alphabet presents a never-ending artistic challenge: How do you do something new and still preserve the letters' essential forms?

"It's a similar sort of urge that a painter or a sculptor or a musician would have who wants to bring something new into the world," says Matthew Carter, the dean of U.S.-based typeface designers and, thanks to a teenage internship at a Dutch printing company in 1955, one of today's few working designers who learned to cut metal type by hand. Carter's creations include Verdana and Georgia, which he designed for Microsoft, and Bell Centennial, the font used in phone books.

Unlike painting, sculpture, or music, typefaces must be useful to someone. Fortunately for designers, the digital age has produced new problems to solve—developing typefaces that work on mobile phones, for one—and enabled better solutions to old problems. In 2001, *The Wall Street Journal* hired Jonathan Hoefler and Tobias Frere-Jones to create a new typeface for its financial tables. The result, called Retina, uses the microscopic precision of digital design to correct for the blurring that takes place when thin ink hits cheap paper at high speed. Designed for tiny agate type, Retina looks bizarre at larger sizes; Frere-Jones compares it to a fish evolved to survive at extreme ocean depths. The strokes of the lowercase t pinch in at their intersection, making them look more like four blunt arrows than two bars. The triangle in the uppercase A bulges slightly inward. The dot on the lowercase i is square and wider than the downstroke, and each curves away from the other. Such distortions compensate for ink blobs, making the font more readable than its predecessors. More recently, the designers created a toned-down version of Retina for *Journal* headlines.

When *The Journal* shrank its pages in 2007, it adopted another font, called Exchange, developed by Hoefler and Frere-Jones for article text. Exchange lets the paper get more on the page while improving legibility. The font works, Frere-Jones explains, by "taking the unique feature of [each] letter—its essence, the thing that makes it this letter and not something else—and turning it up as loud as it can go." The exaggerations are obvious at larger sizes, but invisible to readers of *Journal* articles.

Not all customers looking for new fonts are so technically demanding or, for that matter, so large or famous. Graphic designers, from solo practitioners to large firms, still account for most licenses. Often, they're simply looking for something new, a signature typeface for a publication or corporate client. Helvetica documents the eternal graphic-design debate between partisans of unobtrusive fonts like Helvetica—the reigning metaphor is a "crystal goblet" that contains the words without calling attention to itself—and those who prefer more distinctive, expressive alternatives.

Professionals believe the right font adds valuable nuance to graphic design. Michael Bierut's essay on the AT&T and Bell Telephone logos appears in Bell Gothic, the typeface that Carter's Bell Centennial replaced in phone books.

"That's like a little bit of visual aromatherapy to set the mood," says Bierut. And in these days of PDF files and computer printouts, fonts are one of the few graphic elements that designers still control. "Often you can't pick the paper or the ink," says Bierut. "The one universal thing is the typeface."

At the basic consumer level, the profusion of fonts appeals to a culture that celebrates expressive individualism. Who wants old-fashioned wedding invitations—"Mr. and Mrs. John Smith request the honor of your presence" embossed in black on ivory paper—when you can have paper and ink that match your color scheme, and language you've written yourself in a font that looks romantic? (Of course, your wedding invitations could look embarrassingly dated at your 25th anniversary, or hideously tacky right away.) Mere exposure to the proliferation of fonts creates demand. Once you know you can get a special typeface for $20 or so, you're more likely to want to look for just the right one. Fonts, in this sense, are just like shoes or bathroom faucets. They proliferate because different people have different tastes and identities, and because both creators and users value novelty for its own sake.

With enough patience and up-to-date software, type designers can give their creations just about any look, including the idiosyncrasies of lead type or the individuality of hand lettering. As a Hollywood prop designer, Andrew Leman has often created type that looks old-fashioned, mimicking nineteenth-century newspapers and 1930s telegrams. He has turned some of these partial character sets into fully developed fonts, and four years ago he scored a surprise hit: a font called Satisfaction modeled on hand lettering from 1930s cigarette ads. (The smokes promised "satisfaction.") Its looping curves have shown up in ads for Las Vegas shows, on doughnut boxes in Denver, on a point-of-purchase display for Post-It notes at Staples, and in countless suburban moms' lovingly crafted scrapbooks.

Satisfaction's success came, in large measure, from a new business model created by MyFonts.com. Unlike traditional foundries, MyFonts doesn't act like a publisher, picking the fonts it thinks will do well and paying a royalty to designers. Instead, it takes every font that meets basic technical and legal criteria. Designers set their own license terms and their own prices, and MyFonts gets a 35 percent cut of sales. To promote new fonts, the site features a What's New list of fonts added or updated in the past 21 days. The ones that sell best go on a second list, called Starlets, limited to fonts no more than 50 days old.

Graphic designers are always on the lookout for something new, if only to spark their thinking, so novelty sells. "Believe it or not, there are lots of people who just come and buy lots of Starlets," says John Collins, head of MyFonts and vice president and chief technology officer at its parent company, Bitstream. The automated system keeps overhead low and gives new fonts a shot at the big time. Collins boasts that half the site's 50 best sellers aren't classics like Helvetica but "relatively new fonts that have just come on the scene and have struck a chord in buyers." Satisfaction made the Starlets list in November 2003 and has been a best seller ever since. In its first four years, Satisfaction sold 7,000 copies at $12 a pop, including about 150 licenses last October. "These are not platinum-record numbers." says Collins. "This is a niche business."

That's how it's always been. But by lowering design, production, and distribution costs, the digital age has made many, many more niches economically viable, to the delight of type lovers. Leman now has an easy way to share his love of "slightly crumbly" type with the "gently used feel of old metal," including vintage-style fonts that sell many fewer copies than Satisfaction. As for Satisfaction, says the part-time type designer, "That font pays my rent."

Copyright © 2008 by Virginia Postrel. Published in *The Atlantic*, January/February 2008.

CHAPTER 5

THE ALMIGHTY EURO

BY TODD PRUZAN

✱

The inhabitants of the continental landmass known as Europe know a thing or two about division. European unity is an oxymoron with several thousand years of strife and bickering to back it up, resulting in a fascinating patchwork of languages, cultures, heroes, villains, and wars and treaties and music and architecture and soccer teams.

But commonality is encroaching, following the 1992 establishment of the European Union, with membership extended to the continent's most powerful nations. And from the morning of New Year's Day 2002, the citizens of 11 European countries, from Portugal to Austria, will begin exchanging their own national currencies for new euro notes and coins.

A new monetary lingua franca won't erase national borders, of course; many Europeans are predictably unhappy about having to rally around an untested financial standard uniting their strong national economies with their neighbors' weaker ones. But the issues are hardly limited to economics. A nation's currency—embodied by the design of the notes and coins everyone carries around in pockets and purses—is possibly the most immediate, tangible expression of its culture, history, and identity. So the passing of the franc, lira, peseta, mark, and other currencies may provoke mourning as the 12 billion new euro notes and 80 billion euro coins—most of them lacking any imagery to stir national pride—replace them. To make matters more confusing, there's a new typographic symbol for the euro that ultimately will need to be on nearly every computer keyboard in the world.

The European Monetary Institute, precursor of the new European Central Bank, established the money's design with a contest won, for the notes, by Robert Kalina of Austria's Oesterreichische Nationalbank, and for the faces of the coins, by Luc Luycx of Belgium's mint, Monnaie Royale de Belgique. (Each member nation will supply its own design for the reverse.) Criticism has been extensive of both the currency designs and of Belgian designer Alain Billiet's new euro typographical symbol—essentially an uppercase C with two horizontal bars running through it, evoking the Greek epsilon.

Among those most dissatisfied with the results are European and European-born graphic designers. "It's a great opportunity gone down the drain, as usual," fumes Massimo Vignelli of Vignelli Associates in New York.

"People without knowledge of design, and having done no homework, were in charge of doing a job they're no good at," he says of the Monetary Institute's procedure for selecting a design.

"The right way to do it would be to examine all the good currency in Europe, go to one designer, and ask that person to do it," Vignelli says. "Some great designers have done great money in Europe—number one, R.D.E. Oxenaar in the Netherlands, and Jorg Zintzmeyer, who designed beautiful money for Switzerland rather recently. But this is more a political design than anything, to please everybody—it's very undefined, very blurred. It's just plain corny."

Not surprisingly, some designers in the Netherlands—whose currency has been heralded as innovative and attractive since Oxenaar's designs were introduced— agree with that assessment. (For the record, Oxenaar, himself an entrant in the euro design competition, dismissed Kalina's euro design as "really miserable" last year in *The New York Times*.) Bruno Ninaber van Eyben's existing Dutch coin design, featuring Queen Beatrix, will be revised for the reverse of the Dutch euro, largely unchanged but for a ring of stars, the symbol of the EU, surrounding it.

"I'm not wholly satisfied with the existing coins," he says. "A coin should express a trust in the future, and this coin expresses the border of Europe with nothing inside. What are we uniting? Are we building a fence around Europe? It's really a lost opportunity. I'm disappointed about it."

While some designers can't get into the spirit of unification as a theme, others tried a nationalistic approach with a satirical edge. Lo Breier, a designer at Hamburg's Büro X Kommunikation, proposed a design for Germany's version of the two-euro coin bearing the BMW and Mercedes-Benz logos. Another Breier approach uses a pair of holes—designed, apparently, so the euro coins can be made into buttons. (His proposals weren't selected.)

The European Commission says the face of its new coin was intended to be simple and attractive, with identification possible not only on the basis of prominent numeric denominations but also by size, shape, and color. The 2-euro coin has a diameter of 2.58 cm, with a white ring around a yellow circle; the slightly smaller one-euro coin has a yellow ring around a white circle. And the yellow 20-euro cent coin isn't even exactly round: the EC identifies its shape as "Spanish flower."

The notes are identified by a spectrum of colors as well as varying sizes; the largest, the 500-euro note, is a whopping 16 cm × 8.2 cm. (U.S. bills are 15.5 cm × 6.5 cm.) Each of the notes' seven denominations, identified by a predominant color scheme and numbers expressed in sans-serif type, depicts one historic European architectural style—classical, Romanesque, Gothic, Renaissance, baroque and rococo, the Age of Iron and Glass, and twentieth-century—emphasizing windows, gateways, and bridges, intended to symbolize cooperation and communication.

But anyone traveling Europe in search of these "landmarks" will be crushed to discover that the EMI approved illustrations of hybrid structures rather than real ones.

That, too, has proved a controversial decision. "I think it's a travesty," says Kenneth R. Windsor, executive vice president/creative director at corporate identity agency Siegel & Gale's London office.

Vignelli backs him up: "It's terrible, what they've done with the bridges and buildings that don't belong to any country."

Marc Gobé, the New York-based founder of corporate identity specialist Desgrippes Gobé, disagrees; he feels the design is successful. "You can't be partisan in designing something like this," he says. "I think anyone can identify any of the structures depicted, because the history of architecture in Europe is very common. I can look at a Roman bridge and identify something very similar in France, as would a German, an Italian, and a Spanish person, because we were all at some point occupied by the Romans."

Gobé also appreciates the notes' many cues indicating their value. Windsor does not. "From a design principle, how many variables do you use to create elements of distinction within a system? Do you use size, color, and a graphic element of layout? Or can you keep just one?"

Perhaps the strangest manifestation of this confusion is the repetition of the word "euro" on the note, in Latin and Greek alphabets—despite the fact that only countries using Latin alphabets have signed on to adopt the currency standard. (Russia, with its chaotic economy, and Cyrillic alphabet is not currently under consideration to become a Member State of the EC; Greece may yet drop its drachma.)

Windsor is unsurprised by howls from some parts of the continent: "I can understand the Dutch being a little more critical, because their note design is more forward-looking than the rest of Europe." Still, the problem may demand a larger perspective. "People fear they'll be losing their identity. But what they don't realize is that in ten years we're going to be cashless," he says, predicting an economy running solely on electronic and other cash-free transactions. "Coins and currency will be potentially a moot point."

The currency itself aims to be an enduring institution, even if the cash becomes obsolete—but the design of the euro typographic symbol has encountered some opposition of its own. Many typographers weighed in on the matter on a website run by a Montreal typographer, Neil Kandalgaonkar, who says, "Most people really didn't care who'd done it, but they were annoyed by the fact that it was produced by fiat—produced by a company that apparently didn't know much about typography."

Kandalgaonkar's site documented a host of complaints in early 1998. The symbol, designers said, was hard to draw by hand, requiring three strokes instead of two (e.g., $ and £); it was ugly, particularly with regard to the stems of the horizontal bars protruding beyond the back of the curving C; and, perhaps worst of all, it functioned more as a logo than a new character, unaccommodating to the constraints of varying typefaces. (The EC originally mandated that the symbol's exact dimensions were always to be reproduced identically, regardless of the font it lives in, but quietly backed down from this suggestion in March 1998.)

Typographers were miffed at the EC's lack of understanding on how to integrate a new character into the vernacular of typography, a problem necessitating revisions to existing and forthcoming computer hardware and software as well as fonts. "You can't force anyone to just use one symbol," notes Petr van Blokland, founder of an eponymous design studio in Delft, Netherlands. "If they had made any inquiries about how this kind of thing works in a typographic sense, they would have known."

Still, he may be grateful for the extra work resulting from this special headache. His studio, Buro Petr van Bloklund, has been busy formulating euro symbol designs for its original fonts, including those commissioned by Dutch corporate giants IGBank and Nationale Nederlands insurance. Production costs for the new symbol amount to roughly 90 percent of creating a new font from scratch, he says. (Some hand-drawn fonts' hinting codes, which improve onscreen and laser-printed images of the fonts, will be lost when the font is opened with a commercial font application; a manually drawn hinted character is vastly more expensive and time-consuming to create but is more accurate and precise.) Consequently, most of his clients have opted for the full monty.

The problem is slightly stickier on a larger scale, says Simon Daniels, a typographic engineer at Microsoft in Redmond, WA. His department is concerned with establishing the design of the euro symbol in each Microsoft font. (Another department handles the task of making the symbols printable.) "This is the first time we've altered the code pages, which from the old days have basically contained 255 characters," he says. Whereas Microsoft merely added the new symbol to its code pages,

CHAPTER 5

"The target was to obtain a symbol with non-aggressive lines expressing a large content and an open door to the future."

archrival Apple had no room to do so and instead resorted to replacing the obscure international currency symbol, a circle studded with points at regular intervals.

Another engineer, John Gray in Redhill, Surrey, England, has created extensive notes on how to produce the euro symbol for Microsoft Office software; his paper includes many examples of "euro-enabled" Hewlett Packard FontSmart fonts. In several cases, the euro is based heavily on the uppercase C—including serifs—a character that, like the standard accepted design of the symbol, has been criticized as too wide to function properly in tables of narrower numeral characters.

Of course, the symbol's designer, Alain Billiet, had a formidable task. "The target was to obtain a symbol with non-aggressive lines expressing a large content and an open door to the future," he explains. "I had to consider the fact that it had to be applied to different typefaces"—despite the EC's original intentions to the contrary. "And it has to look coherent to other countries too," he says. "There can't be a double interpretation in India or Japan."

Despite criticism that the euro lacks real meaning, Billiet says his typographic symbol is loaded with significance. "A round symbol gives the idea of an expectation, and the ideal form is open, not a closed sphere. It gives expectations of what the euro has to be in the future—it's unlimited, a circle without limits."

Today, the currency symbol seems to have emerged from the firing line more unscathed than the cash it represents. (Even Kandalgaonkar has softened his stance: "I think the graphic language of typography can accommodate that symbol, the more I've looked at it with some changes.") That's a promising sign. On January 1, the euro became a legal national currency in Austria, Belgium, Finland, France, Germany, Ireland, Italy, Luxembourg, the Netherlands, Portugal, and Spain. By July 1, 2002, national currencies will be good only for exchange at banks. And, ready or not, 370 million Europeans, who have rarely agreed on anything, will be trying to get used to sharing their money.

Copyright © 1998 by Todd Pruzan. Published in *Print*, 1998.

WRITING HISTORY NOW

THE NEW VISUAL ABNORMAL

BY COLETTE GAITER

When I took a commercial art class in high school, I knew that I wanted to become a graphic designer and change the way people perceived the world. Yes, it was grandiose thinking, but it was the 1970s, and changing the world seemed not only possible but immediately urgent to a lot of teenagers at that time. In 1971 the United States was in its sixth year of involvement in the sixteen-year Vietnam War. Black people, LGBTQ people, women, disabled people, Hispanic people, poor people, Native Americans, and everyone else denied American power and prosperity claimed their rights while culture wars raged.

Fifty years later, we are back in crisis mode, confronting similar issues on a global scale that affect every life, plus a pandemic and climate disaster. We survived the seventies, and some conditions did improve. In the third decade of the twenty-first century, designers absolutely can take the lead in accelerating progress for the next fifty years by visualizing a just and equitable future now.

The urgently essential thing visual communicators can do in 2021 is stop normalizing and foregrounding whiteness. Former Black Panther artist Emory Douglas was not much older than a teenager when he started laying out, designing, and making illustrations and cartoons for the Black Panther newspaper. The visual world was changing fast. Just a few years after the Civil Rights Act passed in 1964, guaranteeing fundamental rights for African Americans, mainstream white-controlled media started featuring (although rarely) Black people in ads, on magazine covers, and on television. Previously if Black people were present in the media, we were almost exclusively in subservient roles, primarily as actual servants, especially in advertising. A few Black television characters in the 1950s and early 1960s usually reinforced negative stereotypes or existed solely as sidekicks to the main white characters. There were several firsts when Black female models appeared on the covers of magazines like *Glamour* and *Vogue* in the late 1960s. On November 25, 1967, *Rolling Stone*, an innovator in music journalism and culture, featured the now-iconic Tina Turner on its cover. New images and representations seemed possible.

Magazines were a big part of my childhood and adolescence. *Ebony*, *Jet*, *Vogue*, at least one weekly newsmagazine like *Time* or *Newsweek*, the "big glossies" *LOOK* and *LIFE*, and others regularly arrived in the mail at our house. I loved looking at *Vogue*, with its glamorous full-bleed art-styled photography and spare layouts. The Black Panther (BP) newspaper occasionally came into my household in 1971 when my older sister brought issues home from Howard University. The BP paper's lead artist and designer, Emory Douglas, visualized Black people living in ghettos fighting slumlords, brutality from police officers (drawn as pigs), and the institutions that rigidly enforced racism. I had a range of publications to look at—from establishment-enforcing news magazines to the radically beautiful Black Panther newspaper.

VISUAL WHIPLASH

On one end of magazine culture, in 1971, *Vogue* pictured virtually all white people in its photographs and ads. *Ebony* and *Jet* presented Black people almost as exclusively. *The Black Panther* was full-blown non-assimilationist and anti-capitalist, showing mostly Black people but included other global people of color who joined their fight against Western imperialism in politics and commerce. The Panthers also fought white Western dominance in the American cultural imagination. In the late 1960s, contrasting the Black people in *Ebony* and *Jet*, who were usually meticulously well-dressed and coiffed, with women wearing straightened hair (Afros emerged around 1968), the people Emory Douglas and the other Black Panther artists drew looked authentically Black. Some wore Afrocentric clothing, showing solidarity with Black people fighting colonialism in African countries. Images of people with full Black lips, broad noses, and dark-skinned bodies filled the *Black Panther*'s pages. Douglas said, "The people saw themselves in the artwork. They became the heroes. They could see their uncles in it. They could see their fathers or their brothers and sisters in the art."[1] Lighter skin and straighter hair were preferred on Black people in mainstream media, even

---

[1] Marc Steiner and Emory Douglas. "The Life and Times of Emory Douglas, Minister of Culture in the Black Panther . . ." YouTube. Real News Network, November 14, 2014. https://www.youtube.com/watch?v=hNy_S4z4vpw.

in Black publications, and the ads reflected those aspirations. Douglas's drawings were astonishing in their time because they showed beautiful Black people who had little money and radiated dignity and determination. In Black Panther leader Huey Newton's article in the July 20, 1967, issue of the newspaper he claimed that "strategic revolutionary art," including pictures of people defending themselves against the police, showed "the correct handling of a revolution."[2] The drawings were cathartic as metaphors, encouraging people to arm themselves against internalizing white supremacy by imagining power and control over their lives. At the time, looking at these publications and their oppositional racial representations gave me visual whiplash from observing such a range of culture.

People of color practice cognitive dissonance every day while living in the United States. We know that the mass-mediated world rarely reflects our experiences and ideas. It is not a coincidence that the United States ranks fifteenth out of forty-four countries in effective media literacy education according to the nonprofit organization Media Literacy Now.[3] U.S. diversity complicates finding consensus in education values.[4] The default solution is often to ignore issues that could be addressed by acknowledging difference. Our lack of homogeneity encourages forming myths like the "American Dream" and forcing the dominance of fictional ideals that only work for some segments of the population. In 2021 controversies rage over teaching Critical Race Theory[5] or the seminal *1619 Project* (which explains the country's long and continuing relationship with the institution of slavery).[6] The denial fueling this pushback insists on ignoring the past, limiting progress for the United

---

[2] Huey P. Newton, *Huey P. Newton Reader*. Edited by David Hilliard and Donald Weise. New York: Seven Stories Press, 2002.

[3] Joe Carr, "A New Index Shows That the US Scores Low on Media Literacy Education." Media Literacy Now | Advocating for Media Literacy Education, July 28, 2021. https://medialiteracynow.org/a-new -index-shows-that-the-us-scores-low-on-media-literacy-education/.

[4] Robert W. Kubey, "Why U.S. Media Education Lags Behind the Rest of the English-Speaking World." *Television & New Media* 4, no. 4 (November 2003): 351–70. https://doi.org/10.1177/1527476403255803.

[5] Cady Lang, "President Trump Has Attacked Critical Race Theory. Here's What to Know About the Intellectual Movement." *Time*, September 29, 2020; Kimberlé Crenshaw, one of the founding scholars of CRT, defines it as "a practice—a way of seeing how the fiction of race has been transformed into concrete racial inequities." https://time.com/5891138/critical-race-theory-explained/.

[6] Jake Silverstein, "Why We Published the 1619 Project." *New York Times Magazine*. August 14, 2019. https://www.nytimes.com/interactive/2019/08/14/magazine/1619-america-slavery.html. The New York Times' 1619 Project, initiated by journalist Nikole Hannah Jones, "aims to reframe the country's history by placing the consequences of slavery and the contributions of black Americans at the very center of our national narrative." https://www.nytimes.com/interactive/2019/08/14/ magazine/1619-america-slavery.html.

States on all social fronts. Visual literacy in this country would require focused attention on our relationship with race, past and present. We have not looked at or learned from the ways visual media, starting with early newspapers, deliberately planted images of white supremacy in the American imagination, making racism seem necessary and expected.

UBIQUITOUS IMAGES, BIG LIES

For example, the nineteenth-century lithographers Currier and Ives called their company "The Grand Central Depot for Cheap and Popular Prints." At one time, they produced 95 percent of the engravings sold in the United States.[7] Their engravings included the Darktown series, with over a hundred prints created from the mid-1870s into the early 1890s, primarily by artist Thomas Worth. According to William Thompson, "The series reinforced the widely accepted pictorial stereotype of the African American as a kinky-haired, thick-lipped, wide-eyed, simian creature that could not even pretend to live like white Americans, despite emancipation and the best efforts of sympathetic Reconstructionists—the position to which most late nineteenth-century Americans were retreating."[8] Most of their prints displayed bucolic landscapes and white people who embodied idealized small-town "Americana."

Today the racist Darktown series is usually left out of Currier and Ives exhibitions. Harry T. Peters, the most prominent collector of Currier and Ives prints and related materials, wrote decades ago: "Currier and Ives were businessmen and craftsmen . . . but primarily they [were] mirrors of the national taste, weathervanes of popular opinion, reflectors of American attitudes."[9]

Those attitudes included racism and white supremacy. Images like these justified Reconstruction-era and Jim Crow legal discrimination, visualizing the idea in white minds that Black people did not know what to do with our freedom and did not deserve equality. Emory Douglas's 1960s and 70s illustrations comprised a

---

[7] "Amon Carter Museum Presents the America of Currier & Ives." Amon Carter Museum of American Art, July 15, 2003. https://www.cartermuseum.org/press-release/137carter-museum-presents-america-currier-ives.

[8] William Fletcher Thompson, Jr. "Pictorial Images of the Negro During the Civil War." *Wisconsin Magazine of History* 48 (Summer 1965): 282-94. Quoted in Le Beau, B. F. (2000), "African Americans in Currier and Ives's America: The Darktown Series." *Journal of American & Comparative Cultures*, 23: 74. https://doi-org.udel.idm.oclc.org/10.1111/j.1537-4726.2000.2301_71.x.

[9] Harry T. Peters, *Currier & Ives: Printmakers to the American People*. Garden City, NY: Doubleday, 1942. Quoted in Le Beau, B.F. (2000), "African Americans in Currier and Ives's America: The Darktown Series." *Journal of American & Comparative Cultures*, 23: 71. https://doi-org.udel.idm.oclc.org/10.1111/j.1537-4726.2000.2301_71.x.

WRITING HISTORY NOW

visual antithesis to images like Worth's that sought to reduce African Americans to archetypal caricatures. Worth mocked Black aspiration, making it seem ridiculous, while Douglas's drawings show poor people with their pride and dreams intact. Racist ideas were deliberately and regularly embedded. They can be excavated just as intentionally.

FILLING IN THE BLANKS

As a professor, I am still motivated by my high school revelation that visual media is ground zero for influencing political and social world views. When I first started teaching visual communication and graphic design, I found few examples of non-white or even female designers and illustrators. In the early 1990s, I assigned students a research project and included people like the Harlem Renaissance artists Aaron Douglas and Miguel Covarrubias on the list of potential subjects. I noticed that students (mostly white) always chose the artists of color first. They were intrigued by images of lives that were unfamiliar to them. I added other people of color to my list as I found them, but there were never many because no one had written about them. Later I located the former Black Panther artist Emory Douglas, whose work I had admired in high school, and started interviewing him about his work. I wrote explicitly about his visual work because it was only mentioned briefly in books about the Black Panther Party. I realized that I had to contribute to that incomplete body of texts.[10]

Most visual communications programs include courses that specifically address semiotics and decoding visual media beyond the obvious. I propose that college visual communications programs foreground identity in all learning experiences, requiring students to forget any ideas they had of designing for "normal" or "average" people. Each student is different, as is each audience. I developed and taught new courses (open to all university students of any major) on the effects media, design, and culture have on thinking and behavior. Students become aware that racism, sexism, homophobia, transphobia, and ableism were intentionally built into the mainstream visual media landscape to normalize them as shared national values. Learning about the historical collective unconscious reveals that images people have never personally seen continue to influence contemporary culture through inherited memory and iterative references. Too many people believe that the "isms" (racism, sexism, etc.) are performed in the extreme by only "bad" people. These harmful and antisocial ideas are so innocuously embedded into everyday language and images that they continue unnoticed and even defended by those who

---

[10] Colette Gaiter, "What Revolution Looks Like: The Work of Black Panther Artist Emory Douglas." Essay. In *Black Panther: The Revolutionary Art of Emory Douglas*, edited by Sam Durant, 93–109. New York: Rizzoli, 2007.

scream "political correctness!" at any suggestion that they might be dangerous. Requiring all design and visual communications students to examine their identities (inherited and acquired) and a range of backgrounds and experiences would be a huge step toward building an equitable society. Most people cannot imagine equality because we have never seen it. Visual communicators can lead by modeling behavior that moves toward an elusive ideal. By 2045, when 2020s students influence visual culture at the highest levels, most people in the United States will be of the global majority, who are not white.[11] Design education can anticipate that change.

Despite demographic facts, Western white sensibilities dominate the worldwide popular culture landscape. It is imperative to show young people that biases are specifically taught in sometimes nefarious, but more often, seemingly natural ways. When I ask students to name some of their identities in private writing assignments, some write, "I'm just white," as if that is not an identity. Whiteness is an identity but persists as "default" or "normal" even though demographics tell a different story.

"Whiteness-as-default" aggressively minimizes everyone's interior cultural life, especially for white people. Overrepresented people are usually the ones who believe in "racial color blindness." There is no such thing. Design students of color should never have to defend creating work that does not conform to media-generated ideas of universality. All students consciously and unconsciously bring individual identities into their work, overtly or subtly. Signs and symbols that are not part of the dominant white culture can be translated and learned the same way that young children absorb new words and pronounce them without self-consciousness or prejudice. These practices will expand our visual media literacy and challenge the entire concept of "normal."

THE NEW VISUAL ABNORMAL

The September 2020 issue of *Vogue*, the first after more than fifteen million people internationally protested George Floyd's murder by police, was full of global-majority people[12]—in ads and editorial pages. According to the *New York Times*, "employees at *Vogue*'s parent company, Condé Nast, were publicly calling out what they viewed as racism in their own workplace. At 316 pages, the issue, titled

'Hope,' featured a majority of Black artists, models, and photographers, a first

---

[11] William H. Frey, "The US Will Become 'Minority White' in 2045, Census Projects." *Brookings*. Brookings Institution, September 10, 2018. https://www.brookings.edu/blog/the-avenue/2018/03/14/the -us-will-become-minority-white-in-2045-census-projects/.

[12] Daniel Lim, "I'm Embracing the Term 'People of the Global Majority.'" *Medium*, May 11, 2020. https:// regenerative.medium.com/im-embracing-the-term-people -of-the-global-majority-abd1c1251241.

for the magazine."[13] A painting of a Black woman by African American artist Kerry James Marshall was on the cover. *Vogue*'s editor Anna Wintour publicly acknowledged a history of omissions and mistakes. The public and the fashion industry received her words with both skepticism and appreciation. The important thing is that the pages displayed an adjusted view of the world from the magazine. As I turned pages, I imagined white people writing outraged letters and canceling their subscriptions after seeing the magazine showcase people of color. I also realized that the shift seemed normal and pleasing to my eyes and spirit. I look forward to inclusivity becoming the new visual abnormal.

Copyright © 2022 by Colette Gaiter. Published in *The Black Experience in Design: Identity, Expression & Reflection*, Allworth Press/SVA, 2022.

[13] Edmund Lee, "The White Issue: Has Anna Wintour's Diversity Push Come Too Late?" *New York Times* (October 24, 2020), https://www.nytimes.com/2020/10/24/business/media/anna-wintour-vogue-race .html.

CHAPTER 5

1990s: END OF THE MILLENNIUM

BY STEVEN HELLER

To paraphrase the great Albert Einstein: everything is relative. While in some quarters the 1990s represents a mere microsecond in the time space continuum, in day-to-day earth-time this curtain-closing decade of the second millennium Anno Domini carries more weight. That's relativity. So, although it is much too soon to be sentimental for the comings and goings of 1990s, from an advertising industry perspective these ten short years were consequential in their way. This book is evidence of a distinctly unique American tale of desire and consumption and while advertising-wise the 1990s was not significantly different from the previous two advertising decades, it is definitely not the same, either.

The 1990s marked the tail end of the Creative Revolution and the start of a creative reevaluation based on the advent of digital media, viral strategies, guerilla interventions and the birth of user experiences that lead a new generation of consumers to experience novel technologies. Indeed, this riotous period of boom and bust throughout the advertising industry was a transformative period when traditional ad techniques gave rise to a new wave of media interaction that emerged in the 2000s.

Commercials on network television and a growing new cable TV industry were the pinnacles of practice while print advertising was somewhere in the lower echelons of an endangered medium. If the pundits were not warning of the death of print, they were predicting alternatives soon to be developed, like smart devices loaded with "cookies" that would target profiled-specific ads to malleable and unsuspecting consumers. Perhaps the 1990s seemed to go by so quickly because anticipation of future and its impact on people's conscious and subconscious was moving at breakneck speed.

During the fin de siècle (the 1890s when the nineteenth became the twentieth century) society and culture was plagued by uncertainty, unrest, and social transformation. The 1990s was similarly marred by chaos brought on by a clash of new and old. Advertising was in a state of stylistic confusion and readjustment. Its leaders realized that deploying the same methods from the 1950s through 1970s when under the spell of Big Idea and the minimalist modern design methods was not going to work anymore. Art directors had to make advertising that veered from the old solutions. Advertising design was in a state of flux—no direction known, just like a rolling stone—and the result was that there was no real '90s style but rather a mishmash of the past. While the '90s ads were primarily photographic, they had nonetheless lost the conceptual acuity that distinguished them from the mediocre, pre-Creative Revolution illustrative variety.

This is not to say, they were entirely without intelligence. Craft was at an all-time high. The fact that by the late '90s computers were standard design tools provided art directors with skillsets and capabilities that did not exist earlier. There was indeed a higher level of typographic competency and the level of photography was often exquisite. But this decade's Art Director Club award winners lacked the revolutionary cleverness of the past. Conceptual ideas gave way to moods. Advertising pitch meetings were filled with mood boards, those assembled collections of clipped existing images used to show how a particular campaign might look. The tried and true was dominant and also a sure-fire way to make current ads look like something that had already been done. But there were exceptions.

Among the few campaigns that stand-out for their genuine originality are the inventive "Got Milk" series featuring a gaggle of famous people with milk mustaches, including Lauren Bacall, the cast of the TV show *Frasier*, and even Ivana Trump gave a rather boring beverage an air of class and wit, forcing the average viewer to take notice by anticipating what celebrity would be featured in subsequent ads. Similarly, the Absolut vodka campaign, started in the '80s, continued to pique consumers' interest in the product through a seemingly endless array of iterations using the distinctive liquor bottle in art, architecture, and more. Yet for its no-nonsense curious complexity, "Tell Nuprin Where It Hurts" is arguably one of the most effective of the era's promotions for its brilliant yet understated showing an anatomical diagram mapping where the pain medicine gives most relief to its user.

In the 1990s print was not the primary means to reach the largest audience number of customers. Still, it remained an effective means to reinforce messages that might be lost given the fleeting word and picture of a video commercial. Specifically themed magazines were hungry for ads and ripe for effective placement. Lifestyle, home, fashion, cooking, business, and other niche magazines could ensure a certain number of looks. But the advertisements on the whole, although not as a rule, were more routine solo product shots or models with products or famous endorser portraits than anything too much more creative. Typical of this, for instance, is the Jell-O ad with a photo of Bill Cosby surrounded by children.

Sure, there were aesthetically and dramatically produced photographs, like the one with the empty Häagen-Dazs container lying on satin sheets with the discretely suggestive headline "Who Needs Mistletoe"; or the Wish Bone Olive Oil ad designed to imitate a Picasso painting; or the rather funny Ritz ad showing a light-handed drawing of a couch, with a Ritz cracker on either end and the headline "Perfect for Couch Potatoes." Each had more than a modicum of subtlety, humor, and intellectual appeal. But the vast majority of ads either did an updated iteration of the typical product hack, like Quaker Oats' "A Warm Start To A Healthy Heart" with a photo of the package next to a bowl of the cereal spewing a plume of steam in the shape of a heart, or Cool Whip's "What Could Top Pumpkin Pie?" with, you guessed it, a tasty photo of a wedge of pie with a glob of the whip on top.

Appetite appeal was an important principle in advertising. That glob of Cool Whip was designed to make the viewer's mouth water. It worked, but that was a given. Then there was the ad for Chunky Soup—with the right photograph even a mush of canned processed chicken and vegetables, under the title "A Square Meal in a Round Hole" could make mouths water. It was, however, clever of Taco Bell to show equivalents to other fast-food chains in a campaign where a burger and fries are compared to burritos, tacos, and other Mexican delights. But the average food ad was pretty standard fare, like Lean Cuisine's New Homestyle Baked Fish, which looks phonily delicious although it came from a cardboard box.

Oddly, some of the most sophisticated ads were for the least sophisticated mass market products. Take the advertisements for Trix produced in the Big Idea manner, focusing wittily by self-referencing its colorful little balls of flavor. Jolly Rancher, the fruit candy, also exploited its populist brand fame in the ad that shows a huge apple behind the World Trade Center (a decade before 9/11) compared to a piece of candy above it. The words "Actual Size" sit over the candy, and "Actual Taste" above the apple—an iconic message that projected a sense of monumentality.

Rather than promote ambiguity, which during the Creative Revolution was considered an asset because it made the user think more, and therefore spend more time concentrating on the advertisement, there was a return to pre-revolutionary approaches. Nabisco's "At Nabisco Our Devotion To Making Wholesome Great-Tasting Snacks" puts its entire cracker line on the line. It is their attempt to reinforce the brand's strength. And while there is nothing wrong with the approach, the creative aspects are minimal. Enforcing brand superiority has always been advertising's role and in the 1990s one way to do it was through comic sincerity. For Diet Coke the repletion of a football player drinking a liter bottle in five exact photographs with the headlines, "1st, 2nd, 3rd, 4th, and 4th down!" is straightforward without being too tedious.

In the fashion "space" ads only had to show pretty and handsome models to make an impact. Nonetheless casting the right face to carry the weight of the brand was never as easy as it looked. For the "I Am Esprit" ads, the young redhead was both the girl next door and an object of desire, of sorts. For jockey underwear a gang of snow boarders have dropped their pants to show the variety of Jockey styles. In another provocative add "Is There a Jockey in the House?" three hunks in surgeon garb have dropped their scrubs in a manner suggesting possible malpractice. An ad for the underwear brand Joe Boxer shows a barber and a very long bearded hipster getting a haircut. Both are wearing Joe Boxers over the headline "Change Daily," the ad suggests the brand is for everyone, even though it was originally marked as hip-hop. And for Quicksilver the male model had to seem cool, handsome, masculine and decidedly the epitome of young America.

In the late 1990s there was also more flesh shown than in earlier decades. CK Jeans showed ever sensual Kate Moss in bra and jeans the way every man wants her and every woman wants to be like her. Guess Jeans did not even show the product, just a bronzed, come-hither beauty glaring alluringly at the camera. Gucci made ecstasy into something so matter-of-fact that a consumer could not wait to purchase and wear the garments.

It was the fashion industry, however, or at least United Colors of Benetton that in the 1990s began an engaging campaign that did not sell its clothes but broadly sold its brand and specifically the brand's attitudes about social justice. Beginning with a controversial ad of a white man handcuffed to a black man with only the company logo, the idea of the campaign was to show that Benetton was behind equal justice. It followed up with dozens of ads in the 1990s (including its own promotional magazine, *Colors*), with an ad showing three real human hearts, each one marked with one word, either white, black, or yellow. There was another of angelic little blonde white girl arm-in-arm with a black counterpart. This was not "cause" advertising, but it let the world know Benetton was linked to causes. It further distinguished the brand from the typical model-driven ads for Fendi, Armani, Claiborne, Ralph Lauren and others.

Authenticity (an overly used word) was also key to many advertising campaigns. In ads for Tommy Hilfiger, Fila, and Dockers, models were commanded to be themselves rather than pose for the camera. Of course, this type of faux candid shot quickly became a standard trope.

CHAPTER 5

Liquor advertising was led by Absolut, but Stolichnaya was competitive vodka that found its identity in print through highly stylized illustration. Drawing and painting were not as popular in 1990s ads as they were during the 1950s but a new approach to retro reinterpretation began emerging, that for Stolichnaya borrowed the visual language of Russian Constructivism, while for Hennessy cognac, French deco was employed. The illustration was used to attract a younger audience that appreciated the pop quality of this retro art. Meanwhile, over in the cigarette market, Camel was doing its utmost to wrangle a new consumer basic. Using a comic novel visual idiom it borrowed from Europe, the introduction of Joe Camel, hipster, was drawn and painted as a motorcycle-riding, pimpster whose role was to reel in the teens and even preteens. It met with considerable opposition, and was eventually discontinued, but there is no telling how many new smokers Joe Camel snagged in his web.

The 1990s was also the beginning of the Photoshop era. Retouching was common in the advertising bullpens of America. Airbrush, dye transfers, and all manner of tools and techniques were used for making photo images ever more perfect. The ability to do it on a desktop computer altered the techniques whereby the agency art directors worked. Photoshop impacted color, scale, juxtaposition, and all the other design traits that conveyed and expressed their messages. The impact was incalculable. Costly images were cheaper, complex conceptions were easier. By 2000 the computer and its tools had made massive change in the creative world.

The biggest change was the ability to create imagery from scratch, which gave freedom throughout the advertising industry to work to an even great effect with fantasy. What already seemed unreal was made extraordinarily real. Of course, during the 1990s many of the ads made with this tool were created for the computer and cell phone, which over time will demand as much from designers as it gave to them.

Speaking of common themes in print advertising. In addition to surfeit of computer, phone, fashion, automobile, and food advertising, the ban against cigarette commercials on TV forced the tobacco manufacturers and liquor distillers too, to up their expenses for print—magazines and billboards. Although working on cigarette accounts did not confer the highest creative status, the ads had to sell. And hard selling was the watchword of the decade—and that was the only way to rise above the noise that was 1990s.

Copyright © 2023 by Steven Heller.

WRITING HISTORY NOW

KEEPING TABS: THE HISTORY OF AN INFORMATION AGE METAPHOR

BY EDWARD TENNER

★

How many college students today ever flip through trays of library catalog cards? Some of them may never have used an actual tabbed file. But the tab as an information technology metaphor is everywhere in use. And whether our tabs are cardboard extensions or digital projections, they all date to an invention little more than a hundred years old. The original tab signaled an information storage revolution and helped enable everything from management consulting to electronic data processing.

The tab's story begins in the Middle Ages, when the only cards were gambling paraphernalia. Starting in the late fourteenth century, scribes began to leave pieces of leather at the edges of manuscripts for ready reference. But with the introduction of page numbering in the Renaissance, they went out of fashion.

The modern tab was an improvement on a momentous nineteenth-century innovation, the index card. Libraries had previously listed their books in bound ledgers. During the French Revolution, authorities divided the nationalized collections of monasteries and aristocrats among public institutions, using the backs of playing cards to record data about each volume.

CHAPTER 5

The modern tab was an improvement on a momentous nineteenth-century innovation, the index card.

The idea of a randomly accessible, infinitely modifiable arrangement of data flowered first in the United States. Not that America had more books to organize. In 1820, the Göttingen University library in Germany already had 200,000 volumes; Harvard University had fewer than 118,000 books in 1861, when it became the first major library to use cards. The historian John Higham called the catalog a "revolutionary" and characteristically American tool, which promoted specialization by grouping authorities together under topic headings and integrated the latest books rapidly—features we take for granted now.

It took decades to add tabs to cards. In 1876, Melvil Dewey, inventor of decimal classification, helped organize a company called the Library Bureau, which sold both cards and wooden cases. An academic entrepreneur, Dewey was a perfectionist supplier. His cards were made to last, made from linen recycled from the shirt factories of Troy, NY. His card cabinets were so sturdy that I have found at least one set still in use, in excellent order. Dewey also standardized the dimension of the catalog card, at three inches by five inches, or rather 75 millimeters by 125 millimeters. (He was a tireless advocate of the metric system.)

Even the Library Bureau did not offer a convenient way to separate groups of cards, apart from thin metal partitions that wrapped around them, or taller cards. The tab was the idea of a young man named James Newton Gunn (1867–1927), who started using file cards to achieve savings in cost accounting while working for a manufacturer of portable forges. After further experience as a railroad cashier, Gunn developed a new way to access the contents of a set of index cards, separating them with other cards distinguished by projections marked with letters of the alphabet, dates, or other information.

Gunn's background in bookkeeping filled what Ronald S. Burt, the University of Chicago sociologist, has called a structural hole, a need best met by insights from unconnected disciplines. In 1896 he applied for a U.S. patent, which was granted as number 583,227 on May 25, 1897. By then, Gunn was working for the Library Bureau, to which he had sold the patent. It was to be a perfect match. The Bureau

WRITING HISTORY NOW

was becoming a leading supplier of corporate record-keeping equipment, offering "commercial grade" cards on wood-pulp stock.

The Library Bureau also produced some of the first modern filing cabinets, proudly exhibiting them at the World's Columbian Exposition in Chicago in 1893. Files had once been stored horizontally on shelves. Now they could be organized with file folders for better visibility and quicker access. Tabs were as useful for separating papers as for organizing cards. Since businesspeople were unfamiliar with the new technology, Library Bureau staff provided consulting services as well as equipment and supplies. By 1913, the company was advertising in the *New York Times* that it could supply a credit department with a 16-by-16-by-20-inch cabinet to "keep tab" on up to 14,000 customers. The Library Bureau also worked with Herman Hollerith, whose electrical punch card system later became the foundation of IBM.

James Newton Gunn went on to found one of the first consulting firms focusing on industrial engineering. He became an automotive and rubber industry executive. He helped found Harvard Business School and lectured at MIT, among other places. But the tab is his lasting legacy. And it is ubiquitous: in the dialogue boxes of Microsoft Windows and Mac OS X, at the bottom of Microsoft Excel spreadsheets, at the side of Adobe Acrobat documents, across the top of the Opera and Firefox web browsers, and—even now—on manila file folders. We've kept tabs.

Copyright © 2005 by Edward Tenner. Published in *Technology Review*, February 2005.

CHAPTER 5

THE FORGERY MARKET

BY ANNE QUITO

Her furtive voice is nearly lost in the cacophony of the nearby traffic. "Do you want it to say magna or summa cum laude?" asks the short, stocky woman with the buzz cut. "Are you sure this is all you want? We can do anything." She gestures at a thin 3 × 2 foot (1 × 0.6 m) wooden placard that has been plastered edge-to-edge with an impressive assortment of official-looking papers. Though diplomas are the stock-in-trade here, transcripts, licenses, passports, letters of endorsement, court papers, affidavits, seals, stamps, receipts, cheques, awards, badges, bank documents, and identification cards of all sorts are also available on short order, the possibilities limited only by one's imagination. The prospects are as astounding as the array of papers. Who could I be? What could I be? For a moment, I consider a liquor permit, a pilot's license, or a Reuters press badge, and in an age of biometric scanners and genetic testing, it's alluring to consider that one might still be able to design (or redesign) a functional identity with a few scraps of parchment and plastic. In the end I settle on a diploma from Harvard University, a New York state driver's license, a Philippine birth certificate and a Pulitzer Prize. Forged diplomas produced in the streets of Manila, Philippines. The author paid 400 Philippine pesos (€8.60 or US$9.00) for the "Hardvard" diploma, and 300 pesos (€6.45 or US$6.80) for the Pulitzer Prize, plus 150 pesos (€3.25 or US$3.40) for the research fee, since no original was supplied. The documents were shipped to the Netherlands, where they were framed at the local art store for €192 (US$200).

"Write the name you want printed here," she mutters, her words nearly inaudible under the jeepney and pedestrian noise. As we finalize the deal, a small group of bystanders gathers around her like gadflies. She tries to shoo them off while dashing off a brief text on a battered mobile phone. "Meet me back here tomorrow, but you can pay me half now," she says, before taking the money and disappearing into the crowd.

I am in Manila, the Philippines, in a dubious and sometimes ominous district called Recto where one can order virtually any type of official document to spec. Named after Claro M. Recto, esteemed Philippine statesman and poet, the district commonly referred to as "Recto U" sprang up adjacent to the capital city's university belt in the 1960s, filling the demand for black-market term papers and fake report cards. The operation, reportedly run by a local syndicate, has expanded to specialize in a whole spectrum of spurious credentials, both local and foreign. There is nothing false about the grim atmosphere that pervades Recto even at high noon. It's the kind of place where people wear their backpacks in front and hurry to get wherever they are going as quickly as they can. There are numerous forgery vendors along Recto and on the adjoining streets, nameless pop-up document stations wedged between street vendors that peddle pirated movies, replica ArmaLite guns, and brightly colored dildos. For illegal enterprises, these stalls are remarkably easy to spot, each with a stool, a small desk, and a brazen wooden

Claro M. Recto Avenue is one of the principal commercial roads in north central Manila. Here document counterfeiters openly offer to create fake documents of all kinds. Among the most popular are IDs, birth certificates, marriage licenses, medical certifications, fake receipts, university diplomas, driving licenses and boating licenses. (Photo: Renoir Amba)

sign advertising counterfeit goods in broad daylight. The stalls are really dispatch centers where customers place orders with the street agents or "faces," as they are sometimes called. Upon receiving an order, agents call a central number to obtain price quotes that they can mark up to boost their cuts. Afterwards they negotiate final terms with customers, then hand-deliver the slip of paper containing the specifications to a runner. The sellers on Recto Avenue don't do the forgeries themselves, but are connected via runners to the forgers who do the counterfeiting behind closed doors at an undisclosed location nearby. A university diploma costs 400 pesos (€8.60 or US$9.00), a driving license about 1,000 pesos (€21.50 or US$22.60), and turnaround is about two hours.

The counterfeits are crafted in a factory-cum-workshop nearby, produced by a stable of "master forgers," computer graphics operators who research the documents and then scan, retouch, and print them using Corel Draw and Photoshop. There are also "golden hands," the trained calligraphers and signature forgers whose skillful work with pen and ink is no less vital. With its suite of printers, scanners, laminators and drawing tools, Recto's forgery workshop is much like any other graphic design studio, except perhaps for the heavy security that keeps its illegal activities safe from prying eyes in a less-than-reputable part of town. (Not even the street agents know exactly where it is. "It's probably better that way," one of them says.)

Why then do people venture into a bad neighborhood to do illegal business with an organized crime syndicate? One reason is that despite the risks, it makes economic sense. For instance, obtaining a *sedula* (a community tax certificate that also serves as a legal form of identification) involves declaring one's gross annual income, from which the government levies one Philippine peso (₱) for every thousand earned. But for as little as ₱5, one can buy a forgery printed on an actual official form stolen from the Bureau of Internal Revenue. With the Philippine average annual income hovering around ₱140,000 (€2,800 or US$3,160), every peso saved counts, and the money saved by opting for the counterfeit document is equivalent

The sellers on Recto Avenue don't do the forgeries themselves, but are connected via runners to the forgers who do the counterfeiting behind closed doors at an undisclosed location nearby. A university diploma costs ₱400 (€8.60 or US$9.00), a driving license about ₱1,000 (€21.50 or US$22.60), and turnaround is about two hours. (Photo: Renoir Amba)

CHAPTER 5

to at least a hearty lunch or a tall Starbucks latte. Obtaining a marriage annulment certificate here, in the last country in the world where divorce is illegal, can cost up to a quarter of a million pesos (€4,980 or US$5,640), even without factoring in the cost of missing work to attend months (sometimes years) of hearings and legal procedures. In Recto, it costs ₱225 (€4.50 or US$5.00).

Even in this age of electronic documents, our lives are shaped by colored bits of paper at nearly every step: banknotes, product labels, prescriptions, ID cards, contracts, certificates, warranty cards, traffic tickets. Recto confronts us with the question: how much can a piece of paper document reality? How much can we afford to trust it? Some fake document vendors have other, legitimate businesses, while others hide their forgeries behind dummy business cards and stamps. Documents that can be purchased for bargain prices include fake vendor permits. Most vendors bribe police to stay out of trouble.

Time is also a consideration, and state agencies would do well to learn from Recto's customer-focused operation and fine-tuned efficiency. It generally takes about a week to obtain a copy of one's diploma for employment purposes, up to two weeks to get a birth certificate from the National Statistics Office, and a full day of queues, forms, a mandatory medical examination, and road test to get a driving license from the Land Transportation Office. In Recto, all this can be ready in an hour or less.

Some fake document vendors have other, legitimate businesses, while others hide their forgeries behind dummy business cards and stamps. Documents that can be purchased for bargain prices include fake vendor permits. Most vendors bribe police to stay out of trouble. (Photo: Renoir Amba)

158

A sampling of fake IDs and badges at the Recto Avenue marketplace. (Photo: Renoir Amba)

Sometimes, however, it's a matter of desperation. For a contingent of prospective but under qualified foreign migrant workers, buying a spurious seaman's book or a falsified school transcript from Recto is like buying a lottery ticket with higher earnings as the prize. The Uber driver taking me back to Recto to pick up my documents is another case in point. He had copies of his driving license made so that if a policeman confiscates it (a fairly common occurrence) he can still have the real one safely stowed away, as well as several backups. "I can't afford to miss work," he says. "My family depends on the cash I bring in every day."

Recto's customers are surprisingly diverse, however, and not all of them are attempting to evade the law. There is, for example, the young professional who ordered a duplicate of her original college diploma for her mother to frame. "It's just for her wall, I figured it would be okay. It's cheaper than getting it through my university. The craftsmanship here is really good," she explains, inspecting the dry-embossed seal. I meet my agent, and we repair to a nearby noodle shop with two other agents while we wait for my documents to arrive. Her colleagues appear skeptical, warily picking at the skins of their pork buns and keeping their distance.

"Thank you for inviting us to lunch, but I hope you're not an undercover police spy. It always starts so innocently like this, but you never know where it's going to lead," says one of them, looking me up and down, then straight in the eye.

CHAPTER 5

The agents have ample reason to fear. The mayor of Manila, Joseph Estrada (who incidentally served a term as president of the Philippines before being impeached and imprisoned for embezzlement) has launched a massive crackdown on the illegal document trade. Not only does the black market cheat the state of the taxes generated by legitimate transactions, it also besmirches the city's reputation. In diplomatic circles, Recto's reputation as a global mecca for fake papers is pervasive and pernicious. It's not uncommon to hear of consuls in American embassies rejecting visa applications from Filipinos without even glancing at their paperwork. Does this bother the agents?

"This is just business," barks the woman ("Just call me Tess") sitting next to me. She is the most veteran agent around the table, having been running orders steadily for nearly eight years now. "We have children, debts, many bills to pay," she says defensively. When probed about the stress of being a woman in a male-dominated trade, and a perilous one at that, she softens a little and finally loses her scowl. She shares that over the years, a certain camaraderie has been forged around Recto, a symbiotic circle that includes the police they bribe with a cut from daily transactions in exchange for their tolerance. Before computers and internet access became affordable, Recto-made documents were priced much higher because documents had to be made completely by hand. Business efficiency tools such as Google Image Search or a robust database of diploma templates were not available then. A simple diploma could run up to ₱10,000 (€205 or US$225) and could take days to make correctly.

"The lettering, seals and watermarks, it was really an art back then," Tess recalls. "When it's not busy now, I practice my calligraphy. I have a book in Gothic-style lettering," she says, referring to the Old English typefaces commonly used on diplomas. "Some jobs are easy enough that when the customer is in a hurry, I can just do it myself and earn a bit more from a deal."

Today, pricing for documents is a fuzzy science. The same Harvard diploma can cost ₱500 (€10 or US$11.20) in one stall and three times that at the next. According to the agents, pricing depends on several factors: the kind of document, its physical complexity, the turnaround time, their perception of the customer's ability to pay (dress down and forgo jewelry to get the best deals) and the element of risk involved.

"Birth certificates and sedulas are easy to make and the most popular items," says my agent who never revealed her name (not even a provisional one like "Tess"). "Gun permits and clearances from the National Bureau of Investigation are the trickiest and can run up to ₱5,000 (€100 or US$113) because that's what the police are most concerned about," she says in an even lower voice.

"A certificate of marriage annulment can also be quite expensive because that's a ten-page document," adds Tess, citing the onerous paperwork involved.

"Oh, there's also the reputation of the school to consider. Of course, a Harvard diploma will be more expensive than a University of the East certificate," adds my agent with a sheepish grin, as if to defend the fickle pricing structure. My agent gets a text that a runner has arrived with my documents. She disappears for a minute. When she returns, she drops a small brown envelope and tightly rolled scroll rather unceremoniously on my lap. First, I inspect the birth certificate under the table. It is a fine piece of work, perhaps the best of the lot. The background guilloche pattern, the trademark yellow-green gradient, the blue seal of the National Statistics Office, a clear bar code and a stamped signature have all been perfectly reproduced to the last detail. There's even a notation at the top right, "Page 1 of 1, 1 Copy."

"They have templates, stamps and blank forms back there," beams the agent in response to my compliments. Next, I take out the driving license. At first glance, the substantial plastic card looks impressively authentic, with the correct layout, typographic scheme, and accurate personal information just as I specified. Upon closer inspection, however, I realize that it says "Identification Card" instead of "Driver License," the hologram is flat, and the bar code on the reverse is smeared and misaligned.

Forged diplomas produced in the streets of Manila, Philippines. The author paid 400 Philippine pesos (€8.60 or US$9.00) for the 'Hardvard' diploma, and 300 pesos (€6.45 or US$6.80) for the Pulitzer Prize, plus 150 pesos (€3.25 or US$3.40) for the research fee, since no original was supplied. The documents were shipped to the Netherlands, where they were framed at the local art store for €192 (US$200).

I slip out the Harvard diploma. I quickly notice that the letter-sized parchment sheet has obviously been printed with a color inkjet and that the signatures at the bottom are missing.

"I can sign it," offers Tess.

The major is also wrong; I wanted a degree in theology, but got a B.A. in journalism instead, and for some reason I graduated on March 31, when Harvard Law School's

CHAPTER 5
◆ ◆ ◆

The thriving illegal trade in counterfeit documents forces government agencies to create official documents with ever more advanced security features, which in turn forces forgers to use ever more advanced technology to keep up. (Photo: Renoir Amba)

spring semester was still in progress. And worst of all I seem to have got my degree from "Hardvard," as my diploma declares in large capital letters. With great anticipation, I take out the last item in my Recto sampler, my Pulitzer Prize. I'm imagining an ornate, gilded certificate with multiple seals, ribbons, maybe even large embossed lettering. After all, they did charge an extra ₱175 (€3.50 or US$4.00) research fee. But when I unfurl the parchment, what confronts me is a woefully generic letter-sized template form that anyone with Microsoft Office could output. And it seems that during our hasty exchange, there had been some misunderstanding about the nature of the prize.

"As I said, Pulitzer is not a school. It's a very prestigious award. I thought you researched this." I begin to explain my overall dissatisfaction with my documents. My agent hurriedly scrawls all over the dud certificate, crossing out the word "University," while simultaneously typing a text message.

"Don't worry, I'll get it fixed immediately. It will only take a few minutes. So do you want that to be a bachelor's or a master's degree? What do you want to do about these signatures?" She points to the Filipino names at the bottom of the sheet. "Should we take them off altogether? But then it won't look balanced."

The two other agents are watching quietly. Then Tess offers, "It would have been much better if you brought a sample for them to copy. The artists can do anything as long as you provide a picture."

The veteran agent is right. Graphic artists can reproduce and doctor any credential as long as there is something to work from. On the web, vendors such as BackAlleyPress.com, Cheaper-than-tuition.com, and PhonyDiplomas.com offer higher-quality documents with greater attention to the graphic details, better-quality paper, sharper printing, and correct spelling, not to mention live customer support and money-back guarantees. Marketed as novelty items, the exceptional verisimilitude of diplomas, transcripts, and certificates challenges our perceptions of what is authentic and original. I think about the array of diplomas on my doctor's wall or the impressive collection of certifications displayed by the dentist who once botched my root canal. What differs between these websites and the stalls in Recto is the fact that these companies, many based in the USA, will refuse to print documents that permit one to prescribe drugs (like an MD), or that may compromise public security, (like a pilot's license). Monitored by Homeland Security, these companies will not do business with customers from places like Cuba, Syria, or North Korea (or, curiously, from Connecticut or Oregon either). In bold (albeit tiny) letters, Phony Diploma's "We Don't Print" policy states, "If we have any notion that you intend to use our products against the public interest or public safety, we will refuse your order."

Meanwhile, in the side streets of Recto, rows of etchers are making rubber stamps, engravers are crafting identification badges, and pressmen are rolling out pads of blank receipts, ready for any commission and agnostic to the buyer's intent. Inside the mall where I got my photo taken for the fake driving license there is a legal quick-print shop specializing in rubber stamps, duplicate keys, laminated IDs, branded lanyards, and name badges, an array of identification and credentialing paraphernalia curiously similar to what the street agents were hawking. There is even an album of company logos such as Dunlop, Quiksilver, and DHL that you can use to decorate your custom lanyard or stamp. One wonders where the border between legitimate goods and forgeries actually lies. In this tiny shop, there are two graphic operators toiling at PCs, scrolling through layouts in Corel. I ask what they think of the fake document stalls in the area. One of them responds without looking up from the monitor.

"I can do that too, no problem," she retorts. Inspecting her work displayed in gleaming glass cases, I ask where she got her design training.

She stops, looks up and motions across the street with a knowing grin. "I got a degree from Recto U." She laughs, then turns back to focus on the screen and hits "print" on a sheet of ID cards.

Copyright © 2022 by Anne Quito. Published in *Works that Work*.

CHAPTER 5

THE FAIRYTALE (EXCERPT)

BY JENNIFER KABAT

I grew up in Hollin Hills, a suburb outside Washington DC, of 458 modernist, glass houses. Just beyond the land of federal buildings, marble and granite, columns and porticos and subdivisions of center-hall colonials, Hollin Hills was a place of narrow lanes, shared parks and no fences, of Eames chairs and stainless-steel cutlery. In Hollin Hills, we believed our flatware could change the world.

My parents were Democrats and involved in liberal politics. As a kid, I campaigned at every election—my first was for Jimmy Carter, when I was eight, and I remember McGovern's 72 defeat keenly. My dad devoted his life to building rural cooperatives in the US and abroad. "Owned and operated by the people they serve" was the mantra of my childhood. My father believed that capital should stay in communities and that cooperatives could help everyone, particularly the least privileged. Trained as an economist, my mother worked as a bookkeeper but was mostly a mom. She was the one who chose the house while my dad was working abroad, and they moved in a few months after I was born.

The front and back of the house are all glass, and it perches perilously at the top of a hill with 47 steps snaking up from the street. Hidden in the trees, it looks as if it's suspended in their boughs. Inside, a chimney made of reclaimed brick cuts through both floors and divides the open-plan spaces as if they spiral out from it. My bedroom was downstairs where the house hunkers into the ground, and the windows start at the level of the lawn. I'd often stand before the glass walls at night and wonder who might be on the other side.

I didn't love modernism, not at first. I wanted to fit in, which for me, at my elementary school, meant church on Sunday and a colonial home. The place I wanted to live would have a canopy bed with a ruffled skirt at the bottom, and my name would be "Cabot" not "Kabat." My parents were aghast at these dreams of normalcy and responded by teaching me modernism's principles. In our house everything came with a lesson. The gray Eames chair was "mass-produced and affordable for all." I even knew what my parents paid for it. Seven dollars. Then there was Russel and Mary Wright's *Guide to Easier Living*, a book written by a modernist potter and his wife that provided detailed instructions for a newer, simpler life. The opening pages have drawings of fussy chairs with Xs through them.

With modernism life would be better because it was streamlined. Homes were pared back, and housework would be measured, regulated, simplified, just like on production lines. The factory moved to the domestic realm. Corbusier declared the home "a machine for living in," and said that architecture could solve "social unrest." These homes and their furniture were also going to fix social problems like poverty, as if aesthetics were linked to amelioration.

My parents moved to Hollin Hills around the time that the US started calling modernism the International Style. It was an aesthetic of any place and no place and was applied mostly to corporate headquarters, the UN, and housing projects. In Hollin Hills, nature, sun and light, architecture and design, form and function all represented a new form of idealism.

The community was a kind of utopia. When it was founded, all the residents believed in hope and change. My parents arrived to communal co-ops, collective parks, and collective baby-sitting. People banded together. There were committees for everything from water to trash. A Viennese magazine called it a "colony of intellectuals." The families that came here chose someplace new and different: walls of glass, reclaimed brick, open plan, open lives.

The architect of Hollin Hills, Charles Goodman, described Hollin Hills by saying, "These houses attract the kind of people who don't think the world is perfect." What did that mean? My father believed humanity was ever improving and architecture was part of the process. For him perfection was achievable; that was what progress meant. It went in one direction—better—and modern design would speed us on our way. But how? And how did everyone here in Hollin Hills have such faith? What did they believe was going to happen in these houses? Were they supposed to improve their occupants? Or the world? I wish I could know how Goodman's words sounded then.

I stand in the street and look up at the house where I was raised. I've come back to Hollin Hills to try to understand its magic. My father has been dead for five years, and in the time between his death and this moment, I've found myself rebuilding my parents' modernist home in a remote valley in upstate New York. Clearly their values have a hold on me, so much so that I didn't even think rebuilding the house was suffused with meaning. I didn't think about it at all—not until my architect joked about how I was designing the Oedipal home.

I know it wasn't just my family that lived the modernist dream. Four hundred and fifty-eight other families did too in Hollin Hills. That's more than a thousand people. But what brought them all here? How did they come to idealize modernism? It seems so impossible today, but who wouldn't want to believe something as simple as a seven-dollar chair could make the world a better place?

Only a handful of original residents remain. When my parents arrived in 1956, Hollin Hills was seven years old. My mother's parents helped with the move and when my grandmother got there, she quipped, "Why would anyone want to live in a beach house in the woods?"

I look at the black-and-white photographs from that time. My mother was twenty-nine and had two baby daughters—my older sisters, who were teenagers when I was born more than a decade later. Kids run in the street dressed as cowboys. A mother who looks like a teenager stands in the midst of them in rolled-up jeans and sneakers. Two boys play catch; another swings from a giant tree. It's winter in the pictures. The homes are stark in the landscape, surrounded by bare trees. Spindly black limbs and branches reach for the sky, and those dark lines emphasize the slender white mullions holding up the walls of glass. The homes had high ceilings and low dividing walls, clerestories, and open plans, as if life were moveable and full of possibility.

Hollin Hills was built by Bob Davenport and Charles Goodman. Davenport had been a government employee working in the Agriculture Department during the New Deal and Goodman was a modernist who'd had government contracts during the War and built the National Airport in Washington (now Ronald Reagan National Airport). I grew up hearing stories about both of them: the architect's inflexibility, the developer's generosity. They shared a vision of what they wanted from Hollin Hills and, in 1946, they walked the hills and plotted a suburban development that would be different, that they'd be "proud of." The land, though, was in Virginia—bordering the last vestige of George Mason's original plantation, and not even five miles away was Alexandria, which had been home to one of the biggest firm of slave traders in the country. It's hard to imagine building a progressive community in the segregated South—but that is what they did.

They talked about fitting homes into nature rather than forcing nature to submit to housing. Inside and outside would blur together, boundaries would be frowned upon. To this day, fences are banned in Hollin Hills, and the homes have been sited so the land itself feels shared, while in an act of benevolence that became legendary,

WRITING HISTORY NOW

They talked about fitting homes into nature rather than forcing nature to submit to housing. Inside and outside would blur together, boundaries would be frowned upon.

Davenport deeded parcels to the subdivision for communal parks. More importantly, the only restrictive covenants were to protect the architecture of the homes—not keep people out based on race, like the covenants in many other subdivisions built across the US at this time.

My parents originally wanted to move to Maryland, which was not segregated but politically corrupt. Virginia was the last place they saw themselves living, yet here was a community of like-minded Democrats who all voted for Adlai Stevenson—the last progressive to run for president—living in modernist houses and taking up leftist causes in the most unlikely place.

I stand in my childhood bedroom and pore over the clippings my mother kept about the community. DC punk posters are still tacked on the walls where I'd hung them as a teen. "This is Hollin Hills," announces a sales brochure, with the jaunty self-assurance that assumes we should already know Hollin Hills, or at least want to. Next I find a personal letter from Davenport welcoming my parents to the subdivision. "Hollin Hills," he typed, "is a unique community . . . You like all the others who are now living here or will be here later have been attracted by a new and different type of architecture, far ahead of conventional design."

Far ahead. You are, he's saying, far ahead of the others because this place is ahead of everywhere else.

It's summer and uncommonly cool for Virginia. I walk through the streets and think about the idea of specialness the community cultivated. Roads dead-end in cul-de-sacs, houses are tucked into trees, hidden in the boughs. Ceilings soar, second stories cantilever out. One mimics the line of the roof as if the whole building were leaping into the air. Others have rooftops that wave like a butterfly. Some models, no bigger than a double-wide, come with thirty feet of glass across the side. Another you can see clear through. In one of the communal parks, the trees arch overhead like something out of Ruskin's "Nature of Gothic." A fox darts from the path, and I think about how the earliest residents called themselves "pioneers" to try and capture the sense of adventure that came with moving here—or maybe it was a sense of ordination. For one small second I think of this as "the city upon a hill."

CHAPTER 5

"There was," he says, "a community effort back then. People seemed to do things together."

The more I think about the line, the more it feels like it fits. John Winthrop used it in his sermon to the Puritans on the decks of the *Arbella* when they were about to land in America. He was telling them the world would be watching, and that their new society would be an example to all. The first residents of Hollin Hills also felt like a promised people in a promised land. They were embattled; there was no municipal water, no paved roads, no phone lines, no trash pick-up, no mail delivery. The nearest school was a two-room schoolhouse with a potbelly stove. People had to contend with the land. This language of struggle, of us against the world, of the world watching, this sense of mission, this was Hollin Hills.

My oldest sister Ellen remembers the sense of "freedom" and "openness." These are the qualities she associated with the community as a kid. It was being able to run around in the woods; the homes were open, nature abounding. Today she dates an architect who grew up here as well. He explains that the notion of transparency in the homes carried through to the way you could cut through the neighbors' yards. He not only lives in the community, he lives in his parents' old house. We're in the living room, and I'm sitting on the same leather sofa my parents have. Its teak arms curve out delicately, as if it were an abstracted version of a chesterfield with thin teak legs. The only difference is Roger's is black leather, my parents' a caramel shade that makes me think of the early '70s, and every place I go there's a sense of déjà vu. The homes are all furnished similarly. "There was," he says, "a community effort back then. People seemed to do things together."

How could my father have such faith in progress? His family had escaped the czar's pogroms, and he and his brother and sister grew up in a small town outside Pittsburgh. During the Depression, they had a cross burned on the lawn and their father lost his store. My father and his siblings all served in World War II. My uncle lost his leg to a shark in the Pacific. My aunt was an Army nurse. She'd been at Normandy and the Liberation of Paris, and would say, "The things I've seen, the horrors—" but would never specify what those horrors were, at least not to me. My father was in the deadliest branch of the service, the Merchant Marine, posted in an unarmed ship sailing the most dangerous route in the North Atlantic. In his last years, he'd tell me about the sound of boats around his going down. I don't see anything in those experiences that should lead to an optimism in humankind, but it did.

The year I was born Vietnam was in full swing; Bobby Kennedy and Martin Luther King Jr. were killed, and my mother was wondering what kind of a world she had brought a child into. For her, hope seemed impossible.

In its earliest years Hollin Hills was a place of communal values, but things had changed. Now it was embattled and encroached upon. Soon after I was born a subdivision of traditional homes was built right behind my parents'. Fake gas lanterns hung down over the front doors there as if to suggest a home should look like an antebellum estate, maybe with slaves. Meanwhile in the US—and in Hollin Hills—war divided us. President Johnson started Vietnam and advanced civil rights and social welfare. Come Watergate, traditional politics was tainted and the change everyone had valued seemed far, far away. My dad, though, still believed in fighting to change the world, even with compromises attached.

Copyright © 2016 by Jennifer Kabat. Excerpt of essay published in *Granta*, December 2016.

Biographies are published as books and monographs, feature stories and profiles and as parts of critical writing. A biography is as much a story of an individual (or group) as it is an overview or panorama of particular designs, movements, events and breakthroughs. Biography (and autobiography) will advance history of the genre(s) written about as well as bolstering a reputation with fact and speculation. It may be one of the most difficult and challenging forms of design writing.

WRITING
BIOGRAPHY

CHAPTER 6

LINNAEA TILLETT OFTEN FINDS THAT LESS IS MORE

BY AKIKO BUSCH

✱

"Wait. Wait. Just wait." Such are the words that lighting designer Linnaea Tillett finds herself repeating to her clients time and again. Attuned to the intrinsic connection between light and time, she knows that her work reveals itself slowly, in increments. But if her call for pause feels anachronistic at a time when the pace of modern life seems ever accelerated, that's not the only thing that appears incongruous. As a scholar of illumination, Tillett is unusually engaged with nuances of darkness, aware that human perception is a matter not just of seeing light, but of discerning shadow.

These contradictions have distinguished her work in residential, commercial, and landscape lighting for the last 31 years. Projects executed by her Brooklyn firm, Tillett Lighting Design Inc., range from the High Line, the Franklin D. Roosevelt Four Freedoms Park, and the Battery Bosque in New York, to Shantou University in China and the Icepool in Finland, a collaboration with Lebbeus Woods and Kiki Smith. Throughout, her approach reflects the conviction stated by Junichiro Tanizaki in his classic inquiry into varying cultural ideas of light, *In Praise of Shadows:* Beauty, he wrote, is found "not in the thing itself, but in the patterns of shadows, the light, and the darkness, the one thing against another creates."

Which is to say, Tillett's work is informed by the paradox that seeing more is often a matter of less light. Consider, for example, the fecund landscape of the

Menil Collection campus in Houston, distinguished by its great, leafy trees that dapple the gardens below—and its wash of excessive security lighting. Aware of "the philosophical idea that too much light hinders perception," Tillett specified subtle fixtures interspersed at doorways and entrances and intermittent light on pathways.

For a bicycle and pedestrian bridge over a highway in Albuquerque, she used 450 LED lights to evoke a blue stream of river and sky that takes its shimmer from the galvanized metal mesh of the structure. And for a public park in Syracuse, New York, she programmed 50-plus tiny chips on benches and fountains to blink in seemingly random sequences like year-round fireflies, "reflective, magical animate lights that appear and disappear—delicate, half-light, that are part of our mythology."

Tillett's lineage is one of design royalty. Her parents were D.D. and Leslie Tillett, celebrated textile designers whose bright patterns and designs in the fifties were favored by Jacqueline Kennedy. As a child, Linnaea was accustomed to seeing her parents with their clients, scrutinizing fabrics in different lights. The experience familiarized her with the constant transaction between light and the material world. Each, she found, gives character to the other. That such an exchange might be the basis of a career was something to which she gave little thought, and her undergraduate degree from the University College London was in philosophy. But in the mid-seventies, her sister-in-law—a costume designer—entreated her to help with a theater production.

"We had some old tin cans with lenses, lots of wire, and a good script," Tillett recalls. Discovering the manner in which lighting could support the emotional content of the play, she deferred her plans for graduate school.

When she established her own lighting practice for private homes, museums, and galleries, conversations with her private clients alerted Tillett to the difficulties in speaking about light. "People would say, 'I hate fluorescents,' or 'I want this place bright.' Maybe they had grown up with Depression-era parents who were always turning out the lights. But there was always a lot of raw emotion. And I was trying to read them as people." This eventually motivated her to enroll in the doctorate program in environmental psychology at City University of New York.

As part of her thesis, she worked in a low-income community in East New York, Brooklyn, where, she recalls, illumination was often used as an accessory to authority. This was during the war on crime, and "redlined" high-crime areas were bathed in blinding floodlights. The belief that "having light is like having the police" worked to the benefit of Con Edison and lighting manufacturers, she points out. The doctorate program required that she get 72 credits in psychology and, as she says, "I was always thinking about light. So I got a PhD in how to communicate about light."

Everything, she says now, was shaped by that experience, and the knowledge that lighting conveys an emotional texture. Pure darkness exists only in the imagination. And sunlight is not just about illumination, but a sensation. "It has warmth, it moves, it plays, you feel it on your skin. It is not predictable. It's a more dimensional experience, not just about seeing."

"You try to use very little," Tillett says of her work now. "You ask questions of sensibilities. You ask how you support human development." Certainly she has done that in a current project for an urban waterfront in Connecticut, which includes a highway, train station, and public esplanade. While city planners believed that the dusky area needed more light and more color, Tillett rarely approaches a project assuming that more lighting is what is needed.

"It could be color or signage," she says. "And sometimes I can do more for you if we turn things off. Sometimes it is about suppression. You can see too much. Or there may be too much light in one area, not enough in others."

In this case, standard waterfront industrial structures included the massive concrete pillars supporting I-95, huge boats coming in, container towers, and an electrical tower. Tillett proposed adding uplighting beneath the underpass for the train tracks, but elsewhere relies largely on the use of a reflective paint with a pale coppery glow. It was applied to the underside of I-95, to the stairways, and on the surfaces of underpasses. It shines in the sunlight, she says, and at night it will pick up the glimmer from passing cars, the shine from existing lighting, the shimmering reflections on the water.

"Celebrate what you have," she says. "Use the least amount of materials. Make it legible, vibrant, exciting."

What is happening here is also an example of what she calls "glow"—that social experience of light that occurs when people take in one another's presence; when luminescence is emotionally sustaining and fosters community, perhaps even offering enchantment. To convey this point to her students at Parsons the New School for Design (where she taught for 20 years), she would sometimes take them at sundown to the beds of impatiens planted on Park Avenue's median strip.

"There are different kinds of twilight," she says. "And as the sun sets, our perceptual system shifts in how we see color. Some colors intensify at dusk, others recede. The reds and yellows fade first, then the greens, lavenders, and finally the blues."

Tillett works with the conviction that we are living in a technologically transformative time no less momentous than the advent of gas and electric illumination, which, she says, "changed everything—materials, clothing, the time we work." The technology of LEDs—compact, energy-efficient, cool to the touch, and capable of a wide range of color—allows us to carry light and recharge it. How does this open things up, she asks? "We have to think about it this way—otherwise it is just about tricks, entertainment.

Tillett works with the conviction that we are living in a technologically transformative time no less momentous than the advent of gas and electric illumination, which, she says, "changed everything—materials, clothing, the time we work."

We have to ask: How is this salient to human life? It is profound. It is not just some new engineering tool."

Already, she says, the light on our tablets and phones allows us to reconsider light sources. When things—such as books, cameras, phones—become luminous, it challenges our ideas of what is lit and what is not. But Tillett suggests we need to know more about the brightness of devices. If you are reading at night in bed, the blue light of your device might trigger your circadian rhythm cycle because early morning light is in that blue spectrum. So it might make sense to also have an incandescent light on or to have more ambient light. Or to get a filter.

But if our views to the illuminated world are being changed by new technologies, so too are they affected by disruptions in the natural world, whether it is the decline of bioluminescence in micro-organisms, increasingly erratic weather patterns that disturb the built environment, or conditions of light trespass and the gradual diminishment of the night sky. As a steward for the nuances of darkness, Tillett observes that, before the advent of electricity, we were more attuned to gradations of light, whether daylight, twilight, moonlight, or candlelight. A century ago, we might have been more visually prepared for catastrophic blackouts caused by such environmental disasters as Hurricane Sandy.

Tillett's work increasingly confronts the disturbances of climate change, and the "freakish, unpredictable, chaotic forces that affect us on a day-to-day level, whether it is going underwater, or freezing, or drying out." The bike bridge that she worked on in Albuquerque, for example, was damaged by a violent storm shortly after completion. "We realized that a 100-year floodplain is actually a two-year flood-plain. So you have to think at a level of robustness, and buildings that can withstand a cataclysmic event. Communities change. And people get angry. It changes your thinking."

Part of that shift in thinking now has to do with time, and brings us back to Tillett's conviction that light and time are inextricable colleagues. Light has to do with transience, and portable illumination has become a recent obsession. "There are two ways to use light sustainably," she says. "The first is the use of more efficient sources. But most studies say the more efficient sources we have, the more we use. Because we can! But the second way is to think that the light you don't install is the most efficient. People used to carry light with them. They'd amplify it, use luminous surfaces and reflective materials. We used to paint the bases of trees white. In England, they'd use piles of chalk as road markers to catch the moonlight. So think now about what colors, and what materials, can catch the light. It is a psychological change, learning to be frugal this way."

Tillett is currently devising a system for portable light—not a prototype as much as a way to show clients how compact, movable lighting might be used in a public garden or park. She envisions a rental model not unlike that of the Citi Bike program—participatory, spontaneous, economic, efficient, and part of a larger system. The three issues, she says, are ease of storage, how to mount the unit, and rechargeability.

With its illumination diffused through the fabric, and kinetic in the way that anything carried by hand is sure to be, the mobile lamp comes slowly and softly alive. Consistent with all her previous work, the program is not just about reducing consumption, but about promoting an emotional transaction. "You pick up the lights," she says, "and that changes the internal experience. It's the kind of sustainability that speaks to our need for magic. That's the return here. And we are all still after this enchantment."

Copyright © 2014 by Akiko Busch. Published in *Metropolis*, June 2014.

WRITING BIOGRAPHY

TAKENOBU IGARASHI PUSHED THE PARAMETERS OF TYPOGRAPHY

BY ANGELA RIECHERS

J apanese-born educator and designer Takenobu Igarashi's 20-year creative career brought an architectural understanding of form and space to the world of typography, paving the way for a new field of dimensional type from the mid-1970s to today. His explorations in 3D typography started as axonometric drawings, which he produced by hand using architecture drafting tools. By the '80s, these drawings had morphed into sculptures rendered in complex interlocking forms of folded paper, metal, concrete, and wood, carving up space in pure expressions of shape and volume. The rich surfaces practically beg viewers to run their hands over them.

A new book, *Takenobu Igarashi A-Z*, written by Sakura Nomiyama and edited by Haruki Mori, gives the first major retrospective of his work, complete with process photos, hand-drawn sketches, sculptures, posters, and numerous interviews with the designer. What emerges from all of that material is a portrait of a designer who refused to consider graphic design within its established limits, and instead pushed the discipline's parameters into entirely new territory. Igarashi's deep understanding of form allowed him to consider type as architecture, not just a thin layer of ink on a page. He was one of the first twentieth-century designers to explore more complex spatial roles for typography, even when that type was still part of a 2D printed image.

He became a master of 3D type well before computers became ubiquitous tools in the design industry.

The modular 3D characters Igarashi developed show the influence of early Bauhaus masters, such as Herbert Bayer and Josef Albers, and also looked to the future, paving the way for the explosion of dimensional type that happened throughout the 1970s. During this era, new technologies for phototypesetting and computer-based type systems started to take over all types of publishing, from newspapers and magazines to advertising and signage. Designers began to play with new possibilities in type, now that they were no longer limited to cast metal fonts. Suddenly the world was awash in quirky, non-traditional typefaces that did not follow any established tradition. Instead, they hewed only to the whims of their designers, including Seymour Chwast and Milton Glaser, whose typefaces Blimp and Hologram, respectively, were both published in 1970.

Meanwhile, Igarashi's prolific career was taking off. He taught and founded design programs at Chiba University and Tama Art University in Japan, and the University of California, Los Angeles, and worked for various American and Japanese clients on their corporate design. He employed his hand-drawn 3D type in vibrant and innovative posters for UCLA, TCP Corp Jazz Festival, and Zen Environmental Design. In the 1980s, Igarashi began to collaborate with other influential graphic designers, including Massimo Vignelli and Alan Fletcher, on OUN, a project focused on design education, publications, and new product development, and with Pentagram on posters advertising the newly launched Polaroid Impulse camera in 1988.

In 1984, Igarashi took out a five-year loan to buy three Macintosh computers. He experimented with effects achievable only with this new design tool, adding to his practice of manual, hand-drawn design with its focus on physical construction and process, materials, and methods.

In the same decade, his contemporary in the fine arts world Robert Indiana (creator of Philadelphia's L-O-V-E sculpture) and fellow graphic designer Ivan Chermayeff (whose giant red number 9 stands outside of New York City's Solow building on West 57th Street) were both working with large-scale dimensional letterform sculptures whose main visual appeal is their brightly colored, glossy surfaces. Igarashi's sculptural letters are a different breed entirely: They speak to the complex interplay of void and form first, while maintaining a healthy respect for surface qualities as well. During this time, the designer also advanced into the field of product design, creating flatware and a wildly popular calendar featuring 3D numerals for the Museum of Modern Art in New York. It included 622 individually-designed numerals needed to represent the 365 days of the year—meaning that he designed 4,536 variations of axonometric three-dimensional numerals, based on 84 different ideas. The calendar sold out eight years in a row.

His first type sculptural series began in 1981 with an aluminum alphabet inspired by old radio parts and variable capacitors, as part of a personal design exploration. A side-by-side comparison of his drawing (graphite on tracing paper) for a capital D next to the finished letterform is like seeing geometry come to life, as if a problem from your tenth-grade math book suddenly sat up and decided to assemble itself into an imposing sculptural object. Igarashi's ability to imagine and fabricate precise letters using an analog skill set is all the more remarkable against the backdrop of today's 3D type and motion graphics, where software does much of that work for a designer.

Contemporary dimensional type takes on many forms, from real-world objects to variable 3D effects. All owe a debt to Igarashi. Michael Prisco and Helen Sywalski's project "Type High: Experiments in Dimensional Design and Typography," on exhibit in 2017 at the Cooper Union in New York, falls firmly in the realm of sculpture. "Type High" showcased four-foot-tall letters A, B, and C fabricated from metal and plywood that visitors could walk through, around, and even into. Also in the entirely real camp is Spanish Western, a set of letterforms milled in wood. Designed by Quique Rodríguez, creative director of Spanish design studio Dosdecadatres, the letters were dramatically lit and filmed as opening credits for a public TV documentary. Dosdecadatres has also made some pretty impressive dimensional type from functional laboratory glassware.

SVG technology makes contemporary digital fonts such as Bixa possible, updating nineteenth-century woodblock typefaces whose eye-catching 3D chromatic effects were created for use in advertising. Whoa, designed by Travis Kochel, features an advanced variable 3D effect that makes other commercially-available static 3D fonts look like kid stuff.

By reimagining type (the flattest of flat design) as objects that took up volume and appeared to have mass, Igarashi inspired the design world to envision typography in a brand-new incarnation, and brought a centuries-old tradition into the future. In 1994, he shuttered his design practice and moved to Los Angeles to become a sculptor. Ten years later he returned to Japan where he still lives and works, producing sculptures and graphic artworks for public spaces nationwide. Ongoing design experiments in type and dimensionality demonstrate that as typography continues to advance further into virtual and spatial realms, designers still have much to learn from the groundbreaking work of Takenobu Igarashi.

Copyright © 2020 by Angela Riechers. Published in *AIGA Eye on Design*, October 14, 2020.

CHAPTER 6

VICTOR MOSCOSO'S HALLUCINOGENIC FLASHBACK

BY STEVEN HELLER

Some of you may be here maybe to indulge in a little hallucinogenic flashback. Others are here to celebrate an iconic artist, who helped define the modern aesthetic of his era just as A.M. Cassandre did for his. An artist whose drawings are as fluid and witty as the great cartoon and comic artists of the gilded age, Victor Moscoso's work tends to be locked into a tight timeframe, while in fact, his art is open to appreciation by all generations because of its craft, innovation, and response to social and cultural prompts of his time.

I write this not to relive my counterculture moments—which I don't recall anyway—but to experience a great artist's incomparable work as an abstract storyteller, inventive typographer, and daring colorist.

Victor Moscoso was chief among the tribe of graphic maestros and principal form-givers of the Sixties and into 2020s. He lived through the sixties and is still able to remember it. The Spanish born, Brooklyn-raised, Yale-educated artist stumbled into the counter culture and arose to become its genius of a distinct American music-inspired graphic poster language.

Although the movement's name was not coined by any of the artists, psychedelic aptly underscored the hypnotic letterforms and vibrating color combinations, and retrofitted antique illustrations. They used their visual language as a code that vividly communicated to those visionary—or stoned—enough to see the messages

Victor Moscoso's work tends to be locked into a tight timeframe, while in fact, his art is open to appreciation by all generations because of its craft, innovation, and response to social and cultural prompts of his time.

through the chromatic haze. While many of the artists who were making cheaply printed flyers promoting ballroom concerts were ostensibly self-taught, their respective work unwittingly redefined a large swath of commercial art, graphic design, and fine arts too (even today).

Moscoso was unique in ways that gave him anomaly status among his peers. He was the only formally art school- and university-trained artist in this otherwise grassroots poster movement. He really knew how to draw in a classical sense and understood design theory. He had studied Bauhaus history and early and mid-century Modernism. In short, Moscoso had bona fides as a modernist. But his tenure at New York's Cooper Union and later Yale—where he was taught by none other than the renowned color-master and Bauhausler Josef Albers—was not so much an advantage as a handicap; to work in his newfound counterculture genre he had to reverse everything he learned.

Thanks to David Caraba for bringing the work into the light, and to Victor Moscoso for making an indelible mark on American art and design.

Copyright © 2023 by Steven Heller.

Putting the "I" in design writing has been pervasive throughout the history of the form. It can, of course, be pure conjecture and baseless criticism, but it can also ally with truth and point of view. With the latter, personal design writing can also provide oral history. The rhetorical "I" also serves to denote particular ways of thinking at any given period and when handled without hubris and conceit can be an entertaining subgenre of design writing.

MAKING IT PERSONAL

CHAPTER 7

ROY MCMAKIN'S OVERPOWERING SIMPLICITY

BY EVA HAGBERG

✱

In the summer of 2007, I got on a flight paid for by a magazine to travel from my home in Brooklyn, where I had recently torpedoed my life, to Seattle, where I would meet an artist, or maybe an architect or maybe a designer, named Roy McMakin. I hadn't heard of Roy, which doesn't mean much—I'd just started writing about architecture a few years earlier and was mostly only aware of designers who had publicists, who were based in New York, and who took me to lunch. But I was excited to write about Roy. It was validating to be flown somewhere, and I felt optimistic that my career wasn't over, even though, a few months earlier, I'd published a story in *The New York Times* that had required two corrections, which I thought—believed—made me unemployable, and also, unlovable.

Before flying it seems like I must have gone to the back room of the Chelsea gallery that was then representing McMakin (he wasn't yet Roy, to me), and paged through books that had been handed to me, and seeing immaculately constructed chairs and tables, often bisected with paint, and dressers that I couldn't understand but wanted to think about. McMakin, now 67, had done three shows for this gallery: one a "complete residential environment," one named after his mother, Lequita Faye Melvin, and based on "memories of his grandparents' house in Oklahoma," and one that, to my mind, and maybe also to his, about the heartbreak and the beauty of trying to fit things together.

The latter was reflected in the exhibition "For," in which McMakin, among other moves, combined found furniture with new sculpture, creating pieces made half of the past and half of the present, and it was everything to me, a person who had just realized that I had a past that was intruding onto what otherwise could have been my present. Though in writing this, I realize that "For," in that moment, hadn't yet happened. Not that the detail matters.

My practice then and now involves preparing as little as possible before interviewing someone. I always want to come fresh, and open, and maybe I saw those books after I first saw Roy in Seattle (my past with him, and how it all began, and how it is now—he is my friend, my favorite artist, my subject, my collaborator, my interlocutor, and my wise, slightly elder—is so mingled with the chaos of that time in my life). I didn't realize basic biographical facts, such as the fact that he founded the handmade objects line Domestic Furniture in San Diego, in 1987, and officially opened it as a showroom the following year in Los Angeles, where he lived in Larchmont Village, where tonight my daughter and her father and some friends and I will go out to dinner. Or that he later started the firm Domestic Architecture, or that he had continued to produce fine art that looked like architecture, furniture that operated as art, and art that felt like a house. I didn't realize that I would think about Roy's work for—at this point—the rest of my life. Instead, given what was, as they say, going on for me, I thought, How little can I get away with?

I was supposed to write about a house designed for an art-collecting couple, whom I thought at first had hired Roy to design their house, a phrase that's really doing the bare minimum here. What they did, or what I came to see, was that they had commissioned Roy to do a piece for them, and the piece happened to be—or had to be, or could only be—in the form of a house: a complete residential environment, overlooking Lake Washington.

During that trip, Roy picked me up from wherever I was staying and we drove to the house. At first it seemed sort of normal, a mix of Victorian and craftsman (not that I know anything about either of those styles—not my century). Inside, I realized there was something else going on.

I had been writing about nice houses for long enough by then that I had a routine, which is likewise followed by many design journalists: I would ask about what the clients wanted, and then about what ideas were embedded into their home, listening while feigning a sense of curiosity and delight. But here I was out of routine. I was curious. I was delighted. The house itself was both open and delineated; rooms at once swept into each other and separated themselves. There were tables angled together and plushly upholstered chairs that looked like things my Corvallis-based, then-alive grandmother would have had, but tweaked, somehow, into furniture that made you look twice if you looked hard enough the first time to detect something was just slightly unexpected.

CHAPTER 7

In the primary bedroom, two windows were right next to each other. One had small frames that opened, providing an obstructed view of the lake that offered the capacity for transformation, and one was embedded in a single large frame, and inoperable: no visual obstruction, but no fungibility. The wife had wanted one style and the husband another; Roy had found a way to both draw attention to these differences, and to soothe them. It all exemplified how everything in Roy's world, it seemed, was ratcheted up to the nth degree of execution, and also, I would come to learn, of emotion.

That night, the owners took us out to dinner and maybe they invited me, or maybe I invited myself, but somehow I ended up sleeping in the guest wing that night, in the lower level of the house, in a room that was delineated with at least two paint colors that cut through the bed, ran through the bedside table, and made the entire room a work of art by drawing attention to things I had never thought about, like beds always being one color. As I went to sleep, I thought about the room as a work of art, the way in which the bedside table was two colors, and how that evoked inclusion and exclusion. The next day I flew back to New York. I wrote my piece, giving it my best instead of my least, and it was published and life went on.

I figured that I would never see Roy again because that was the nature of this kind of assignment. But that is not what happened. We kept in touch. It was probably Roy, whom I've learned is very good at keeping in touch. One of my favorite things about him is that when I send him a text message he responds with a phone call, usually within two minutes.

Roy came to my wedding. Later, I talked to him about my divorce. He did a book event with me in Berkeley, when I'd just started grad school and published my second book, about nature and architecture, in which I included that Seattle house. He moved to San Diego, where he built an extraordinary collection of works of art—a house, complete with his furniture, for himself and his husband, Mike; a complex of rentals. After a while, I figured out that he was no longer tied to Seattle. Sometimes I would ask him if he missed that city. Eventually he would graciously say, "Well, it's been a long time," which reminded me that a lot of time had passed, and that we were still in conversation.

I want to tell you about Roy's work, but at the same time part of me wants to keep it to myself, which is fueled by my inherent selfishness, which isn't the vibe. Roy is generous. His work is generous. And his capacity and imagination to distill the weird, stupid, awful, wonderful, extraordinary fact of being alive into three- and two-dimensional forms is astonishing.

I will tell you that in his house, right now, there is a room in which there are eight dressers, four for Mike and four for Roy, all slightly different. On one of the dress-ers—one of his—is a series of objects he has collected, silently resting there. They made me think about conversations we've had about his work and how little there often is to say, because there is just so much to feel.

For instance, in 2008 he made a piece called "Untitled (a small chest of drawers with one drawer that doesn't fit)." It's a maple dresser, with five drawers, and one of them doesn't fit so it sits on top. The piece, to me, is wrenching. It reminds me of all the times I didn't fit, and also all the times I assumed I didn't fit but maybe actually did.

He made another piece, called "4 photographs of 4 sides of a green chest of drawers (cameras the same distance from each side) with Mike, and another green chest," in 2011, which is a grouping of four photographs, two featuring himself and Mike, crouched together behind chests. To me, it's about Mike's love for Roy, and Roy's love for Mike, and Roy's desire for other people to get to feel the kind of love that he feels for Mike and Mike feels for him, and also the way in which dressers, for him, became love. The dressers are central to these photographs; Mike is central to these photographs; Roy is central to these photographs. That's why I keep thinking about his work.

Another piece, "Untitled" (this one with no parenthetical subtitle), from 2018, and from the same Garth Greenan Gallery show as the photographs, is an enameled maple dresser, white, six drawers. At first blush, it's plain, and I think maybe it's about the craft of maple or the process of enameling. Then I realize that there are no pulls on the drawers, that I don't know if they can open, and that it's unlikely that they're push drawers. And so the functional dresser becomes a sculpture and the object asks me to look at it differently, to consider volume and form and ridge and edge line. That is another trick of Roy's heart: to invite us to glance, and then to look, and then to really, really look.

By now you have probably realized that dressers, and chests, are a large part of Roy's work. When I asked him why that is he said that, when he was younger, he found solace in dressers. Furniture became an object onto which he could imprint his love: the love he came here with, the love we all show up with, the love that gets torn out of us or slowly leached out of us, the love that maybe we want, or at least, that I want.

When I asked him a few years later to talk about that again, because I felt like I was the opposite—I have lost so much physical material in my life; I have decided not to care—he talked about his work being more than a chance for him to imprint his own love. It's a chance, he said, to give some of that love to someone else.

The way he sees it, or maybe it's just the way I see it and have imprinted onto him, is that it isn't only about the dresser he loved. It's about how he loved that dresser and getting someone else to love a dresser, too. Or it's about feeling loved by a dresser, by the fact of it having been made by someone. We are all alone and we are all loved.

CHAPTER 7

Roy's work is what they used to call "deceptively simple," though there is nothing deceptive about it. Actually, it is so honest and so direct and so straightforward that it is almost too much to process, too hot to handle. To be honest, I thought about how simple I could make this story. Part of me thinks that I have not told you enough about Roy. But when I told him I was writing this and asked if he wanted to be involved, he said maybe for fact checks, sure, but that this was my thing, and that's the thing. One of the things.

Roy performs very little on the surface and accomplishes multitudes beneath it. He talks about love, and collecting crap, and art, and how much he loves Mike—he loves Mike, so much—and within that simplicity and that clarity comes the oceanic feeling. When I talk to Roy, and when I think about his work, I am often overcome because there is so little to hold on to that I am overwhelmed. His work reminds me of all the pain that I have experienced and all of the love that I have been given next to that pain. It shows me that even in my solitude, I am not alone. That particularly in my loneliness, I am not alone.

I love Roy's work and I love Roy. Sometimes people say they love someone when what they really mean is that they think they're fine, or that they met them one time, or that they know they're supposed to say that about them. But really, I love Roy. And maybe in many ways this whole essay is just an attempt, by barely glancing across the surface of what I could say, to show what this one love has looked like. How it has felt.

Copyright © 2023 by Eva Hagberg. Published in *Untapped Journal*, September 11, 2023.

MAKING IT PERSONAL

WHAT THE "WHOLE EARTH CATALOG" TAUGHT ME ABOUT BUILDING UTOPIAS

BY ANJULIE RAO

✱

My mother threw away her copy of the *Whole Earth Catalog* long before I was born. Having endured so much use, it was in shreds, she tells me as I sit in the kitchen of her home near Golden, Colorado. She first purchased the manual when she was fourteen, growing up in the flower children era. She was deeply drawn to it, calling herself a devotée, she says, "because of the zeitgeist I was unconsciously a part of: that whole Aquarian Age," prompting a "return to the earth."

A compendium that reads like a scrappy, ad hoc Sears mailer, the *Whole Earth Catalog* featured products, books, and tips for those seeking a life defined by self-sufficiency. Published several times a year between 1968 and 1971 (and a few times afterward) by its technofuturist co-founder and editor, Stewart Brand, the volumes offered insights and instructions for tasks such as building geodesic Bucky Domes, constructing solar arrays, operating weaving equipment, and performing first aid. Received with great excitement by hippies and futurists, the catalog's contents informed a social revolution characterized by experimental living communities and the age's countercultural mantra to "turn on, tune in, and drop out." To my mother, the notion of going back to the land meant freedom: building a life on her own terms.

Open the first issue and you'll find a commandment: "The user should know better what is worth getting and where and how to do the getting." At the time of the *Whole Earth*'s emergence, what was worth getting was away—from a hyper-capitalist culture characterized by a *Leave It to Beaver*-esque, Buick-in-every-driveway pattern of consumption.

Last fall, more than fifty years after the catalog debuted, almost all of the *Whole Earth* library was digitized and made available online, for free. Newly accessible to younger generations, its readers can once again define "what is worth getting" for themselves.

In our current era—one defined by climate collapse, international conflict, and the decline of democracy—the question of the utility of the *Whole Earth Catalog* is fraught. Is it now simply an archive of a lesser-tech era, the subject of a mythology perpetuated by the unduly optimistic Silicon Valley–types who idolize its publisher while building their lavish bunkers? Can we ever fathom dwelling in self-sufficiency, or imagine a new path to utopia? I felt compelled to dig around for answers.

My parents didn't raise my sister and me as *Whole Earth* children. We lived in a small suburb of Boulder, Colorado; not in a commune or "on the land," by far. But there were elements of our existence that hinted at my mother's past: A frequent shopper at Crystal Market natural grocers, she fed us seaweed snacks and bulgur, and enrolled us in children's meditation classes. At 14, I began working for the local community garden's youth program, where I spent every summer for the following four years learning about high-desert irrigation, growing organic produce, and how to operate an aging tractor, while selling our harvests at the farmer's market.

There, in some ways, my mom's adolescent Aquarian values began to resonate with me. As a teenager, she went to Ipswich High School—a "hippie school," she calls it—and later attended the Habitat Institute for the Environmental in Belmont, Massachusetts (now called the Habitat Education Center and Wildlife Sanctuary). Students there visited intentional living communities attempting to develop self-sustaining habitats in nearby places such as Cape Cod, where residents grew their food and farmed fish. In 1976, she moved to western Massachusetts to live on a New Age spiritual commune that was loosely affiliated with the Renaissance Community (once called the Brotherhood of the Spirit).

By then, my mom had been reading the *Whole Earth Catalog* for almost a decade (though the first *Whole Earth* issue, she stipulates, was far superior to those that came later). She loved them because they offered access—to information including recipes for granola (a novel food at the time), Japanese construction techniques, herbalism, and more.

They also offered access to people attempting to build a world aligned with self-sufficiency—most notably Buckminster Fuller and Paolo Soleri, whose dome forms were emblematic of communal life. In one issue, she read a review of the 1970 book *Living on the Earth*: a consequential guide for members of the back-to-the-land movement that was beautifully hand-written and -illustrated by nineteen-year-old Alicia Bay Laurel. My mother immediately purchased the book, and to this day, it remains one of the most influential titles in her life.

I contacted Laurel, now seventy-four, to get a better understanding of the context from which her book emerged, and to hear how she thinks about it now. She told me she wrote it as a way to document what was necessary to survive while residing at Wheeler Ranch, a Northern California commune made notorious by neighbors who complained of drug use and unsanctioned buildings, and that housed dozens of residents who sought a life outside of cities and post–World War II American culture.

"All of a sudden, the United States was the most powerful country in the world," Laurel says of the time. "And it wanted to not only stay that way, but increase its military. Everything was about consumerism."

The Vietnam War intensified as her generation became teenagers. "Here was this society," she continues, "that was willing to grind up its young men and turn them into corpses."

This horror, coupled with LSD usage, which Laurel credits for inducing a feeling of universal interconnectedness, spurred many to leave behind the structures and rules that would fuel a culture of violence. Building their own societies for living communally required skills that both *Living on the Earth* and the *Whole Earth Catalog* could teach. (Though similar in content—the former provides instructions, for example, for making soap and for building a kitchen in the forest—Laurel says that the books, "were related, but not the same.")

"Stewart Brand was not particularly interested in living rurally and doing subsistence farming," Laurel says. "He was more interested in information systems. The catalog, for him, was [about] trying to make available all the materials that people like me and my friends might find useful."

Laurel lived happily at Wheeler Ranch until her book was picked up by Random House, in 1971 (its first version was released by Book Works, a small Bay Area publisher), and was made wildly popular by the *Whole Earth* review. She left Wheeler Ranch shortly thereafter, using her earnings to continue writing and making music.

Meanwhile, my mother didn't stay long at the Habitat school. "People got in each other's way, and not in a healthy way," she says. "Some communes were like dictatorships, or more like cults," while others, like hers, made decisions by consensus. She eventually returned to her hometown of Columbus, Ohio, and enrolled at Ohio State University to study social work.

On page 81 of the *Whole Earth Catalog*'s 1968 issue, to the left of a recipe for "beautiful natural grain cereal" is a letter from a reader, detailing the conflicts inherent to utopias. The author, known only as "ORO, El Cerrito, Calif.," writes that he had spent more than 20 years in the "Hippie Movement," living in communes "based on anarchistic freedom" as well as in ones "based on religion." The communes based on freedom failed within a year, he notes, while "those communities based on authority, particularly religious authority, often endure and survive even against vigorous opposition from the outside world." In other words, we could return to the land in search of freedom only to be met with failure; countercultural success requires replicating the same hierarchies found in society.

Laurel tells me that the problems in the communes that ORO mentions were inherent to experimentation. "All of those places were social experiments: whether we could provide enough food, enough whatever we needed, to live peacefully."

While those social experiments, like many in the U.S., didn't last, my mom maintains that the counterculture movement didn't die off; instead, its values got baked in to our culture. The small-scale obsession with health foods, natural textiles, and naturopathic remedies can be found in modern mainstream grocery and hardware stores, and Amazon, YouTube, and Google can be thought of as extensions of the access provided by the *Whole Earth* enterprise. Reading the catalog today with any semblance of seriousness, I begin to feel not like a countercultural Aquarian but like a prepper, gathering supplies and honing skills in anticipation of an inevitable apocalypse, reading in order to shield myself and my immediate family from harm.

Such prepping feels eerily similar to living in a commune. I briefly lived in one outside Lyons, Colorado, after finishing college, in 2008. I was brought there by a Craigslist ad placed by a group of homesteaders seeking additional residents. I spent time on their land—dirt paths wound through dense coniferous forest; hand-built houses were surrounded by greenhouses, vegetable gardens, and animal pens.

It was a gorgeous place founded in darkness. The colony's matriarch, an older woman who would zip around the rocky valley on an electric scooter, had established the mountain refuge under the shroud of "peak oil"—a theory that we would soon run short of fossil fuels, and be violently forced into civil war and agrarian life. She spoke of buying some yaks, which would someday tow obsolete cars that people would retrofit as wagons.

The thought of peak oil gave me slight shivers of paranoia at a time immediately preceding a global financial meltdown and amid a seemingly endless Middle East war. Returning to the land to manage the everyday struggle of staying alive seemed like a viable possibility at a time when the future felt inconceivable. Today, the concept speaks to me as a now vanished countercultural impulse: the longing to build something cooperatively out of care for each other and the planet—not out of fear—and despite communism's pitfalls.

Maybe that's what separates my generation's desires from those of the Whole Earth-era audience's: aspirations driven by fear and anxiety about the future, rather than an ethos of togetherness. Sure, those communes based on freedom generated conflict, and many failed, but perhaps the spirit of self-sufficiency was driven by a collective effort to build something better.

Laurel says that the idealism of the *Whole Earth* texts remains intact in global ecovillages, but what they and the rest of us—facing endless natural disasters, war, and illness—might deduce from the catalog today is the notion that building a community, like building a whole new society, requires skills and care.

This understanding entails recognizing that the failures of supposed utopias past—both those based in anarchy and those rooted in religious zeal—failed, in part, because of their separateness from broader society. (It's no wonder we look at the visions of present-day technofuturists, with their bunkers and dreams of erecting new cities in the desert or on other planets, as a prepper's heartbreaking wet dream. Rather than feeling liberating, self-sufficiency starts to look like a lonely endeavor.)

Instead, the "urban utopia" could be characterized by expansiveness: opening ourselves up to others and sharing our bounty and our safety without prejudice. We see glimmers of such ideals in our cities, where community gardens, tool libraries, mutual-aid networks, and other more informal methods of providing access are generated by our collective efforts, allowing everyone to share in what can be built from such resources. Rather than ignoring civic and structural ills, we must tackle them together. What we seek doesn't require going back to the land, but rather going back to the cities and neighborhoods we live in now—and reorienting them around elements that serve us all.

"Once there's a center, different kinds of structures grow from it, and they aren't necessarily farms out in the country where middle-class kids are taking drugs," Laurel tells me. Communal living doesn't require a commune, but simply communing.

We might not be able to live as the *Whole Earth* and its followers intended. We might be better off embracing its mythology—its core ethos of access to skills and care—and building our own utopias right here.

Copyright © 2024 by Anjulie Rao. Published in *Untapped Journal*, February 26, 2024.

CHAPTER 7

BLONDE AND DANGEROUS

BY PUNE DRACKER

In a time when women were still expected to perform traditional gender roles that reflected puritanical American values, Marilyn Monroe and Anita Ekberg rose to fame for representing sexual beings who enjoyed sensual pleasures. For having bodies and enjoying them. For dressing and undressing.

Though they were very different—Marilyn was deeply involved in crafting her persona, while Anita once claimed she found the idea of a sex symbol to be "stupid"—both were operating within the confines of a male-dominated industry. How did they embody the blond bombshell persona, and what can they show us about being a woman in the late 1950s? A look at their most iconic performances and outfits through the lens of dress as situated body practice—Marilyn in the "subway dress" in Billy Wilder's 1955 film, *The Seven-Year Itch*, and Anita Ekberg wading in the Trevi Fountain in an evening gown in Federico Fellini's *La Dolce Vita*—aims to provide some insight.

> "Cool and clean, in a dirty, dirty city"
> —Costume designer William Travilla describing the legendary dress he designed for Marilyn Monroe in *The Seven Year Itch*

As a designed material object, there is much to say about the dress known for being lifted up by a breeze as its wearer stood atop a subway grate. The bias-cut cocktail dress features a halter-like bodice with a plunging neckline that exposes

MAKING IT PERSONAL

the arms, shoulders, and entire back. A self-belt crisscrosses about the waist, ending in a small, tidy bow. The gently pleated skirt falls to mid-calf, unless of course there is a wind machine nearby. The dress was once owned by actress Debbie Reynolds and sold at auction for $5.6 million in 2011. It's what Marilyn impersonators wear, it's a classic Halloween costume, and it's never shown in its entirety in the iconic scene in the film.

The closest to a full-length view is the medium long shot when Marilyn and Tom Ewell are outside the cinema, walking toward the camera—Marilyn chopped off at the ankles. From there on her dressed body is bisected, decapitated, sliced off at the legs or just below the bust through a series of camera tilts and edits that follow Ewell's—and the intended male viewers'?—lecherous gaze. Choice cuts include:

- A medium shot that cuts at crotch-level, emphasizing the belt tied around Marilyn's waist, the pleating of the fabric framing the breasts

- The camera tracking close and creeping down her body, ending with a chunk of her lower torso filling the frame

- The frame filled with her skirt rising and billowing, exposing the legs mid-thigh

- The camera tracking upward and resting on the upper torso, mid-breast level; Ewell lurks in the background and gazes downward, presumably at the calves and thighs.

It's too easy—yet not inaccurate—to label this as one of the most famous and creepiest objectifications of women, in which Marilyn is reduced to a collection of body parts, and stop there. But it's not so black-or-white. Yes, there is a passivity about the actor in this scene, standing still and allowing her body to be acted upon, the skirt billowing, revealing, having its way, without her initiating this move-ment—as if the dress has more agency than the body wearing it. A reading of the scene as a woman's lived experience of dress provides a more nuanced perspective.

Isn't it delicious?

In *Thinking Through Fashion*, Dr. Llewellyn Negrin points to Iris Marion Young's analysis of the gendered nature of corporeality.

"It had been assumed that women's pleasure in dress is a secondary one which derives from them vicariously placing themselves in the same position as the puta-tive male spectator," writes Negrin. "That is, they would only experience pleasure through their internalization of the objectifying male gaze, seeing themselves as others see them."

Negrin shares Young's argument that there is a pleasure in dress that transcends the male gaze—the pleasure of touch. Marilyn's character is clearly enjoying the cool breeze from the subway on a hot, humid evening—facilitated by the dress she is wearing, of a particular shape and volume to collect and circulate the air, the skirt touching and then not-touching her legs. This would not be possible if the dress were more restrictive (think wiggle dress, in which the hem is narrower than the hips) or one made of a different fabric. Travilla was quite intentional in his selection of rayon-acetate crepe, "heavy enough to swing as she walked, but light enough to catch that all-important breeze." I would argue that Marilyn's genius performance of sensual pleasure, of her *delicious*-ness, has allowed this scene to stand the test of time. What if we read it as one in which Marilyn is wearing the pants, as if the pleasure is more hers than Ewell's?

Which is not to say that Marilyn was unaware of the objectifying male gaze. Indeed, there were actually two scenes featuring the dress, both shot at the same time—the one directed by Wilder, and the press conference attended by thousands of fans and male photographers directed by, ahem, Marilyn herself. As Wilder shot fourteen takes of the scene at 2 AM, in between Marilyn was posing for the cameras, crouching down with her thighs pressed demurely together, left hand framing her face, holding the skirt up to expose the entire length of her leg. In another photograph from the event, Marilyn's knee is bent a la flamingo, her left buttocks and underpants in view. And another: mid-laugh, closed eyes, lips parted, she holds down the front of the skirt up at shoulder level to reveal her entire lower torso. In contrast to how she "wears" the dress when standing above the subway grate, here she is acting, rather than being acted on, moving in ways that suggest a collaboration with, at times a command of, the garment. The dress works on Marilyn's body as she in turn manipulates the dress.

None of this is evident in Wilder's footage of the scene, which had to be recreated and reshot on a Hollywood soundstage due to the noise of the crowds. Yet there is an interesting dichotomy between the still and moving images, in a way each containing Marilyn's invisible labor for the other.

Also invisible: the emotional labor that haunts this dress. In a 1984 interview with Tom Ewell, the actor recalls he and Marilyn were not informed beforehand by Wilder that there was going to be a powerful fan under the subway grate "that would blow them sky-high" the first time they walked over it. Marilyn's husband at the time, Joe DiMaggio, was one of the 5,000 fans in the bleachers and was infuriated—he felt it was exhibitionist. During a break he asked her not to do it again, and she refused. She went on to film thirteen more takes, and according to *The New York Times*, "Later that night the couple had a screaming fight in their room. The next morning, her hairdresser covered up Ms. Monroe's bruises with makeup. Three weeks later, Ms. Monroe filed for divorce."

In this chilling example I am reminded of Entwistle's seminal essay: "Dress lies at the margins of the body and marks the boundary between self and other, individual and society," she writes, referencing Mary Douglas's idea that, since "the boundaries of the body are dangerous, it is therefore no surprise that clothing and other forms of adornment, which operate at these 'leaky' margins, are subject to social regulation and moral pronouncements."

In this case, the parts of Marilyn's body that polite, sexually uptight society required women to cover at the time were not. It was "that silly little dress," as Travilla once called it, that set and ignored these boundaries. This theoretical framework enables me to see force of Marilyn's artistic integrity and professionalism, given she had full awareness of her image and, though she didn't call it that back then, *brand*.

A dress so dangerous it got the wearer beaten up.

The character in La Dolce Vita *who embodies goodness and innocence, and who wholeheartedly revels in the beauty of life, is Sylvia... a sort of Swedish-American fertility goddess transcending mere voluptuous sexuality through boundless exuberance and generosity of spirit.*
—Film theorist Michael Joshua Rowin, "Party Time in Fellini Land"

While the boundaries between body and dress can be spaces of danger and unsafety, these "leaky" margins can also be exciting and life-affirming spaces that provide fashion its power as a catalyst for social change. And in the case of Federico Fellini's fountain scene in *La Dolce Vita*, the margins are not only leaky, they're waterlogged.

Swedish actress Anita Ekberg, in the role of American starlet Sylvia Rank, wades into the Trevi Fountain in the middle of a moonlit night, clad in a velvet evening gown with sweeping gossamer-like underlayers. Created by Italian fashion and costume designer Fernanda Gattinoni, the strapless dress with sweetheart bodice was said to be inspired by the black satin sheath dress worn by Rita Hayworth in 1946's *Gilda*—which in turn was said to pay homage to John Singer Sargent's 1884 *Portrait of Madame X.*

While Gilda wore the dress to perform in a nightclub, and the socialite Madame X was dressed for a portrait, what makes Sylvia's version of the black dress different is *context*: it's unruly and disruptive to bathe in an eighteenth-century Roman fountain, and additionally inappropriate—and certainly impractical—to wear a velvet evening gown while doing so. As Entwistle explains, ignoring societal dress codes leaves people feeling awkward or embarrassed. She uses the example of a bikini, appropriate on the beach but not at the boardroom, but also think of showing up to a traditional wedding in a white dress if you're not the bride, or wearing street clothes and street shoes to an exercise class.

CHAPTER 7

Dress worn by Anita Ekberg in Fellini's movie *La Dolce Vita* (1960) in the hall dedicated to Federico Fellini at Rome's Cinecittà Studios, Italy, on January 31, 2018. Photo: ABACAPRESS/Alamy

"Dressed inappropriately we are uncomfortable," writes Entwistle. "We feel ourselves open to social condemnation."

I must also mention there are different what's-appropriates for different bodies. Sylvia's voluptuousness, for example, made her automatically subject to additional scrutiny. If women are historically and culturally associated with the body—with emotions and feeling and a kind of animal wildness—a hyper-sexual body carries those qualities multiplied. This means the spectacle of Sylvia in the fountain, spilling over the dress, is even more inappropriate.

And powerful. It begins with her delight in seeing the fountain, as she holds up the train of her dress to protect it from getting wet, and then just as soon lets it go. The sensual pleasure conveyed in the close-up as she stands under the fountain is innocent, palpable, almost sacred—even Marcello cannot touch her, his hands tracing the space between her face and throat as if there is an aura, an invisible boundary, around her body—nude as it appears in this shot. Unattainable, not because she's too famous, but too good, too pure. There is nothing uncomfortable about her rule-breaking. In this scene, it is natural for a woman to do whatever it takes to experience pleasure.

The scene further illustrates what is gained when analyzing fashion as a situated body practice, which Entwistle notes has been absent in fashion studies.

"Either the body is to be self-evidently dressed (and therefore beyond discussion)," she writes, "or the clothes are assumed to stand up on their own, possibly even speaking for themselves without the aid of the body."

Take a look at the dress, on display here in January 2018 in the hall dedicated to Fellini at Cinecittà Studios in Rome. Indeed it is void, mute, maybe even parched and cold after its giddy week in 1960 of being soaked and penetrated. Understand that dress also contains, but cannot speak about, the invisible labor by the film crew surrounding its care. Over five nights of filming, the dress had to have been carefully dried, preserved, underlayers fluffed and straightened, made as new again. It even took extra crew to carry the train so that it would be perfectly splayed for the long shot. And then the extra physical labor of Ekberg, who recalls how cold the waters were, as the scene was shot at the end of January and beginning of February.

"I was freezing," she said. "They had to lift me out of the water because I couldn't feel my legs anymore." Marcello, on the other hand, was reportedly drunk and wearing fishing boots.

In my mind I replay the footage, see the long shot of Marcello leading Sylvia out of the fountain, the train of the dress a silken monster. Feel that the dress takes up so much less space now, without her. Lost its splendor, though gained a sense of "costume." Much like Entwistle's description of Issey Miyake's fluid designs as "activated by the body of the wearer," without Sylvia's body, the dress is *inactive*, unplugged, without spark or electrical current.

CHAPTER 7

These case studies explore the haptic experience of dressed performing bodies. Ultimately, I cannot say that Marilyn Monroe experienced pleasure at the feel of the breeze from the subway, but the character she played appeared to. It is interesting to think of what it is about this dress, and the body wearing it, that makes people who see it want to recreate it with their own bodies, play tribute to it, sploof it.

While Marilyn's subway dress costume is available in adult and children sizes starting at $29.98, I think that masquerading as Sylvia is less about fashion and more about action, creating mood and spectacle. In fact, many a tourist and Roman alike have replicated the scene, including a 64-year-old woman who, on a hot day in 2016, waded into the Trevi Fountain in an evening gown and fur stole and waved to tourists. This is one of several *La Dolce Vita*-inspired instances that resulted in the 2017 decree that banned bathing and swimming in any of Rome's Baroque fountains. There's something about this that makes Sylvia's action and persona even more legendary, knowing her carefree, joyful action and celebration of sexual freedom and sensual pleasure is against the law. And feeling a cool breeze of the subway could never be as revolutionary. Things are too complicated for that now.

Copyright © 2023 by Pune Dracker. White paper from the online exhibition *The Fabric of Cultures*, 2023.

MAKING IT PERSONAL

TOXIC NOSTALGIA

BY ANGELA RIECHERS

"I LOATHE nostalgia!" The provocative opening sentence of the legendary magazine editor Diana Vreeland's 1984 memoir, *D.V.*, would find few supporters today—as a culture, we currently ADORE nostalgia. Design, from I.D. and the digital world to graphics and architecture, is drowning in it. Every era has borrowed and repurposed visuals from previous times, but lately design recycling has reached a new high. The endless archives of the internet allow us to continually review and mine the past with great ease; as a result, we now often cloak the new in the forms of yesterday, even when these forms no longer serve any purpose except as wistful reminders of a world gone by. Does this create a progressive visual culture, or does it impede real progress? In short: has nostalgia become a toxic force in design?

Modernism strove to eliminate ornamentation and retain only an object's pared-down, essential form, introducing typefaces without cluttery serifs, and industrial design and architecture stripped of the merely decorative. By contrast, the packaging of some contemporary products uses old-fashioned elements at the expense of function. A good example is Churchkey beer, which eschews the useful pop-top in favor of flat-topped steel cans that require a separate opener. The company's tagline reads, "It's worth the effort. The harder it is to achieve your goal the greater the satisfaction."

Churchkey's website features a helpful video demonstrating how to correctly open a beer with the strange historic device (the churchkey) included with each six-pack. Having to watch a video to open a can does not feel like progress.

CHAPTER 7

We miss the weight of objects, the sounds of gears and levers, the clicks and thumps, the ringing bells and clacking keys—and so we have a whole range of modern skeuomorphs, or derivative objects that retain ornamental design cues to a structure that was necessary in the original. Noisy Typer adds the sound of typewriter keys to a computer keyboard, and USB Typewriter ("A groundbreaking advancement in the field of obsolescence!") allows any manual typewriter to be converted to a keyboard for an iPad or PC. Several iPhone covers are available that mimic the look of a vintage Leica or Hasselblad film camera. Instagram filters turn digital photographs into imitation Polaroids. None of this adds functionality. Nearly every one of the iPhone/iPad's built-in apps uses an icon that refers to an outdated, much earlier version of itself: the Frank Sinatra stand mike, the vintage tube television, the spiral-bound address book, the envelope. Yet many smartphone users are too young to have used most of these objects in real life (consider the inconvenience of carrying them around); the nostalgic design of the interface feeds upon a set of reconstructed memories divorced from the experiences that generated them, creating a culturally shared yearning for lost golden moments. The latest iteration of Apple's iCal looks like a desk blotter—an item that's been obsolete since we stopped writing with fountain pens. Ask ten people under the age of thirty if they know what a desk blotter is or what it was used for, and see how many have a clue what you're talking about. Nostalgic design serves as a kind of safekeeping, preserving images of beloved objects so they don't completely disappear from the collective unconscious.

Maybe we pine for outdated mechanical items because featherweight digital objects and applications lack soul. Quickly obsolete (the average lifespan for digital products is 18 months before a new version becomes available), they acquire no patina, remaining devoid of the gentle signs of wear and tear that prove they were used and even loved. The Singer Company's 160th-anniversary limited-edition sewing machine—made mostly of plastic, with digital components—borrows its look from the company's iconic cast-iron machines from decades past. There's no significant downside, looks-wise; the anniversary edition is a lovely homage to the Singer heritage. But consider how many Singers from the early part of last century are still in use today, working flawlessly—then try to imagine this latest version still operational in 2112. Its nostalgic design is tinged with even more sadness than usual; it becomes an unintentional memorial to a vanished age of durable products.

Most vexing of all from a design perspective is the particular flavor of nostalgia best described as a fantasy trip to the imagined past. If years gone by are continually portrayed as better times, how can we hope for actual better times to come? For one dispiriting example, compare the Obama campaign's graphic design for 2012 to his 2008 efforts. The first iteration introduced the distinctive Gotham O logo, promising a new path to the future. This year's "Betting on America" combines the O with folksy-feeling retro typography that seems to look backward, evoking the design of fruit-crate labels from the early twentieth century. It is a pastoral, farmland version of a simpler America—one that couldn't comfortably exist in today's economy.

Both recently constructed baseball stadiums in New York City fall victim to this nostalgic fantasy approach, too; the Yankees have brought back the old manually operated scoreboards in left and right field (a feature last used in the 1960s), while the Mets' Citi Field has a facade loosely modeled on Ebbets Field, the beloved former home of the greatly missed Brooklyn Dodgers. Even the dark green color of Citi Field's seats was copied from Manhattan's extinct Polo Grounds, where the New York Giants and the Mets once played.

In the advertising world, Peroni beer has created devastatingly beautiful commercials set on Lake Como or in Italian ski resorts, honey-tinged reflections of the 1950s and '60s complete with soundtracks featuring cover versions of classic hits like "My Girl" and the Temptations' "Get Ready." Flirty women wear heavy eyeliner on their lids and old-fashioned curlers in their hair as they swan around in structured little bikinis. Laughing men drive classic wooden speedboats and lounge in swim trunks reminiscent of Cary Grant on the Riviera. There's nothing wrong with any of this—except that the world shown is long gone. A viewer comes away thinking, "I wish I'd been there . . . it looked better than what we've got now." Nearly all good design is aspirational, showing us that better possibilities exist, but using lost eras to project images of perfection seems unfair—we can never duplicate the past, no matter how hard we try.

Perhaps the problem is that we stopped believing both in a better future and in design's ability to further it. The thread is broken; terrorists have shoe bombs and bioweapons, and we've lost hope in the promises of flying cars and glittering cities hovering in the sky. The world's climate and environment seem headed on a crash course to ruin. And so we cling to design that relentlessly references days gone by because we know what to expect—the scary challenge of the new has been removed from the equation. We seem to want design to give us the reassurance found in the recognizable. For those wishing to discover something new, however, all this unending nostalgia begins to provoke a feeling very close to nausea. Diana Vreeland wrote in *Allure*, "This book isn't about the past. I'm looking for something else. I'm looking for the suggestion . . . of something I've never seen."

Shouldn't we, too, keep trying to shape that unseen future? Shouldn't we refuse to accept that it only resembles the past?

Copyright © 2012 by Angela Riechers. Published in *Print*, July 26, 2012.

It is every designer's duty to engage in constructive commentary for that is how students learn and professionals learn to do better. The critical voice is a significant part of the process. It cannot be ad hominem or shrill. No ranting, please. It needs to be incisive, direct, and authoritative, and generous. Critical discourse is common in education, but the profession also benefits from judicious public conversation, debate, and oratory that take fellow designers to task for bad craftsmanship and unoriginal conception.

REVIEWS
AND
CRITIQUES

CHAPTER 8

GIVING AND TAKING CRITICISM

BY CHAPPELL ELLISON

✴

I firmly believe you can be a critic while being kind and open-hearted. I don't even care if that sounds naive. Most people think the number one goal of a critic is to judge whether work is good or bad. They are wrong.

The number one goal of a critic should be to make things better. That's it. None of this binary good/bad stuff. Lots of people would disagree with me on this.

Criticism only succeeds when everyone wants things to be better. The moment you sniff out that a critic's goal is not to help you make things better, see ya.

How do you know if they don't want to make things better? You know when a troll is a troll. They reveal it through their lack of curiosity about your work. Leading up to an Apple event, I once saw a prominent tech writer and critic tweet, "Can't wait for another boring design from Jony Ive." Why wouldn't you want Jony Ive to do the best he can? Why wouldn't you want the next iPhone to be the best thing of all time? Why wouldn't you want everything to be amazing? It might not be, but give it a minute. As a critic, if I'm not open to the possibility of my mind being blown, what's the point?

To be a good critic, you don't have to start a blog or write essays. But you must stay curious and look for ways to make things better.

Universities teach you how to give criticism. They've been doing it for centuries. They supply all sorts of texts so that you can cough up fancy words and names to support your argument.

But the thing is, no one teaches you how to take criticism. This is ridiculous. It's like teaching construction workers about nuts and not bolts.

As it turns out, it's really hard to teach people how to take criticism.

That's because everyone is human and naturally defensive and very sensitive and we all have a secret emotional space where we're in a constant state of dying inside.

Usually, when we face criticism, we concern ourselves with one question: Is my work good or bad?

You've got to stop asking yourself this. It is torturous. It will make you sad. Instead, focus on this question: What is the next step I can take to make my work better? And then, focus all your efforts on taking criticism that helps you answer that question.

I used to work for the New York City government. It was the best, hardest, most rewarding, most nightmarish job I've ever had. I worked in an office of 1,400 people. My twelve-person design and communication team was often referred to as, "The weird art kids."

The people that I delivered presentations to each day weren't designers or coders. They were accountants, lawyers, and secretaries. They grew up in Trinidad, Pakistan, Queens, and Estonia. And by working with non-designers, I learned some very important lessons.

Most people still don't understand what designers and tech people do. And therefore, most people are scared of what designers and tech people do. They won't ever let on that they're freaked out. But they are. You'll know this because they'll call you things like, "The weird art kid." They'll look at you like you're selling snake oil.

The criticism and feedback you get from other people is often propelled by this fear. But fortunately, it's called taking criticism for a reason. You get to choose whether or not to take it.

And this choice is what we need to practice.

There are some things you can do when facing criticism. One of those things is to stop and ask yourself: Is this helpful or not helpful? Is this person saying something that's helping you move forward or not? I'm about to give you an example of putting that in use. But first. Another problem.

When giving feedback or criticism, people rarely say what they mean. We're just complicated like that. We're humans. For example, when someone asks you how you're doing, you often respond, "Fine," when you really want to yell, "THE WORLD IS A GARBAGE FIRE SO I'M NOT DOING GREAT."

To understand criticism is to be a translator. Not only do we have to ask ourselves in the moment, "Is this helpful or not helpful," we must also listen to the person, then try to understand what they truly mean.

This isn't easy. And not everyone's brain is wired for this.

CHAPTER 8

To understand criticism is to be a translator. Not only do we have to ask ourselves in the moment, "Is this helpful or not helpful," we must also listen to the person, then try to understand what they truly mean.

At my government job, my creative team had one of those clients who was definitely always right. In a meeting, while scrolling through a website, a logo my team made for this client appeared on the screen. Our client stopped everything, pointed to the logo, and he looked at me and said: "What do you think of this?"

At this point, I turned on my mental translator. I knew this client well enough to know he wasn't feeling particularly positive about the logo. And perhaps, he just needed someone to listen.

So, I asked the client what he thought about the logo. He answered, "I just don't like it."

Talking about subjective stuff like design is hard. It's deeply personal. It can make you feel exposed. When people say they don't like something, without any further explanation, what they often mean is: "I'm afraid my explanation will sound stupid."

So now, I'm asking myself—is this helpful? If I go back to my team and tell them the client just doesn't like it, will it improve our work? Nope. In fact, it will just make my team angry. So, something very important to do at this point: Stay curious.

I press him. I say, "Can you tell me what it is that you don't like?" Then he says a classic line: "It looks like something my three-year-old could've done."

Interpreting this gets slippery, but there's an underlying subtext to this common response. And that's, "This thing you've made doesn't make sense to me at all—am I missing something?"

You know that thing I said about people fearing designers? That plays a role here. People are always suspicious of designers. Even designers are suspicious of designers. Is this helpful feedback? If I take that feedback to my designers, their online portfolios will suddenly be up to date as they look for new jobs.

So, I asked our client for specific things he didn't like. After some thought, he responded. "It's the primary colors. I don't like them. They feel juvenile to me." Finally. Finally? Finally! Is this helpful? Yes. I can work with this. My design team can use this feedback to inform their future color choices.

I'm not saying translation is a science. I'm not always sure what people truly mean. But the process of taking criticism is about empathy. It's about imagining how others think and feel, and using that to guide your curiosity without inciting your own defensiveness.

Taking criticism is often described metaphorically as standing in front of a firing squad. Being a helpless target. But it's not. It's an empowering practice. It requires just as much work as giving criticism.

Taking criticism is the search for actionable feedback.

No one loves taking criticism.

It can make you feel frustrated.

And small.

But I'm going to tell you a secret, one that critics won't tell you.

You have as much power as your harshest critic. That's because you hold the power to decide whether or not to take someone's criticism.

We have the privilege to make things for people that can improve their lives. And by listening to others we can figure out the next step to making everything better.

Copyright © 2016 by Chappell Ellison. From a talk to the employees of Vine given July 2016.

CHAPTER 8

OUT OF THE SHADOWS: WOMEN ARTISTS AND ABSTRACTION AT MoMA

BY KEN CARBONE

★

The gloriously exuberant painting by abstract expressionist Joan Mitchell at the entrance of *Making Space: Women Artists and Postwar Abstraction* at MoMA builds anticipation for good things to come. The exhibition is wonderful and the only disappointment at the press preview was how few men were present. Was this shameless disregard or were they just busy? In any event, the show is well worth a visit.

Making Space highlights the outstanding work of relatively under-recognized women artists from between 1945 and 1968, a period that saw the end of World War II and the dawn of the Feminist movement. Organized by Starr Figura, Sarah Hermanson Meister, with assistance by Hillary Reder, of the Departments of Drawing, Prints, and Photography, the show is ripe with new work, some never before exhibited. Among these are early works by art legends that are stylistically uncharacteristic in addition to numerous pieces by artists that were previously unknown to me.

REVIEWS AND CRITIQUES

Drawn entirely from the MoMA's collection, the exhibition features nearly 100 paintings, sculptures, photographs, drawings, prints, textiles, and ceramics by more than 50 artists. Featured are works that range from the muscular compositions of Helen Frankenthaler, Lee Krasner, and Joan Mitchell; to the precise minimalism of Agnes Martin, Anne Truitt, and Jo Baer.

Given the quality of this show I can imagine that MoMA would still dominate the world of modern art and never need to borrow from another institution. The museum's centennial in 2029 might provide the ideal moment to flex their essentiality to art with a yearlong retrospective on the institution itself.

One work in the exhibition that caught my eye was a postcard-size collage of cut paper, cloth, and string by Anne Ryan that was a rich composition of subtle color and formal vitality. In another case, a grid of black and white patterned rectangles by the grand dame of Japanese art, Yayoi Kusama, from 1962, was surprisingly restrained compared to her brash later work.

Although splashes of color could be seen in most galleries Kusama's print exemplifies my general impression that muted tones, grays, and monochrome dominate the exhibition. Additionally, the creative tools of geometry, high contrast, reduction, and materiality these artists used have informed modern art and design ever since.

Women have been producing great art for centuries and their ancestors in primitive societies, much longer. Whether it is female hand stencils in ancient caves, the bravado of Artemisia Gentileschi in the fourteenth century, or Cecilia Beaux, Gabriela Munter, and Louise Nevelson in more recent history, their collective contribution to art is undeniable. Nevertheless, it is always wise to reinforce this fact due to the tireless debate about gender equality in society and art. *Making Space* is not a politically motivated exhibition and it doesn't appear that the women represented saw gender issues as a driving theme. What is clear, from the outstanding quality of what has been assembled, is that these artists stood shoulder to shoulder with their male counterparts of the period and focused on one thing: making great art.

Copyright © 2023 by Ken Carbone.

CHAPTER 8

TOURIST/PURIST

BY JARRETT FULLER

✸

Virgil Abloh is moving. A recent scan of his Instagram feed shows images from Paris, Chicago, New York, Vancouver, and Spain. The multidisciplinary designer, creative director, DJ, and artist travels 310 days a year; each trip meticulously documented on Instagram for his 4.2 million followers. As the menswear artistic director of Louis Vuitton; proprietor of his own label, OFF-White; collaborating with everyone from Ikea to Evian, Tamara Murakami to Nike; DJing at Coachella; and for ten years, as Kanye West's creative director, designing the covers for *Yeezus* and *Watch the Throne*, art directing tours, and designing merch, Abloh seems to never be still. His iPhone is his studio, WhatsApp his conference room.

A mid-career retrospective of this work, curated by Michael Darling titled *Figures of Speech*, is currently on display at Chicago's Museum of Contemporary Art. The accompanying publication is as unusual as its subject—more than a simple exhibition catalog, it was designed and edited in close collaboration with Abloh, includes texts from people like Michael Rock and Taiye Selasi, a conversation with Rem Koolhaas and Samir Bantal of AMO (who also designed the MCA exhibition), and a visual index of everything Virgil's worked on dating back to his thesis as an architecture student at the Illinois Institute of Technology in Chicago. Seeing his work organized around medium (graphic design, fashion, photography, fine art, product, etc.) and theme (race, social commentary, readymade) a new reading of his work begins to emerge. His highly visual, pop-culture-referencing work can, at times, obscure the thinking behind it all. Indeed, his trademark typographic gesture—all-caps Helvetica in quotes (never smart quotes!)—suggests an ironic distance that hides the depth of his process. But in the pages of *Figures of Speech*, Abloh's deep knowledge of design and art history are front and center. Looking at this work in one-sitting, however, I was struck by the consistent train of thought that runs through an at-first-glance schizophrenic body of work. The portrait of an artist reveals itself.

Abloh, the son of Ghanaian immigrants, grew up in Chicago, obsessed with punk music, skateboarding, and art. Originally studying engineering as an undergraduate to please his immigrant parents with a suitable degree, he tried to find a way to express himself artistically. Architecture was a logical way to build upon what he learned in engineering school. While in school, he started designing his own t-shirts and upon finding out the printshop where he worked part-time and printed his own designs was also the shop that printed Kanye West's merch, he purposely left a few of his designs out in the open when he knew West's manager would be there. As hoped, his designs caught his eye and made their way back to the then-rising Chicago rapper. Abloh started to design shirts for West, gaining more autonomy, and ultimately becoming West's Creative Director, designing everything from stage sets to album covers. When West got interested in fashion, it was Abloh who interned at Fenti with him, learning the ins and outs of the industry, preparing him for the career he was beginning.

Abloh's architecture background should not be overlooked; this origin story comes up again and again in the texts in the book and clearly influences everything he has done since. The conversation with Koolhaas and Bantal is, in the end, a conversation about the expanding nature of architecture and how Abloh, through thinking like an architect, applies this education to everything from garments to album covers to runway shows. Much like Koolhaas, in fact, Abloh sees architecture as an expansive discipline, not reserved for simply building buildings. (His 2015 talk at Columbia was called "How Architects Can Change the World by Not Building Buildings.") If architecture, then, is a way of thinking, a way of seeing the world, Abloh's taking this approach and applying it to everything he can.

This is, perhaps, the model of the new designer. The silos in the design industry are falling away—fashion designers need to understand graphic design, graphic designers should look to architecture, architects are looking at product design. The cross-pollination of industries and mediums creates new types of designers and new types of work. The old-fashioned ideas of the multi-hyphenate designer or the 'designer as X' suddenly seem antiquated. For Virgil Abloh, it's all one and the same. It's all design. He moves between mediums; blends high and low; a relentless self-promoter, skilled at social media; well-versed in both art and design history and contemporary culture.

CHAPTER 8

"Off-White," explains Virgil Abloh of the name of his fashion brand, "is about the grey area between white and black." Abloh's entire oeuvre, of course, lives in this grey area: not just in medium or discipline but also high and low, insider and outsider, historically aware and culturally attuned, accessible and exclusive. He calls himself a tourist and a purist—simultaneously touring other fields while bringing his own background with him, both student and teacher, novice and expert.

"When you touch on so many different creative activities, none of them can really be seen as central. To be 'OFF-' then is a kind of working philosophy," said Michael Rock when he introduced Abloh for a lecture at Columbia, "It means OFF-track, OFF-tune, OFF-message, OFF-balance, OFF-kilter. At the heart of it, to be OFF-White is to be OFF-center. And Virgil proves over and over, we should forget the center, the edge is where the action is."

What Abloh seems to get better than many of us is that we're all postmodern now. We all blend references; we borrow and remix. The next generation of designers, already savvy brand builders on social media, aren't interested in disciplines, or historical movements. To them, it's all the same, free for the taking. Abloh's described his design philosophy as changing something by at least three percent. "Duchamp is my lawyer" he's famous for quipping. But this too, of course, isn't new at all but rather a reclamation of an older type of design practice. Until this generation, designers were always polymaths. Think Munari, the Eames, Malholy-Nagy, Albers. These designers' careers are equally hard to classify, moving between architecture and graphic design and children's books and photography and painting and teaching. Abloh isn't merely remixing, borrowing, adapting, he's also reclaiming an older definition of design, updating it for a new generation.

Off-White, then, is a metaphor, a symbol of the thread that connects an otherwise disjointed career. To be on the edges is to constantly be shifting between groups and tribes, styles and movements, disciplines and mediums. The only way to find the edges is to keep pushing, to exploring, keep moving. "What is the marker of good design?"

Copyright © 2019 by Jarrett Fuller.

REVIEWS AND CRITIQUES

THE LEGACY OF RACISM IN THE MAKING OF CITIES AND COMMUNITIES

BY ALICIA OLUSHOLA AJAYI

✳

The highly anticipated exhibition at the Museum of Modern Art in New York, *Reconstructions: Architecture and Blackness in America*, takes its name from the historic two decades that followed the bloody Civil War. Yet, despite the reference, the show (through May 31) isn't a call to a return—the aim is to reflect on the legacy of a country attempting to redefine itself. While the works commissioned from ten prominent architects, landscape architects, designers, and artists place a critical lens on systems of racial oppression, "the premise is not to press for solution-based designs," according to the co-curators, Mabel O. Wilson, professor of architecture and Black studies at Columbia University (and 2019 RECORD Women in Architecture honoree), and Sean Anderson of MoMA. Instead, the process of interrogating the past and the present, as a way to insist on liberating futures for Black lives, gives a new understanding of what architecture can actually do.

The opening of *Reconstructions* has come on the heels of a year we can't wait to put behind us. Still, the show's challenge is not to take its timeliness for granted. The contributors' work confronts the very structure of the design field and offers insight into the often-overlooked motivations of many BIPOC architects who have actively fought against the profession's ambivalence toward engaging social issues, especially those relating to race. Though using such conventions as plan, elevation, and section—as well as video, collage, and sculpture—the designers foreground new ways of making. In all of the work on view (and in the accompanying catalog, which serves as a "field guide"), the tension between time and Blackness serves as a baseline for spatial speculations, rooted in the history of ten American towns, cities, and communities, each of which is explored by one of the contributors.

Formed as the Black Reconstruction Collective (BRC), they include Emanuel Admassu, Germane Barnes, Sekou Cooke, J. Yolande Daniels, Felecia Davis, Mario Gooden, Walter Hood, Olalekan Jeyifous, V. Mitch McEwen, and Amanda Williams. A video installation by David Hartt is also included. While the subjectivity of each individual is as varied as the shades of black (expressed in Williams's recent project *What Black Is This You Say?*), the collective's manifesting statement deviates from the objectivity of the vested architecture canon, conjuring a new directive:

> *The Black Reconstruction Collective commits itself to continuing this work of reconstruction in Black America and these United States. We take up the question of what architecture can be—not a tool for imperialism and subjugation, not a means for aggrandizing the self, but a vehicle for liberation and joy.*

The manifesto, in bold black letters on a 10-foot by 10-foot hanging canvas, covers the namesake of MoMA's architecture gallery, the department's founder and a respected architect who was also a well-known fascist. The statement itself may read as a new call to action, but, for many, the call draws its strength from the continuation of the labors, desires, and catalytic ideas of those who came before. The generations of calloused hands that built this country understand the work has never ceased, and the statement rallies behind those who have done the construction and will continue to build.

Inside the gallery, rebellious spirits work at multiple scales. Mario Gooden's *The Refusal of Space* is a "protest machine," reconfigured from a Nashville streetcar, made of black painted aluminum and wood. Adorned with a blackened Confederate flag and using photography, video, and sound, the structure reimagines the occupation of segregated space by Nashville student protestors in the 1960s. As Pittsburgh's Hill District currently prepares for an upending development in the near future, Felecia Davis's hanging soundscape sculpture allows a reciprocity between the body and the environment, to suggest a practice of collaboration and co-construction with the community. The Black Panthers' Ten-Point-Program from 1967 is the source for Walter Hood's invention of ten towers—materialized as black, human-scaled models—to regenerate an Oakland, California, neighborhood neglected by systemic disinvestment. Amanda Williams confronts the intersection of legal ownership, property, and Black spaces in Kinloch, the first historically Black town

The work is complex, exhaustive, and inspiring. The gallery is overwhelmed by unknown history, enlivened with each piece; the installation is visually commanding and rigorous, stretching back to the past while illuminating possible futures.

established in Missouri, by showcasing a letter-sized patent, along with maps and video, for "a method for navigating to free Black Space" from the U.S. Patent and Trademark Office.

An investigation of material staples in the Black community, such as hot sauce and the beauty-salon basin, makes its way into Germane Barnes's suspended exploded axon of a kitchen—a key Black space in Miami's diverse Black landscapes. V. Mitch McEwen incorporates video of Black women dancing and delivering architectural fantasies for the city of New Orleans. McEwen's piece, inspired by artist Kristina Kay Robinson's *Republica: Temple of Color and Sound,* hinges on the counterfactual and ponders what the city might have looked like as a Black nation-state if an enslaved uprising had succeeded. (Mid-video, the feed is abruptly interrupted to give a "Warning Advertisement" of the danger of being in the white space of MoMA.) J. Yolande Daniels's *the BLACK city* creates a glossary to recount the contributions of African Americans to the founding of Los Angeles. One such figure is Bridget "Biddy" Mason, a formerly enslaved woman who used the spatial tactics of buying properties to aid her in her philanthropic work. A new series of Olalekan Jeyifous's speculative futures visuals repurposes the existing, troubled Metropolitan Transit Authority as the Main Threshold Access, to better serve Black Brooklyn's mobility. Finally, with all the style and grace of a DJ, Sekou Cooke uses elements of hip-hop to remix the tragic history of displacement of Black residents in Syracuse, New York, with a new proposal for place-keeping tactics in public spaces.

The work is complex, exhaustive, and inspiring. The gallery is overwhelmed by unknown history, enlivened with each piece; the installation is visually commanding and rigorous, stretching back to the past while illuminating possible futures.

In trying to peel back the layers of Blackness and architecture, the show challenges the blinded perception of the discipline as innately progressive, as the field continues to falter under the weight of structural racism. The profession's lack of reflection is heightened by the country's obsession with what was and what is to come, while obscuring whatever present realities engulf us. Blackness often falls victim to this cycle of memory and time. The temporality of the white gaze on the Black experience comes and goes, rising at the breaking points of pain for Black and Brown folks. The most recent cycle of the gaze—due to the renewed momentum of the Black Lives Matter movement—has been more demanding of our attention. Expressed empathy becomes interchangeable with taking action, making claims that Reconstructions is a timely endeavor. However, the voices showcased in the exhibition declare that Reconstructions was inevitable because the work for Black freedom was never prioritized—so the task never ceased. This poignant and needed work is not only a living archive but a celebration of the continued fortitude in bringing consciousness to the profession. By engaging the labor of resistance against the oppressive systems within the field, the show demands that architecture take an active part in remaking American society. *Reconstructions* and the BRC, which plans to continue its efforts beyond this moment, is not a new wave of architectural thought; it is the field and MoMA that are just now catching up.

Copyright © 2021 by Alicia Olushola Ajayi. Published in *Architectural Record*, March 2021.

REVIEWS AND CRITIQUES

DRESS SENSE: WHY FASHION DESERVES ITS PLACE IN ART MUSEUMS

BY VIRGINIA POSTREL

✱

On May 7, the rich, famous, and beautiful will parade into the Metropolitan Museum of Art wearing their best, or most interesting, clothes, pausing for photographers along the obligatory red carpet. Once inside, the 700 guests—actors and models, designers and socialites—will dine and dance and preview the museum's newest exhibition, *Poiret: King of Fashion*. The occasion is the "party of the year," the Met's Costume Institute Benefit Gala. Co-chaired annually by *Vogue* editor in chief Anna Wintour, usually with a movie star (Cate Blanchett this year) and a fashion designer (Nicolas Ghesquière), the party is not just a chance to wear and admire beautiful clothes; it's a lavish and efficient fundraising machine. Tickets start at $6,500 per person, with tables for ten running as high as $100,000. Last year's gala raised $4.5 million for the museum's fashion department.

While only the Met commands that sort of glitz, fashion collections throughout the country are enjoying a new prominence. When the Philadelphia Museum of Art opens a new building this spring, its space for costume and textile exhibitions will nearly triple. Boston's Museum of Fine Arts recently devoted its main special-exhibition gallery to a display of straight-off-the-runway selections from ten Paris houses, the first costume-department exhibit to occupy that space since 1989. For the first time in its 28-year history, the Museum of Contemporary Art in Los Angeles included fashion in an exhibit, *Skin + Bones*, which examined connections between architecture and clothing design. The Meadows Museum in Dallas is currently featuring a retrospective of Basque-born couturier Cristóbal Balenciaga's mid-century work, across from galleries devoted to such Spanish masters as Velázquez, El Greco, and Goya.

But despite huge public interest—or perhaps because of it—fashion departments still find themselves constantly required to justify their existence. Dennita Sewell, the Phoenix Art Museum's curator of fashion design, sputters her frustration with presumably sophisticated New York critics who seem to begin every review of a fashion exhibition not by asking whether the show's concept is valid or the pieces are good but whether museums should show fashion at all. "Somebody has poured their heart out working on this show, and the first question is 'Why are you in here?' Gosh, can we move on from that? It just—I mean, the collection has been here since 1966. Why are we still discussing this?"

The Boston exhibit's comment book records a debate between fans, mostly women, who praise the museum for displaying an "inspiring" and "seldom seen" art form and detractors, mostly men, who decry its descent into commercialism. "What's next? Victoria's Secret's Xmas Collection?" writes one.

"People in the museum world complain that fashion is not art, and they think it is unworthy of being in an art museum," says Valerie Steele, the director of the Museum at the Fashion Institute of Technology. "Fashion is really seen as the bastard child of capitalism and female vanity."

Behind the criticism of fashion as an artistic medium is a highly ideological prejudice: against markets, against consumers, against the dynamism of Western commercial society. The debate is not about art but about culture and economics. Critics who decry fashion collections are less troubled by the prescribed costumes of dynastic China or the aristocratic dress of baroque France than by the past century's clothes. With its fluctuating forms and needless decoration, fashion epitomizes the supposedly unproductive waste that inspired twentieth-century technocrats to dream of central planning. It exists for no good reason. But that's practically a definition of art.

Prejudice aside, it's hard to come up with objections to fashion collections that don't apply to other museum departments. Fashion is mass produced? So are prints and posters, often more so than haute couture. Ephemeral? So are works on paper. Utilitarian? So are pots and vases. Customized to an individual? So were suits of armor. As for the fickleness of fashion, the history of Western art is a story of changing styles. And however much critics may despise commerce, many undisputed masterpieces were works for hire. "Paintings were marketable goods which competed for the attention of the purchaser," writes the historian Michael North in *Art and Commerce in the Dutch Golden Age*. Michelangelo and Ghiberti got paid.

REVIEWS AND CRITIQUES

The real question is not whether museums are too good for fashion but whether they're good enough. Clothes are unique sculptures, dependent on a supporting human form and created to move. Yet museum mannequins stand still. Clothing is made to be seen and touched—the tactile qualities of fabric are as essential to the art as a garment's color or shape—but light and fingertips dim colors and degrade fabrics. The first rule of fashion exhibitions is Do not touch.

Any fashion exhibition is thus a compromise. But, of course, altarpieces weren't meant to be ripped from their candlelit sacred context and put up on museum walls to be admired by nonbelievers. The Elgin Marbles were supposed to be on the Parthenon. For many works of art, a museum is an artificial setting—a zoo not a natural habitat. Some zoos, however, are worse than others.

Take the Costume Institute's permanent galleries in the basement of the Met, where garments are displayed in dimly lit glass cases lining the walls. Visitors can see each object only from a single angle. But clothes, like sculpture, are three-dimensional art. An evening gown's plunging back may contrast with a modest front—think of Hilary Swank's dress at the 2005 Oscars—but you can't appreciate the relationship if you can see only one side. No wonder the recent exhibition of the late socialite Nan Kempner's extraordinary wardrobe seemed less like an art retrospective than a series of crowded shop windows, a tribute less to Yves Saint Laurent's or Madame Grès's work than to Kempner's buying power.

Elsewhere curators have mostly dispensed with the glass, relying on decorum and guards to keep corrosive fingers off the clothes. The result is a much fuller experience of the art.

"If it is lit well, you can really see the details, and you can see the surface and hand of the fabric," says Steele. No photograph can adequately convey the cascades of seemingly weightless pinked ruffles and the precise yet delicate pleats of the Rodarte evening gown on display in Phoenix. Like an impressionist painting, it has to be seen firsthand.

The best of fashion, like the best of fine art, offers not only nuance to the connoisseur but also immediate pleasure to the uninitiated. The familiarity of clothes makes fashion exhibits accessible, but that very familiarity also highlights the difference between daily dress and museum-quality garments.

"At the time when people are getting fatter and dressing more casually than ever before—jeans at the opera!—there is an increase in interest in very fashionable dress," notes Sewell, the Phoenix curator.

The challenge for fashion curators is to balance aesthetics and history, pleasure and meaning. The Met's 2001 exhibit of Jackie Kennedy's White House wardrobe was wildly popular, but it made little sense in a museum dedicated to aesthetic masterworks. Kennedy's clothes were derivative of French fashions, interesting for

CHAPTER 8

what they reveal about the first lady's self-conscious image-building but not for any fashion innovation. They belonged in a history museum.

If museums treat fashion purely as art for art's sake, however, they risk draining the medium of what makes it distinctive and meaningful—not only its aesthetic elements but its connection to history and the human body. Fashion is, as Steele has insisted since she was a Yale doctoral student, a part of cultural history, and the relationship goes both ways. No history of business or chemistry explains the appeal of aniline dyes as powerfully as coming upon the 1860 purple-and-black striped dress in FIT's current exhibition on color in fashion. (One of FIT's two exhibitions is always historical, for the benefit of fashion students.)

Three years ago, the Met's *Dangerous Liaisons* exhibit showcased eighteenth-century costumes in the museum's period rooms, creating dramatic vignettes of mannequins socializing in naturalistic poses. The clothes were not only beautiful but, shown in their physical and social context, culturally understandable despite their extreme artifice. The clothes, furniture, and interior design became not just displays of luxury and handcraft but tools for seduction and self-expression, relating the unfamiliar setting to universal human behaviors.

Emphasizing romantic intrigue, says Harold Koda, the Costume Institute's curator in charge, "is a way in which one can get a contemporary audience to look at eighteenth-century dress that doesn't look like Cinderella."

Great fashion, like any museum-worthy art, is both timeless and time-bound, recalling the tension between the classic claims of art and the work's origin in a specific time and place. As Steele says: "We are trying to convey the story of fashion, the appeal of fashion, the experience of fashion. Fashion is about change. It is about changing silhouettes, and it is about new ways of presenting yourself to the world." It is, in short, an ideal art form for modern times.

Copyright © 2007 by Virginia Postrel. Published in *The Atlantic*, May 2007.

REVIEWS AND CRITIQUES

THERE'S TOO MUCH DAMN CONTENT, AND SLICK UX DESIGN IS MAKING IT WORSE

BY CHAPPELL ELLISON

Over the past decade, everyone—and I mean everyone—with an online presence felt the pressure to become a content publisher. Coca-Cola. Costco. Tiny midwestern lawn care companies. Because attention can often lead to revenue, companies produce articles, videos, and podcasts in hopes of engaging with consumers, and a rapidly maturing UX design industry answered the call. Like sweeping dust under a rug, we hooked readers with infinite scroll and hid pages behind hamburger buttons. Designers helped new publishers make their site look as if it was bursting with content when, in fact, it might've only contained 10 articles. Or maybe 1,000 articles? It was hard to tell. It still is. We've now gotten so good at designing the web that it practically pours out of our screens, lulling us into a stupor where we abandon all notions of time and space.

Today, technological advances in digital products enable us to hide all the edges and seams, smooth corners until they're unidentifiable. But designers across all industries have long been in the business of concealing seams. At companies like

CHAPTER 8

Now, we're so invested in designing interfaces that provide a seamless delivery of content, we aren't considering user mindsets that teeter into decision paralysis when confronted with infinite content.

Apple and Ford Motor Company, industrial designers develop beautiful, unibody casings to cover the guts of laptops and trucks, respectively. This isn't just about aesthetics. We've been cloaking the inner-workings of our greatest inventions since the Industrial Revolution and World War, when new, mechanized objects demanded protective casings to prevent human injury.

By the 1930s, casing was an art. Desk-mounted pencil sharpeners looked like atomic airplane engines. Clothing irons seemed poised to win the Grand Prix. And we don't even have time to go into what was happening with television cabinet design in the 1950s.

At some point in the late '90s, our adeptness at concealment transferred to the design of websites. Cascading Style Sheets (CSS) control how html elements—fonts, colors, formats—appear in browsers. Before CSS, the look of the web was mostly an incidental result of webmasters and developers pushing information in whatever way seemed most logical for the time.

Now, we're so invested in designing interfaces that provide a seamless delivery of content, we aren't considering user mindsets that teeter into decision paralysis when confronted with infinite content. Because the fact is, there's just so much damn content. Everywhere you turn. It would take you more than 11,000 years to watch Netflix's current catalog. Buzzfeed reportedly publishes 222 pieces every single day. As Amanda Hess wrote for the *New York Times*, "Movies do not begin and end so much as they loiter on screen. And social media is built for infinite scrolling. Nothing ends anymore, and it's driving me insane."

Because the fact is, there are only so many hours in a day, and we've reached our capacity. A quote from a report released by media and technology analysts at MIDiA Research states: "[E]ngagement has declined . . . suggesting that the attention economy has peaked. Consumers simply do not have any more free time to allocate to new attention-seeking digital entertainment propositions, which means they have to start prioritizing between them."

It's a privilege to bemoan abundance. We should all be so lucky to worry about having access to too much information, rather than too little. But that doesn't erase this predicament. Through recent years, we've seen what too much online content can do. It obfuscates truth. It breeds falsehoods that damage human connection and empathy. It exhausts us.

And for many of us, myself included, endless content overwhelms, resulting in decision paralysis (also called analysis paralysis). It's that feeling of scrolling through Netflix for twenty minutes, only to give up and turn off the TV. The search for the edge of content—where seams reveal information as surmountable—becomes an obsession to relieve anxiety.

But what if, to combat this anxiety, designers were in the business of revealing seams? Tired of his industry's race toward seamless design, computer scientist and theorist Matthew Chalmers proposed the idea of seamful design. In his paper titled "Seamful Design and Ubicomp Infrastructure," Matthew Chalmers defines seamful design: "Some features that we designers usually categorize as infrastructure problems may, to users, be useful interactional features. Examples include the edges and gaps. ... Seamfulness is about taking account of these reminders of the finite and physical nature of digital media."

It turns out that limitations, or "reminders of the finite," as Chalmers calls them, are critical to helping people avoid decision paralysis. Many studies have concluded the importance of limitations in decision making, but among the most famous is the Iyengar-Lepper study from Harvard Business Review:

> In 2000, psychologists Sheena Iyengar and Mark Lepper published a remarkable study. On one day, shoppers at an upscale food market saw a display table with 24 varieties of gourmet jam. Those who sampled the spreads received a coupon for $1 off any jam. On another day, shoppers saw a similar table, except that only six varieties of the jam were on display. The large display attracted more interest than the small one. But when the time came to purchase, people who saw the large display were one-tenth as likely to buy as people who saw the small display.

Retail companies found the same principle to be true. When Procter & Gamble went from twenty-six kinds of Head & Shoulders shampoo down to fifteen, they saw a 10 percent increase in sales.

Limitations can also deepen our connection to a digital product. In his paper, Chalmers also explains that seams are a moment of orientation—they can help a user understand the thing they're engaging with and remember their relationship to it. One of the best examples comes from the fan culture surrounding Mario 64, the first title released for Nintendo 64 in 1996. Fans have carefully documented the game's many glitches, one of which occurs in the first level when Mario lands a wall kick jump over a seesaw platform. The camera drops under his feet and reveals the construction of the entire level to the player. It feels like opening the hood of an old car—the architecture behind the game is revealed.

Glitches are the result of unresolved engineering. They're rarely intentional, often the product of limitations of time and technology. But with whole forums dedicated to documenting these glitches, fans don't see it as a failure of the game's design. In fact, the discovery of limitations can deepen our connection to a digital product and give users a comforting sense of ownership. They can inspire new exploration of the tools the game offers and encourage community development.

We aren't designed to live in the world we're creating. The human body isn't designed to have 24/7 access to electricity, food, and information. What we are biologically designed to do is satisfy hunger, thirst, and curiosity as soon as possible. Not satisfying these urges requires discipline and willpower, which is something we like to think we've evolved to develop but truly, we're just humans.

But that doesn't mean we aren't trying. Sort of. We have algorithms to help focus our attention a bit—Spotify's Discover Weekly, for example, provides a customized entry point that is much less overwhelming than their catalog that contains millions upon millions of songs.

Then there's the Calm Tech movement, championed by Amber Case. Calm Tech is the practice of building the minimum amount of technology to solve a problem, with as little ambient distraction as possible—that means no endless phone notifications or pop-ups. While it's catching on in leadership circles, we've still yet to see its practices take hold in consumer design.

Netflix is considering adding a random episode button to take the pressure off decision making, and companies like Blinkist specialize in ways to help you read nonfiction books in fifteen minutes. While I appreciate the effort, auto-selection and hyper-abridgement seem like dismal prescriptions for symptoms of a greater problem.

But times are changing, and perhaps the internet as we know it today will look vastly different in a decade. Paywalls are starting to go up. Distribution companies like Netflix are showing signs that they can't continue to pour endless money into content. Investment capital will shift—the internet is simply not a safe bet anymore. What company wants to put their content on a platform next to racists screaming slurs?

For now, the burden falls on us to decide, every day, how to spend our few, precious free hours. You can find me on my living room couch, remote in hand, anxiously scrolling through thousands of movies I will never watch.

Copyright © 2019 by Chappell Ellison. Published by *AIGA Eye on Design*, July 30, 2019.

REVIEWS AND CRITIQUES

THE CANON OF CHICAGO (AMERICAN) MODERNISM EXAMINED

BY STEVEN HELLER

CHICAGO MODERNISM & THE LUDLOW TYPOGRAPH:
Douglas C. McMurtrie and Robert Hunter Middleton at Work
By Paul F. Gehl

A dvertising designers from the early- through mid-twentieth century America were not revolutionaries. While some of them may have admired the radical design approaches practiced in Europe, most homegrown American commercial artists stuck to a rigid playbook that was at times novel in form but routinely practical in function. In a capitalist system, selling goods was the goal and advertising was the means. Advertising's job was to attract consumers by following mannerisms and fashions dictated through trade manuals and journals supported by vendors. However, certain American graphic designers and typographers believed messages could be presented more contemporaneously yet also with an air of futuristic dynamism. These were not "Modernists" in the European sense of rebelling against tradition; nonetheless they were modern in that they were in and of their times.

Modernism is, after all, a slippery term. For some it meant the passe was rejected, for others the past was revived and reapplied. To be Modern, Modernist or (lower case) modernistic meant that antiquated stagnancy was anathema. Among the leading type designers there was a mandate to conceive products that had eye- and sales appeal. Despite the various socio-political symbolism implied in the term "Modernism," most type designers were resolutely practical. And the type foundries could expect nothing less.

In Europe Modern sans serif and certain slab serif typefaces were linked to radical art and design movements. In the United States type design was pegged exclusively to consumer culture—it was a highly competitive culture too.

For over five years I have been researching how Europe's "New Typography" (a.k.a. Neue Typographie, Elementare Typographie) movement was interpreted by designers and foundries in America for talks and essays. In Europe modern type took two intersecting directions: An austere, geometric, sans serif approach on one side and what we'll call the modernistic manner on the other. The former was simple, unadorned, and asymmetric, the latter was contemporary, vivaciously imbued with decorative characteristics.

Much had been written about both the Modern and modernistic during the 1920s and '30s in professional periodicals, including *The American Printer* and *Inland Printer*, as well as in detailed style guides and manuals. Very little of this material that I can find has been republished or sourced for recent historical surveys. I have spent many hours reading and annotating these articles, wondering all along why so little research has been done. That is until now.

Chicago Modernism & The Ludlow Typograph: Douglas C. McMurtrie and Robert Hunter Middleton at Work, by Paul F. Gehl (Opifex Publisher, 2020) is a very refreshing history of early American modernism (meaning prior to what is now called "Mid-Century Modernism" influenced by the Bauhaus, et al.) and two of its leading proponents. Both McMurtrie and Middleton designed some of the era's most emblematic display and novelty faces. They were responsible for marketing them and ensuring levels of popularity among designers and printers. Given these men were so prolific it is curious that Gehl's overall text is comparatively short but there is not a misplaced phrase, and his research is excellent. Avoiding the palaver common to some standard type and printing histories, Gehl's compact approach is both readable and enjoyable.

Having done my own research on this typographic era—and engaging with some of the same source materials—I am pleased to report I find only a little redundancy in our respective findings other than the predictable repetition of many specimen sheets and type catalogs.

By focusing on McMurtrie, who was an avid advocate of Jan Tschichold's "New Typography," and Middleton, who as type director of Ludlow was a prodigious inventor of new and novel form, Chicago (e.g. American) modernism is explained through the personalities of these individuals not through pedantic theory or fashions alone.

There were other type founders in Chicago, notably Barnhart Brothers, but The Ludlow Typograph company is the other important aspect in American modern and modernistic phenomena. Working for the company, McMurtrie and Middleton were encouraged to make emblematic "modern period" type, including Square Gothic, Ultra-Modern, Stygian Black (McMurtrie) and Stellar, Karnak, Tempo Bold (Middleton), among others that spoke to the contemporary eye.

Gehl's contribution to the narrative of American modernism comes at an interesting time when so-called "de-colonization," "de-canonization," and "people's history" is broadening the design historical landscape to include underrepresented people, places, and ideas. All well and necessary. Gehl's book is firmly rooted in a somewhat Eurocentric canon, yet it is nevertheless a very welcome missing addition to be sure.

Copyright © 2020 by Steven Heller.

CHAPTER 8

CAN A TYPEFACE SELL AN IDEA?

BY ANDREW McQUISTON

Centered within an empty field of black, the photographic image of Earth shot from space is featured on the cover of a worn magazine. Above the silvery blue sphere, the prominent title, "Whole Earth Catalog," sits with resolute being. Relying on a graphic serif font that spreads across the cover, its presence is emphasized by bold letterforms which somehow manage to both flow delicately and bump awkwardly into one another. Below, the phrase "access to tools" floats as a smaller, subtle counterbalance. Apart from the Fall 1968 date and price, the remainder of the cover is left blank—providing a sense of reflection in its simplicity.

Print magazines often fall to the category of ephemera; read once and then promptly dropped into a blue bin to be recycled at the end of the week. Outside of collectors and archives, the *Whole Earth Catalog*, an ecologically driven counterculture magazine released between 1968 and 1972, mostly finds itself lost to time, but not in memory or impact. The cover alone has become a compelling design artifact, one that has been reinterpreted ever since it was first published, from an issue of *New York Magazine* and book covers to graphic t-shirts, and even reimagined as a woven blanket. The inclusion of the Earth, and specifically one of the first released images of our shared planet, became a powerful symbol intended to evoke a mutual sense of universal destiny. But symbolism was not solely driven through the *Whole Earth Catalog* cover image. The font chosen for the masthead, Windsor, proved to define its own equally powerful role in establishing perceived meaning.

Typography is regularly viewed through the lens of capitalism. We are presented with a kaleidoscope of fonts daily through advertisements, branding, and commer-

REVIEWS AND CRITIQUES

cial signage. Many become background noise and are quickly ignored, rarely standing out among the graphic clutter. Where Windsor falls in this spectrum is somewhere between the hand drawn vernacular of street signage and the corporate stiffness of Helvetica. This placement leaves it with a potential separate from many other typographic styles, one less ordained to a life of commerce, and more towards an unbound fluidity.

Windsor's magnitude is best understood when considering the work involved in creating a typeface. Typeface design typically embarks through a process of seemingly endless sketching. The weight and curve of every line are thoughtfully placed onto paper, each stroke establishing individual characters through careful consideration. All these newly drawn forms, and the relationships they begin to develop, are slowly brought together as a whole. Through experimentation, adjustment, and refinement, letterforms begin to take shape and develop life. The uniqueness of the typeface becomes reflective of the creator's intention, delicate brush strokes, and time spent.

Windsor is a typeface that magnifies its own uniqueness at every opportunity. Its creation can be assumed as a purposeful journey, articulating ideas into concrete forms. The result in this case has been viewed as both elegant and oddly unconventional. Created by the British type designer Elisha Pechey, Windsor was released in 1905 by the London type foundry, Stephenson, Blake & Co. Pechey began his career in 1846, where he apprenticed as a printer and bookbinder for his uncle. He later moved to London to work as a proofreader at the publisher Cox & Wyman, eventually becoming one of the founding members of the London Association of Correctors of the Press, a longstanding trade union representing proofreaders in the United Kingdom. In 1863 he began working for Stephenson, Blake & Co., where he worked for nearly 40 years. In *Typefounders and Typefounding in America*, the American writer William E. Loy described Pechey as, "a designer of ability, a man of artistic temperament, and a patient and skillful draftsman," in an obituary published only a few years prior to Windsor's release.

Windsor is both a showcase of Pechey's artistry and incredible patience, as the majority of his characters offer distinct features and personality. Its ability to feel refreshingly active and simultaneously neutral is emphasized by the sense of nature drawn forth by the typographic forms. Produced at the turn of the twentieth century, the influence of Art Nouveau's organic aesthetic on the typeface can be found in many of its stylistic details. This is illustrated most prominently in the round bowl of the "R," the sharpness of the serifs on the "E," and the gentle curls created within its numerals. Especially dramatic in this effect is the ampersand of Windsor Light, the tail of which twirls over the body of the form like a dancer spinning.

While the name "Windsor" alludes to nobility—you may picture a timeless wooden chair, necktie knot, or stone castle—these features create a quirky typeface and one that many typographers struggle to use well. The reliance on loose and flowing forms embodies the curving shapes observed in natural floral patterns and provide Windsor with idiosyncrasies, playfulness, and warmth. Art Nouveau's presence, inspired by the craftsmanship, quality, and ideals of anti-industrialization from the Arts & Crafts movement, then becomes notable in its directness as an ideological and political stance imbued through its creator.

Typographer and graphic designer Bethany Heck described Windor's characters as both "bulbous and egg-shaped" in her review for *Font Review Journal*. This quality of the egg, hinting towards a symbol of life itself, again offers a nod to "Mother Earth," reinforcing the nature-like characteristics of the typeface. This is immediate when observing the capital "O," its weight and proportion fresh from the dairy case of the local grocery store. It is no wonder that the typeface found a home on Sainsbury's egg packaging and McDonalds breakfast marketing used in the 1970s, further securing the implied "natural" meaning we have grown to perceive.

Heck explains that Windor's usage on the *Whole Earth Catalog*—certainly one of the most widely recognized applications—permanently associates a time period and cultural mindset with the typeface. The counterculture and youth-led movements of the 1960s became tied to this typographic style and were subsequently compounded through its repetition and use. This is seen in similar font choices used for protest posters, show flyers, and record covers from the time. It is recognized as a typographic branding element for Woody Allen, used in nearly all of his movie title sequences since *Annie Hall* in 1977, and on the cover of his essay collection, *Mere Anarchy*. New Yorkers may also recognize Windsor from the signage for Max's Kansas City in Manhattan—the 1970s nightclub and restaurant frequented by both Andy Warhol and Patti Smith. Cooper Black—another boldly rounded, visually similar serif typeface released in 1921—gained wide usage and popularity as Windsor's refined and slightly more conservative younger cousin. The suggested meaning that became ubiquitous fifty years ago, associated with sustainability and environmentalism, and the counterculture's feelings of rebellion, is now being renewed through a freshly flowing spring of typography. Perhaps designers, motivated by recent U.N. Climate Reports and an increased global mood of climate realism, are being reminded of their capacity to provoke and inspire.

The Climate Science, Risk, & Solutions program from the Massachusetts Institute of Technology uses Windsor as their logo and display typeface across their website. The page explains, prominently typeset in Windsor Bold, that their goal is to summarize the most important "evidence for human-caused climate change." The application suggests the designer felt the typeface generated a meaningful connection to climate change and environmentalism. A more direct reference to the *Whole Earth Catalog* is also apparent in the masthead of *Emergence Magazine*.

As a contemporary printed example, the editorial strives to "share stories that explore the timeless connections between ecology, culture, and spirituality." Windsor again is used to support their mission through the symbolism it embodies.

This use can be seen commercially, as well. The fashion brand Jam, founded by Sam Jayne in 2018, also relies on Windsor for their logo. Marketing the brand as one that "delves into themes of nature," Jam leans heavily on images and motifs that evoke nature—including the circular image of the earth. These choices compliment the typeface and capitalize on its design aesthetic. It has been used as a tool to sell a collection of consumer wearables from a number of brands, floating between a smart graphic reference and predictable cliché. Even fashion giant Nike has capitalized on the implicit meaning through apparel designs for its outdoor collection ACG—All Conditions Gear. The landing page for a recent collection went so far as to suggest that the clothing will aid in "connecting with Mother Nature."

Within these use cases, Windsor demonstrates the development of its own subliminal code. Like a newly unveiled image of Earth, it has the curiosity and depth to maintain a power of its own and shapes the way content is viewed. Born from a simple formal element, then evolved into a series of typographic characters, Windsor not only holds the capacity for language, but the ability for symbolic expression. But Windsor also presents us a with paradox. Does its overuse aid in its superficiality, sterilizing a once radical font? Or does its resurgence breathe new life into the utopian ideals championed through an ephemeral publication?

Copyright © 2021 by Andrew McQuiston. "Approaches to Design History" seminar, MA Design Research, Writing & Criticism at School of Visual Arts, October 2021.

CHAPTER 8

THE REBRANDING OF AIR INDIA

BY ROSHITA THOMAS

In the landscape of global aviation, where airlines strive for a distinctive brand that echoes both relevance and familiarity, the recent rebranding of Air India has emerged as a poignant chapter. Last year the airline announced a massive rebrand and new identity rollout. The iconic Maharaja mascot, once synonymous with the airline's face, now stands at a crossroads.

While initially exciting, the Air India facelift took an unexpected turn by opting to sideline historical nuances in favor of positioning the airline within the "global market." The rebrand seems to turn away from what could have been a very significant change. Travel is a market that feels akin to quicksand, undergoing constant change, where preferences oscillate between consumers and corporations, and budgets redefine scopes overnight. Designers face the intricate task of delicately balancing brand legacy with the desire for a new and innovative approach. The Air India rebrand prompts us to explore not only the transformation of a logo and wordmark but also the deeper implications of cultural distinction being turned into consumable morsels for the West in the name of progress.

Founded by J. R. D. Tata, an industrialist, entrepreneur, and India's first commercial pilot license-holder, Air India (originally known as Tata Airlines) established itself as an independent company in the country's aviation sector, launching its first aircraft in 1933. If you came of age in India during the early '90s, the aviation scene was characterized by simplicity, with only a handful of airlines dominating the skies. Among them stood the Maharaja mascot of Air India, first conceived in 1946 by Bobby Kooka, Air India's commercial director, and illustrated by Umesh Rao, an artist at J. Walter Thompson. Characterized by a potbelly, distinctive oversized curled mustache, sharp nose, striped turban, and a calm expression, he stood as a symbol of the nation's hospitality etched into every Indian's memory forever. The identity before the rebrand showcased the Flying Swan silhouette and the Konark wheel within, complemented by a deep red wordmark and Devanagari script. It marked Air India's distinctive presence in the aviation sector and encapsulated an era when air travel was a novel and privileged experience—a time when aviation in India was synonymous with wonder and wealth.

Initially establishing itself as an independent entity, Air India bloomed in India's aviation sector before being acquired by the government of India in 1948. After operating under government ownership for roughly 70 years, Air India was reacquired by the Tata Group in 2022. In December 2023, Tata announced the rollout of a new global brand identity for Air India, led by the London, UK, office of Futurebrand in collaboration with its Mumbai counterpart. The rebrand also seems like a valid step to distance itself from the negative pushback accumulated during decades of government management. But the agency charged with redesigning one of the oldest airlines in India was left with a research task that must have been both daunting and exhaustive.

Air India's historic fleet of iconic Boeing 747s, nicknamed "Your Palace in the Sky," featured interiors curated by Tata himself. The fleet epitomized luxury travel's golden age, with the renowned Maharaja Lounges and a first-class cabin adorned with Indian motifs, vibrant bandhani print uniforms, Gupta period art, murals from the Ajanta caves, and Kashmiri textile patterns. The white facade and red 'jharokha' windows became a signature. Air India was known for amalgamating heritage and meticulous design.

While the history of the aircraft featured so many elements to draw inspiration from, the new identity seems to limit itself. The updated logo and livery feature a revised color palette and typeface, and the airline's mascot now assumes a predominantly subdued role confined to the premium classes. As a component of the rebranding effort, the airline has launched a fresh website and app, along with initiatives such as round-the-clock customer service, full lounge access for premium passengers, and a revamped loyalty program.

The logo underwent a major overhaul, replacing the previous red swan and Konark Chakra with a gold window frame symbolizing a "Window of Possibilities." The wordmark appears impressive along the entire length of the fuselage. While the custom type family designed in collaboration with Fabio Haag Type, Air India Sans, is a crisp addition to the identity. The new visual system features deep red, aubergine, and gold hues, along with a chakra-inspired pattern and the main element i.e., "The Vista" graphics.

Inspired by the 747's jharokha window, the Vista graphics use the window as a framing device. Though neatly executed as an animation, the gradients and chakra patterns seem force-fed into the system. The sarees, designed by celebrity designer Manish Malhotra, are sharp and don't dilute the essence or authenticity of the uniform but rather transform it.

While the new identity aims to position Air India as a globally recognized brand, some critics argue that it might have diluted its distinct cultural elements. Introducing a more minimalist logo, featuring a gold window frame, deviated from traditional symbols like the red swan and Konark Chakra, potentially disconnecting from the airline's rich heritage. The shift in the mascot's role, with the Maharaja appearing predominantly in premium classes, signaled a departure from its historical international prominence.

The public reaction to the Air India rebranding in India has been a mixed bag. While some individuals appreciate the airline's efforts to change its image, others have criticized the changes for potentially disregarding cultural nuances. Positive feedback emphasizes the modern and vibrant aesthetic, considering it a step towards aligning with global standards. However, there are concerns about the potential loss of the airline's distinctive identity and whether the rebranding adequately honors its rich history.

When comparing Air India's rebranding with other global airlines, it becomes evident that the pursuit of global standards often leads to a certain level of homogenization in identity. In an interesting development, the new branding of Air India bears a resemblance to another airline, Vistara, also owned by Tata. This similarity is not coincidental, as Tata Sons and Singapore Airlines have agreed to consolidate Air India and Vistara by March 2024. This consolidation highlights the challenge of maintaining distinct brand identities while aligning with global standards in an industry marked by increasing convergence.

In an article titled "Are rebrands starting to look the same?" writer Elizabeth Goodspeed phrased it right: "While designers might debate the intricacies of truly unique branding, beneath these immediate concerns, there's an underlying truth: what's seen as popular often holds a key to broader appeal and effectiveness."

The tension between global aspirations and cultural preservation is a challenge faced by many companies seeking international recognition. Air India's rebranding reflects a broader trend where the quest for global standards (aka recognition from the West) poses challenges in maintaining cultural nuances. Air India's rebrand underscores the delicate balance required to navigate growth strategies while preserving the unique cultural fabric that defines its identity.

Copyright © 2024 by Roshita Thomas. Published in www.printmag.com, February 7, 2024.

REVIEWS AND CRITIQUES

HEADS TOGETHER: WEED AND THE UNDERGROUND PRESS SYNDICATE, 1965–1973

BY STEVEN HELLER

✱

"If you remember the '60s, you really weren't there" is the oft quoted saying attributed to different people, referencing the counterculture mantra coined by LSD guru Timothy Leary: "Turn on, tune in, drop out." I've deluded myself that not having touched weed or psychedelics, I thwarted any memory loss and can vividly recall the counterculture era in all its split fountain shades and black light spectrums. After spending hours engaged with this chaotic collection of covers, articles, and ads drawn from dozens of anti-design, poor design, and emblematic underground papers and then reading David Jacob Kramer's illuminating introduction in the profusely illustrated book *Heads Together: Weed and the Underground Press Syndicate, 1965–1973*, I realize there was a chunk of Sixties youth culture I missed.

The Australian-born, Los Angeles-based author, Kramer, who was born in 1980, a generation after the day the music died, has written a revealing history of the period, peppered with quotes from many of the key editors, publishers, and stoners of the era and printed on such lightweight paper that you could roll it up and smoke with it. Although *Heads Together* is by no means a definitive legacy of the underground press, it is an illuminating snapshot (his word) of a history that I lived through and have chronicled in my memoir *Growing Up Underground*. It gives truth to the lie that just because I could lay claim to two out of three keywords, "Sex, Drugs, and Rock 'n' Roll," having made the choice not to bogart that joint or blow my mind with weed (and its derivatives) wiped out a major chunk of my Sixties experience.

The design of the book takes a little getting accustomed to. It is not an exact replica of an underground, but it means that design is like a run-on sentence, difficult to navigate. Since most of the illustrations are clips from the actual newspapers, the layouts are very raw and untidy. With the notable exception of the comics artists, the papers show designers who lacked the training to do more than Yale students.

Kramer's most admirable feat is how in his essay he weds drug culture and smoking marijuana to the leftwing revolutionary issues of the day—anti-Vietnam War, Black Power, feminism, police brutality, American racism, J. Edgar Hoover, and Richard M. Nixon. As a tactic, propagating the power of weed, he says, was aggressively and positively both mind shattering and world changing as an atomic bomb.

The bomb in which all this energy was harnessed, was The Underground Press Service (UPS), founded by the activist and pot entrepreneur, Tom Forcade, founder of *High Times* magazine. UPS began with five leading underground papers—which grew to 500 around the U.S.—that maintained their own identities while sharing their respective contents. UPS enabled national distribution through a national network of indie headshops, where dope apparatuses were sold.

Quoting John Sinclair, leader of the political band MC5, "Dope was like the link between the neo-beatnik culture, which we had been involved in prior to 1966 and the new hippie culture, which was just beginning to spring up."

Smoking pot had other significant consequences; it was construed as an act of solidarity with the soldiers in Vietnam, where most soldiers "were being introduced to it for the first time along with PTSD," Kramer notes.

In 1913 weed sales or possession was already criminalized along the southwest American border towns as Mexicans fled their own Civil War; it was outlawed in California and Texas, and the laws were used to enforce racist persecution elsewhere in the U.S. Most jazzmen in New Orleans, for example, were Black and consumed large quantities of what Louis Armstrong called the "Viper." By the 1930s, marijuana was the preferred name for cannabis because it sounded Mexican.

REVIEWS AND CRITIQUES

At the same time, Kramer discusses the acrimonious rift within the Liberation News Service (LNS) that supplied weekly content to papers around the globe. As LNS founder Ray Mungo is quoted: "The two factions were at violent odds, the political wing he called Vulgar Marxists and the pot heads he called Virtuous Caucus."

Many of the freaks who believed that drugs would save the world helped run UPS into the ground, to be replaced by The Alternative Press Syndicate (APS) also founded by Forcade. He conducted market tests using government statistics indicating that 20 million reefer smokers lived in the U.S. and invested his own "weed money" into *High Times*, which is claimed (pipe dream?) had a peak circulation of around 400,000.

As unlikely as it was in the Sixties and Seventies, weed had made it through the gates of the capitalist citadel. What *Heads Together* does so well is to place this continuously fought battle in its early context of mobilization when the underground conscripts began fighting an existential war which at first terrorized middle Americans, and today is possibly the most non-partisan issue in state legislatures to make WEED more than a battle cry but an issue of how best to make it legal—and profitable. Gummies anyone?

Copyright © 2023 by Steven Heller. Published in *Print*, November 30, 2023.

Ask designers questions about form, content, aspiration and process and you'll get many similar and many dissimilar answers. A wide spectrum of editors, writers, scholars were asked many of the same questions as well as those tailored to the specific work of the individual author. The results serve as a to-do, have-done, and self-critique of the education of a design writer.

WHERE, WHEN, HOW, AND WHY

I WRITE:

**WRITERS / EDITORS / DESIGNERS
ANSWER QUESTIONNAIRES**

CHAPTER 9

THE POLYMATH

★ TOD LIPPY ★

Founder, Editor, Publisher of *ESOPUS*

Q. *You are truly a polymath. Why so many different skills?*

I'm not sure, to be honest. I just love being creative, and as long as I'm not failing miserably at a discipline I've decided to try my hand at, I'll continue to pursue it.

Q. *You have written about a lot of cultural phenomena. What prepared you for this kind of writing career?*

I've always loved art, music, film, theater—as did my parents. I guess the fact that they exposed my sister and me to all of these cultural activities early on—and encouraged us to participate not only as audience members but as practitioners—probably got that ball rolling.

Q. *Esopus is the magazine you founded and edited for twenty-five issues. It was a lavishly designed publication, which you did yourself. How did you balance your writing with the rest of your responsibilities?*

I didn't do a lot of writing for Esopus, and that was on purpose. For one, I was loathe to "overexplain" any of the magazine's contents—the idea behind the publication, always, was to let readers approach the visual content on its and their own terms. And while I did pen an editor's note for, say, every other issue (especially if the issue was themed), I tried to keep these short and sweet for the same reason. It's funny, but the bulk of the writing I did in relation to Esopus, which was a 501(c)(3) nonprofit publication, was for the hundreds of grant applications (and subsequent final reports) we submitted over the years to the NEA and many of our other public and private funders.

WHERE, WHEN, HOW, AND WHY I WRITE

Q. *What determines whether you warm to an essay or not?*

As long as an author offers an unusual perspective; an introduction to a unique, memorable subject; or—perhaps most important of all, a real engagement with the topic at hand, I am immediately interested. All of those factors can make even the most poorly written first draft something worth tackling.

Q. *You work as an editor, molding and orchestrating words; what are you trying to do? Rewrite or simply get the piece in a readable state?*

My goal with editing is to create a polished, eminently readable piece of writing that, above all else, reflects the voice of the writer. In some ways, it's almost like working as a translator.

Q. *Is a magazine meant to have a dominant authorial voice? And when you get that, is there any room for variety and improvisation?*

I think it depends on the publication, and I think "authorial" should probably be replaced by "editorial." I can think of many magazines whose editorial tone or voice is essential to their success: *The New Yorker*, *Spy*, *The Economist*, *McSweeney's*. But that still leaves room, if the editors (and the art directors) really know what they're doing, for a variety of authorial voices. In the same issue of *The New Yorker*, you'll find a cartoon by Roz Chast, a hard-hitting investigative piece on abortion by Jia Tolentino, and a short story by Salmon Rushdie. Yet they all feel very much like *New Yorker* material.

Q. *As the magazine editor, can you also be your own editor?*

I think you can. I write in stages: my first draft is always messy, scattershot, and filled with "t/k" gaps in information and transitions. For that reason, my process as a writer requires me to be my own editor as, draft by draft, I refine an essay into something readable. But just because you can be your own editor doesn't mean you necessarily should be. It's near impossible, I think, to edit one's own work with the impartiality and objectivity required of the best editors, copyeditors, and proofreaders. And I guarantee you'll miss at least one typo if it's your own piece of writing.

CHAPTER 9

KNOWING YOUR AUDIENCE

★ LIZ DANZICO ★

Lead of AI Microsoft

Q. *How and why did you become interested in writing about design?*

I founded my own newspaper, *The Greenridge Gazette*, complete with articles I wrote and illustrated after interviewing neighbors, all at age seven years old. Issues could include articles about the design of an object like a neighbor's hat, the latest pet parakeet, or neighbor's trip to Bermuda. Breaking news! The masthead was in my own hand-lettered calligraphy based on a class I was taking with my father at the time. Years later, as a college student, I had a writing internship that focused on teaching excellence, and I was writing about the design of a classroom and the design of its course based on student feedback. I remember the specific day I became interested. I was staring at my writing in PageMaker: the words on the page together with black-and-white illustrations. Having the opportunity to write about design, and lay out the article, and illustrate it brought me so much joy, I nearly couldn't contain myself. I remembered my childhood newspaper, and it was then I became convinced of the inseparable nature of design writing and design itself to communicate and make an impact to audiences. If one makes writing clear, one could make a difference to critical communities like teachers and students with lasting impact.

Q. *Can any writer write about design, or is there a singular talent or skill one must have?*

Any writer can write about design yet there is a particular skill one must have that makes it easier—noticing. Noticing can occur with any one of the five senses—but it's non-negotiable that a writer sharpen the breadth, depth, interestingness, frequency, scale, and measure to notice over the course of their career. It is the noticing of the design in concert with humans that elevates the writing to a place that is new to the reader. Noticing takes time as well.

Q. *What constitutes effective design writing?*

Early on, someone told me that Kurt Vonnegut once said to write for only one person. Diligently, I chose carefully one audience member, and wrote everything I could with that person in mind. It wasn't until years later that I learned that Vonnegut meant, for a different sort of writing, that one should write for yourself.

Yet effective design writing is indeed knowing your audience. Writing with your audience in mind will help create context that starts where they are and takes them on a journey. If they don't already understand what Bauhaus means, you have to start there. Yet if they were a student of the Bauhaus, you can start at a higher level. Your role is to create details that exist beyond the imagination of the reader and round out their understanding. Yet to know how to frame those details, you have to consider your audience in the first place.

Q. *Should design writing be "entertaining"?*

No. Clear design writing should not entertain. It can, and if that is what's necessary, get to the point, and let the entertainment follow.

Q. *Is it best not to be a designer when writing about design or does this not matter?*

John Dewey, the American philosopher, once wrote, "Recognition is perception arrested before it has a chance to develop freely." It's not best that a non-designer write about design, but it sometimes can help. Our perception is so often arrested, and we become so familiar with contexts that we lose the perspective necessary to describe and translate meaning to others.

I once wrote the user manual for the Samsung washing machine. In order to do such a prestigious and important job effectively, one must take part in the process as follows: receive an unmarked box from the company containing one washing machine in a nondescript box with no instructions. It is then up to you, as the writer, to figure out everything on your own, from unboxing to washing. The idea behind this quasi-bizarre process of writing for humans— and much of professional/technical writing—is that writing can be more user focused, more centered on the person, if it comes from the point of view of someone who can directly empathize.

Early in my career I described washing machines, telephones, computer software, and other pragmatic devices—always from the users' point of view. These experiences have never left me as I moved through my career, considering how to write in a way that honors the audience I write for.

Q. *Do you draw a distinction between professional and creative design writing?*

Professional writing and creative writing are as different as classical and jazz music. There are overlaps and crossovers and even misconceptions—yes, I do draw a distinction between the two. Professional is classical, of course, having its set tempo, dynamics, chords, and harmony. Professional writing can be creative, but its purpose is quite distinct; its job is to create clear and simplified communications across media. It need not be creative, but it does take creativity oftentimes to be simple. Creative design writing is quite different; it's jazz music. It need not be about clarity or simplicity (although it can be), and in fact, can be the opposite should the occasion call for it. Creative design writing can be a call and response with its intended audience and even improv at times.

And for what it's worth, *Kind of Blue* has been known to get one unstuck in both professional and creative design writing when played in the background on low.

Q. *You have written for your blog and for publications, is there a marked difference for writing on these two platforms?*

Writing for a blog is like being an editor with a journal, where you can control the topics for the reader. Writing for a publication is pure writing. With a long history as an editor, I also have trouble separating my editor mind from my writing mind, and as a writer for your blog, you are, in fact, the writer, editor, designer, art director, and technologist, and social media expert. Oftentimes for publications, you are the writer period, and sometimes are asked to participate in social media efforts.

On a personal note, I was surprised at how prolific I could be on a blog, but how little I could produce if commissioned for a topic by a publication. Just the act of someone giving me a constraint of a topic, rendered me without the ability to write. On the other hand, constraints of word count, which publications also give, were thrilling to me. It pays to explore which constraints a publication is seeking, and which constraints work for you.

WHERE, WHEN, HOW, AND WHY I WRITE

Q. *Do you insist that students and/or the designers that you oversee write as well as visualize?*

I do indeed. When I started the SVA program, MFA Interaction Design, one of the things I had found when I did research on the gap in the industry ahead of time, is that there was a gap in designers who could communicate about their design. Students were graduating in design but could not tell great stories about the great design work they had done. We made it a core pillar of the graduate program to teach writing and presenting design writing. No matter the pushback, we insisted. Likewise, we insist in the professional work we do that people use clear language, and started a UX writing team who could help people who cannot help themselves.

Q. *Are design writing and editing viable disciplines?*

We're at a step change in the world of design and technology. Much like we were at the introduction of the web browser, the design of the iPhone, and now generative AI. With this movement of AI, writers have a new opportunity to be the authors and directors of a new creative direction for writing. While there is no value in dwelling on the short-lived, but early used phrase, "prompt engineering," that act is one of writing and will help writers hone skills that can help propel them into creative leadership positions to direct what is being written and read. What will we do with the opportunity?

One of the most valuable industries, according to the market, right now is AI. And most of that market is made up of words. Many of the design interfaces we use today, and the most intriguing interfaces that are making it clear they will change our world, are mostly text. People are consuming design writing and relying on text-based interfaces to perform functions like no other time.

Design is writing. And design iteration is editing.

247

CHAPTER 9

EVERY DAY BEGIN AGAIN

★ KIM TIDWELL ★

Managing editor, www.printmag.com

Q. *How and why did you become interested in editing design writing?*

As with many multifaceted creatives, nothing about my career has been linear. We often don't fit neatly in boxes. But one consistent thread has been art and design: I've hovered around visual communication like a groupie. My particular strength has consistently been articulating what I feel and see and finding solace in connecting people and ideas—writing was a natural fit. Even so, whether by societal script, family of origin, or some combination, I never thought I could write for a living. At most, I thought of writing as a hobby, something I could bring to enhance my ability to do another role. It took me decades to embrace the idea that I am a WRITER, not just a designer-marketer-brand manager who writes.

What I love about design writing (and editing) is that I can indulge my inner polymath. Deeply considering design, art, and makers is an ongoing education in sociology, psychology, anthropology, language, science, and math. It exposes me to incredible thinkers who surprise me and zhuzh my thinking. Putting your aesthetic and practical design knowledge on the line can feel vulnerable. But sticking to safety won't serve my growth. I learn more every day about how I see the world, and writing about design helps me crystallize my point of view. This craft also offers a chance to change my mind.

Writing can take many forms. Being a writer doesn't always mean that you have to publish books, though that's an aspiration for many of us. Writing is simply about weaving accessible stories for your reader (whether short-form blog posts, long-form articles, research papers, book-length fiction or nonfiction, personal essays, what have you). As with all creative endeavors, collaboration is part of the process, and so is friction (resistance and what-ifs can

WHERE, WHEN, HOW, AND WHY I WRITE

help us refine our work). Enter the editor. What I love most about editing is that I can cultivate the bigger picture while helping writers bring their ideas to life.

Q. *Can any writer write about design, or is there a singular talent or skill one must have?*

To effectively write about design, I believe a generalist's sensibility is your most effective tool. Influential design writing isn't necessarily about the process behind (or construction of) a campaign, typeface, or brand identity, though that is one aspect. Memorable design writing evokes what it means to be a human in today's world. The writer pulls from the zeitgeist of the time to encapsulate something essential about our lives. It's about articulating something about our broader culture and our place in it.

Q. *What constitutes effective design reporting and writing?*

Curiosity is most fundamental. Second is a willingness to see past your own biases. Call up your knowledge of contemporary design and design history, but don't let the past dictate how you view the work. Progress depends on the uncomfortable, the uncategorizable, the indefinable. As design writers, we must first rely on our ability to look at design work and wonder about the many decisions that created it. Then, we can ascertain whether it is effective, not based on our specific aesthetic preferences, but on the work's context, audience, and purpose (the why).

Q. *Is it best not to be a designer when writing about design or does this not matter?*

A foundation in what you want to write about is always a good thing. At the same time, an outsider's perspective can be a design writer's secret weapon. All of life involves design. We can all quickly decide whether we like or loathe a particular piece of visual communication. We have instincts about whether something is compelling or not. We can sniff out the authenticity of the voice and the earnestness of the effort (or lack thereof). Humans recognize human (yes, even in this burgeoning age of AI). We all are capable of visceral reactions to aesthetic forms. Whether we have the industry language to go along with these innate abilities is moot. When I was getting my master's in art history, I remember approaching my advisor during a moment of intense imposter syndrome.

249

I'll never forget what she told me: "You don't need the jargon. Speaking and writing about what you see in a clear, accessible, human way is a superpower." Sometimes, entrenchment in an industry can work against you. Like International Art English, design has a language that obfuscates and distances. The writing that breaks through is the stuff that touches a nerve across industry lines, the universal things that make readers— even non-designers—stop and reconsider something they previously held.

Q. *What differentiates reportage from commentary from punditry?*

The delineation for me lies in the lens. Reportage is a specific skill set based on the framework of journalism (impartial, truthful, accounting). On the opposite end of the spectrum is punditry, or expressing opinions about something because you've claimed some topical expertise. The "expression of expertise" is the key here. Punditry isn't inherently wrong; it's just that it should come with a label: this is the truth, in my opinion. Commentary is your sweet spot for design writing. Commentary involves some accountable expertise, which affords you the narrative perch to observe, review, and critique the work in question. Opinions can be part of commentary, but a shared knowledge bank informs them. That shared knowledge invites and is part of an ongoing conversation.

Q. *Do you draw a distinction between professional and creative design writing?*

I might have a controversial belief, but I don't think there's a distinction. Maybe it's simply my itchiness about the loaded subtext behind "professional." Professional and creative are not at odds with one another. Design writing is creative. Good design and excellent writing about it always operate a little outside the script. And when we talk about creative and professional in separate boxes, it has an "othering" effect—that creative people cannot or are not inherently professional.

I prefer to focus on the lens of the writer. Are they coming to this piece of writing as someone who is also a practitioner? Are they coming to it with different expertise, as an observer, an appreciator, or someone who wants to further the conversation?

A design writer can come with both of these.

> WHERE, WHEN, HOW, AND WHY I WRITE

"You don't need the jargon. Speaking and writing about what you see in a clear, accessible, human way is a superpower."

Professional and creative can also be used to distinguish paid writing from non-paid. As any working writer (or designer, for that matter) will tell you, all the output, whether for a client, for *Print*, for a future book, or hidden away in a journal, is professional. This creative output helps me develop my craft and learn to articulate my thoughts. In our society, pursuits that don't earn an immediate paycheck are often labeled frivolous. But as with any creative craft, many hours of skills-building, practice, and refinement don't see the light of day. What crosses our screens or lands in our hands as an object to admire is years in the making. This growth and continual learning is the very picture of professionalism.

Q. *Are design writing and editing viable disciplines?*

Of course! I'd love to help dismantle the subliminal messages that say design writing isn't lucrative, viable, or preferable. I advise students wanting to pursue these disciplines to take the meandering path. Try a lot of things. Seek out varied experiences. Consume many different visual and sensory media: fine art, plays, movies, ads, illustrations, books, graphic novels, applied art, essays, reportage, and music. Develop your creative intersectionality. Hone your writing all the while.

All these diversions will give you perspective, your career texture and heft, and your voice its singular flavor.

On a broader scale, the world needs people who can connect the dots, articulate big ideas, and help people connect with visual culture. Great design writing can do all of these things. Go forth!

CHAPTER 9

ORAL TRADITIONS

★ MICHELE Y. WASHINGTON ★

Writer, critic, historian

Q. *How and why did you become interested in writing about and editing design?*

My interest in writing is rooted in oral storytelling traditions, much like spoken word. Starting from this orientation helps me frame my thoughts before putting pen to paper.

Q. *What constitutes effective design writing?*

For me, the real question is, what is design? What are the ways in which we communicate today? Is it through social media, where our words are short quips strung together?

Q. *Should design writing be "entertaining"?*

Of course words need to bounce and sing from my lips.

Q. *Are there subjects you prefer or do you think of yourself as a generalist?*

While I do have subjects that I love writing about, such as food and its connection to sensory modes, it's the act of writing itself that fuels my soul. I think it's good for me to broaden my range to embrace areas outside of what I usually write about. After all, it's a good learning experience and helps expand my scope. I love writing about food and its sensorial mode.

WHERE, WHEN, HOW, AND WHY I WRITE

Q. Is it best not to be a designer when writing about design, or does this not matter?

It doesn't matter if the person is not a designer. After all, fiction writers can naturally craft their words into visual dialog while developing their characters. For me, Toni Morrison paints her words on the page. Poets like Nikki Giovanni weave rhythmic phrases that sing. Sun Ra's masterful sonic fusion free form and improvisational style. His sounds were a syncopated stream of beast composed into words. Missy Elliot riffing.

Lesley Lokko, a Ghanaian-Scottish architect and academic, stepped away from her career for twelve years to write fiction. She has written ten fiction novels, including *Soul Sisters*; *Sundowners*; *Rich Girl, Poor Girl*; and *Private Affair*. Her writings explore racial and cultural identity, love, and family histories.

Q. Do you draw a distinction between professional, academic, and creative design writing?

Each of these writing areas differs and has its own set of criteria. However, weaving words together forms comprehensive sentence structures. Although each of these form the backbone of effective communication in writing disciplines.

Professional writers I tend to think of in the world of journalism, roles such as newspaper or magazine editors and reporters. Other areas are content writers, bloggers, or podcast producer.

Q. Are design writing and editing viable disciplines?

Absolutely. Each has the ability to enhance one's ability to communicate and become a stronger communicator. The big question is, under which department is best suited for offering design writing as a discipline.

CHAPTER 9

ON
EXPLORATION

★ ALAN RAPP ★

Editor, book packager, and content curator

Q. *How and why did you become interested in editing design writing?*

Writing and design are two interests that came together in a logical way–
through books. I took my love of reading/writing into the very first jobs I could
get as a teenager, as a bookseller, and in college I worked at one of the top
architecture and design bookstores in the country. That job opened my eyes
to those worlds, and I have been involved with design, writing, and publishing
professionally ever since.

Q. *Can any writer write about design, or is there a singular talent or skill one
must have?*

Absolutely any writer can do so—through the modes of analyzing function or
aesthetics, and certainly through speculative generation (a major aspect of
worldbuilding is tech/design ideation). It starts with close observation, but
then the skill comes in articulating interrelationships and effects of systems,
seeing the complexity in ostensibly simple things.

Q. *What constitutes effective design reporting and writing?*

Conditions on the ground in the present analysis; a sense of historical context
in the longer view; a personal point of view that synthesizes this all.

WHERE, WHEN, HOW, AND WHY I WRITE

Q. *Is it best not to be a designer when writing about design or does this not matter?*

If anything, designers should explore writing, as it's another mode of generating critical thought. In design MFA programs I designed writing courses that were meant to help students use writing as a creative avenue to inform their practice, but also challenge them to articulate what they were trying to do and stake their claim in the larger worlds of design and culture.

Q. *What differentiates reportage from commentary from punditry?*

Boiled down, reportage is based on timeliness and topicality within the development of projects. Commentary is often timely but is not constrained to a single project or situation; it can take an expanded view, a larger context. Punditry can be as expansive, personal, and interpretive as you want...but since the concept is so often funneled toward politics and society, let's not lose why the idea of punditry has such a negative charge these days. But this can be redeemed through cogent, informed, and defensible writing.

Q. *Do you draw a distinction between professional and creative design writing?*

Yes, but I respect when those boundaries are blurred. Is the distinction ever problematically unclear for the intended audience? This reference will date, but any horror fiction based around the detailed flaws of a Cybertruck would serve as both modes of design writing.

Q. *Are design writing and editing viable disciplines?*

As it is phrased, this question works within a binary of an earlier time. The answer is yes, but we need to take into account how much the editorial (print and web) and book publishing industries have changed since the turn of the millennium, as well as the change within the online platforms and social media outlets. "Viability" in this context is enormously self-generated.

CHAPTER 9

A METEOR CRASHING EXPERIENCE

⋆ COLETTE GAITER ⋆

**Professor Emerita in the Departments of Africana Studies
and Art & Design at the University of Delaware**

Q. *How and why did you become interested in writing about design?*

Just as I did with my academic career, I came to writing serendipitously and through a side door. I knew what I wanted to do since taking a high school graphic design course. I went on to college and absorbed a traditional design BFA undergraduate education at Carnegie-Mellon University, where I learned the design canon that later became the basis of my teaching. I am a century- and millennium-straddling baby boomer. I was always one of the few people of color working and teaching in graphic design and later digital media.

I am still motivated by my high school discovery that visual media is ground zero for influencing political and social world views. It was the late '60s and early '70s. Everything was changing in a post-civil rights/early women's liberation world, especially for me as a formerly-Negro, becoming-Black teenage girl. Graphically, the world was more colorful, messy, and organic compared to mid-century/early '60s straight lines and huge sans-serif type.

At my first job after college in Pittsburgh, I wrote articles and designed an internal magazine for one of our small Black agency's clients. I don't remember a discussion about my writing qualifications. I was a design major, but they were happy with my writing. The agency's principal had been the editor of the *Pittsburgh Courier*, a nationally important Black newspaper.

I started teaching graphic design and computer graphics in 1986 at the Minneapolis College of Art and Design, after ten years of design practice in

Pittsburgh, Washington, DC, and New York City. A colleague asked me to write an article for a design newsletter he edited. I remember laboring over an article I wrote about artists using new media for *Forecast's Public Art Review* in Minneapolis. I contributed to *Bad Subjects: Political Education for Everyday Life*, an online defunct but archived magazine. I was always writing something while making new media art that incorporated graphic design.

In the mid-1990s, for a new course, I assigned design students a historical research and presentation project. The list of designers and illustrators they could choose from included the Harlem Renaissance artists Aaron Douglas (African American) and Miguel Covarrubias (Mexican). I was surprised that the mostly white students always chose the artists of color first. Maybe they were drawn to perspectives from people who were unfamiliar to them. I added other people of color and more women to the list as I found them, but there were never many because no one had written about them—not that they did not exist.

I realized that I had to contribute to that incomplete body of texts. As the writer Toni Morrison said, "If there's a book that you want to read, but it hasn't been written yet, then you must write it." After I sent out an internet query about designers and illustrators of color, a colleague helped me locate the former Black Panther artist Emory Douglas, whose work I had admired in high school when my older sister brought the Black Panther newspaper home from Howard University. I interviewed Emory in San Francisco about his work and time with the Panthers in 2004. I wrote specifically about his visual work in 2005 (at Steven Heller's invitation) for *Voice: AIGA*, the online journal for the organization. Books about the Black Panther Party discussed Emory Douglas and the Black Panther newspaper. Still, they did not elaborate on his bold illustrations, newspaper layouts, and their significance to communicating the Party's messages.

A meteor-crashing experience occurred in my life over the years in the late 1990s when I worked on a master's degree in liberal studies at Hamline University in St. Paul, MN. The program, for working professionals, guided me toward more informed writing through reading and discussing texts I had never encountered. Since I graduated college more than twenty years earlier, so much had happened in the humanities. They became inclusive (which was then controversial), postmodern and structuralist theory became influential, cultural studies became a popular discipline, and semiotics made a comeback. Even Marshall McLuhan was back in style. Our thesis was called a synthesis project, and mine—an artist's book about my early life—used images and text to compare the external social and political events of the mid-twentieth century to my unusual childhood. It won the Most Creative Synthesis Award for the program in 1999.

When I began writing about Emory Douglas in 2005, most people in the mainstream design world did not know that he led a team of talented and prolific illustrators, cartoonists, and designers for thirteen years. There were similar teams at Black newspapers and publications across the country. People of color have always been designers and visual communicators. Until recently, they worked in segregated spaces that were mostly disconnected from white designers and environments.

In 2015, Emory Douglas was awarded the AIGA medal for lifetime achievement in the field. He was the first living African American to receive the award for "individuals who have set standards of excellence over a lifetime of work or have made individual contributions to innovation within the practice of design." Two other Black designers before him, Sylvia Harris (2014) and George Olden (2007), were awarded the medal posthumously.

Q. *Can any writer write about design, or is there a singular talent or skill one must have?*

The best writers illuminate an idea, experience, or object by comparing aspects of it to something familiar or relatable to their readers. This is especially important when writing about design. The college professor part of me wants to say that a person should have some visual media background, but maybe not. What happens when a musician writes about design? They could make enlightening observations that others (even designers) might miss.

A good design writer should love design.

Q. *What constitutes effective design writing?*

Effective design writing engages people whether they formally know anything about design as a discipline or not. The writing should not be primarily about whether the designed thing followed the rules or employed specific approved methods or aesthetics. The questions to answer are, "How does it affect people?" and "Does it understand the assignment?" There is always an assignment that may not have been completely articulated in the initial project brief or conversation. When I moved to New York in 1980, I took a course at the School of Visual Arts taught by Milton Glaser. He told our class of professional designers, "You should give your client what they want—and more." The best design writers see what most people might miss, but once it is pointed out, it cannot be unseen.

Because I am a Black woman and acutely aware of American society's shortcomings in terms of social justice, I am drawn to writing that looks critically at how design influences understanding of society, culture, history, and individual lives. I believe that design is foundational to true and lasting social change. All designed artifacts draw from societal and cultural visual languages, vocabularies, and symbols that have meanings attached. Those meanings are fluid and can change as a society changes. For example, Confederate flags and monuments are slowly disappearing from the American landscape as the "Lost Cause's" symbols are called out as signifiers of racism, anti-Semitism, xenophobia, and other dangerous and threatening human proclivities. Before 2020 and a highly mediated racial awakening, "rebel" flags were hiding in plain sight everywhere because unchallenged distorted perception normalized them.

Q. *Do you draw a distinction between professional, academic, and creative design writing?*

First, the terms should be at least loosely defined. In my mind, professional might mean expository, critical, or both—such as an article in a design magazine about a practitioner, company, studio, or trend. Because design publication is less prolific than other disciplines and is still growing, academic writing on design has the chance to escape established research traditions that require extensive theoretical and methodological references. The absence of a PhD as a terminal degree requirement for teaching design also offers an escape from potentially limiting expectations. I would love to read more creative design writing. Design the writing formally and conceptually.

I believe that the boundaries of "design" should be more elastic. Many people who were historically known as painters, illustrators, or craftspeople were also designers. Under-represented groups (including women) were more often multidisciplinary because of the difficulties finding traditional design work in an institutionally segregated and sexist society.

Q. *Should all design writing be "entertaining"?*

Engaging and illuminating writing can help people appreciate more about design's sometimes mysterious and often invisible aspects. Design writing should be accessible, yes—frivolous, no. Glitz, glam, and celebrity are always in the same zip code as design but should not move in next door. The writing should not be elitist and never mean-spirited. It can definitely be humorous— slight smile or head-back-eyes-closed funny.

CHAPTER 9

Q. *Are there subjects you prefer, or do you think of yourself as a generalist?*

I just wrote about a Midwestern white male poster designer from the 1930s who made beautiful pastel lithographs of New York City for the New York Central Railroad. When I accepted the assignment, I was concerned that there was nothing much more to say than that his litho technique made the images look like watercolors and that they were impressively big. I was not sure how I would connect with the work and, by extension, understand its significance beyond its bucolic and pretty first impressions that seemed like the formal opposite of what New York actually looks like. After researching, I could contextualize the posters as designed to create a deliberate counterpoint to New York's unsavory reputation at the time. That reputation was fueled by the persistent manufactured American fear of "others" and the more reasonable skepticism of unnatural vertical landscapes, which had not yet reached most of the country.

I took on the project because I liked the posters. I suppose I am a generalist because I will always try to find my way into a topic from a perspective that makes sense to me.

Q. *Is it best not to be a designer when writing about design or does this not matter?*

I believe that non-designers and designers can have important insights and observations about design. Both points of view—from inside and outside—are necessary for the most complete body of literature for the discipline.

Q. *Are design writing and editing viable disciplines?*

Of course!

Q. *Are they essential or optional for designers and design students?*

I recommend that students read various design writing examples and do observational writing to help them look more deeply at a designed artifact. In the digital world young people have grown up in, everything seems flat, similar, and interchangeable. In some ways, this flatness makes the world accessible and is a phenomenal innovation. However, texture and volume can be metaphors for what can be seen in real life versus on a screen. I think asking students to record their impressions and speculations on design could be essential to design education.

WHERE, WHEN, HOW, AND WHY I WRITE

STRUGGLING TO FIND THE RIGHT WORDS

⭐ ELLEN LUPTON ⭐

Chair, MICA Design, Curator Emerita, Cooper Hewitt

Q. *How and why did you become interested in writing about and editing design books?*

When I studied art and design at the Cooper Union in the early 1980s, post-structuralism was in the air. The intricate language of Roland Barthes and Michel Foucault intoxicated my young mind, and so did the rigor of art and architecture criticism. Alas, there wasn't much to read about graphic design back then. Critical theory exposed untenable binaries, consumerist myths, and the physicality of text and typography. As a student, I began applying these insights to graphic design. I became curator of Cooper Union's Herb Lubalin Study Center after I graduated. There, I began to write, publish, and grow my own voice.

Q. *Can any writer write about design, or is there a singular talent or skill one must have?*

Writing is a skill AND a talent. Some people enjoy playing with words, and others struggle to find the right ones. However, with conscious effort and training, most people can learn to use words to communicate. It's better to be clear and direct than ornate and academic. Good writers are curious and patient. Writing takes time. We are shaped by what we read, so writers should absorb fiction and journalism, not just academic research.

CHAPTER 9

• ✦ •

Q. *What constitutes effective design writing?*

Effective design writing conveys credible, verifiable facts. Effective design writing also has a point of view: a perspective or angle that connects readers to the topic and brings something new to the conversation. I read about design because I want to learn about designers and design movements (contemporary or historical) or design issues (like the dangers of AI or how to expand the design canon). I also want to learn how to do things, like improve my typography or my camera skills. Flowery, bombastic, or convoluted writing has surface appeal, but if the content isn't compelling, I won't keep reading.

Effective design writing tells stories. Stories engage our senses and emotions. Stories create images in your mind. Stories unfold in time, making us wonder about the answer to a question, the struggles of a person, or the life and death of an idea. Every sentence tells a story by delivering an action.

Q. *Should design writing be "entertaining"?*

Alas, most design writing isn't entertaining. Most design writing is well-meaning and dull, including my own. But don't you love it when a speaker at a design conference makes you laugh? Humor flows more easily from the stage than the page because the speaker has risked humiliation, exposing their physical self. I am an entertaining speaker, but I battle against the formality of text. So yes, design writing should be entertaining, but that is very hard to do.

Q. *Are there any words or phrases that you will NOT use in your writing?*

I'm trying to avoid words like "always," "must," "never," "don't," and "no." I have probably used half of those words in this interview.

Q. *Is it best not to be a designer when writing about design or does this not matter?*

Designers are good at writing about design because they have lived experience. If you love what you do and want to understand it more deeply, write about it!

Q. *What differentiates commentary from punditry?*

I had to look up the word "punditry." According to the Oxford Learner's Dictionaries, punditry is "the activity of giving expert opinions on a subject in the media." Pundits are retired from their active professions yet are revered for their opinions. Journalists sometimes ask me to say something about fonts, even though I have never designed a font, which makes me a pundit. To answer your question: punditry is for muggles; commentary is for insiders.

Q. *Do you draw a distinction between professional and creative design writing?*

Both genres sound deadly to me. Professional writing is filled with phrases like "innovative," "deliverable," and "innovative deliverable." Creative writing is loaded with first-person pronouns and florid descriptions. Escaping cliches requires constant effort. Why is ChatGPT so good at generating credible prose? Because writing is predictable. Let's try to be less predictable.

Q. *You are also a pioneering design curator, what is your "style" or approach for writing for public consumption, notably for catalogs and wall labels?*

The phrase in my mind when I write a museum label is "clear like water." A museum label should make sense to a third grader, a grad student, and your Uncle Fred. Imagining these readers as you write will help you build simple, direct sentences. Have empathy for readers. They don't know the same things you do. What do they want to know? Recently, I visited MoMA's astonishing permanent collection. I was disappointed by the lack of narrative labels. I'm an educated person yet I wanted to know more about the people and ideas behind the art.

Q. *Is there a marked difference for writing with a museum audience in mind and a more niche audience?*

A niche audience already knows a lot. However, it's unkind to assume that our brains are carrying identical baggage. Many of my students come from China, Korea, and India. These brilliant designers know lots of things I don't know. When writing for designers, I try to fold in the "explaining parts" in a way that isn't condescending. We see this in movies all the time. When some guy with a white board explains libel law or money laundering, he is explaining it to us— the viewers—not just to his grandson or the local cops.

Q. *Are design writing and editing viable disciplines?*

Rarely, but if you play your cards right, you could become a pundit.

CHAPTER 9

WRITING AND EDITING

★ ADRIAN SHAUGHNESSY ★

Designer, writer, and co-founder of Unit Editions

Q. *How and why did you become interested in editing and design writing?*

I've always had an interest in written language. It started with fiction (and the writing on cereal packets, album covers and comics), and as I got older, I graduated to literary, film and music criticism. I didn't go to university, but I've always felt that reading critical writing was my education. If you'd asked me in my teenage years what I wanted to do in life, I'd have said I'd like to be a music critic. I also had a strong interest in visual art, and I stumbled into graphic design. After some dead-end jobs, I co-founded a studio and spent every waking hour for the next fifteen years, fixated on graphic design.

In the 1990s I found myself endlessly writing proposals. Firms would ask us to pitch for business and my response was to decline to do visual work and instead, provide a written proposal. I became obsessed with making these documents as clear (and persuasive) as possible. I'd do one, sometimes two, every week and this gave me the confidence to start writing about design.

Another incentive was the '90s design discourse. It was in full spate, and I wanted to be part of it. When I gave up studio life in 2003, I devoted most of my time to writing, blogging, and editing. And in 2009, with two friends, I set up Unit Editions, a publishing company dedicated to producing books about design and visual culture. To date, we've published over fifty titles, and this has allowed me to write longform texts about design and designers.

WHERE, WHEN, HOW, AND WHY I WRITE

Q. *Can any writer write about design, or is there a singular talent or skill one must have?*

The easy answer is that any writer can write about design. The more difficult question is, will the result be any good? I often think about the similarities between the acts of writing and designing. In many ways they are remarkably similar. Writing is having something to say and finding a way to express that thing. It's the same with design—you have a message, and you find a way to visually articulate that message. The difference is that with design you are usually expressing someone else's message. The act of creative writing means the writer must have the message.

Q. *What constitutes effective design reporting and writing?*

Clarity, objectivity, and an understanding of the craft of design are essential components of good writing. But I'd also add cultural awareness. Design does not exist in a vacuum. It sits in a dense web made from economics, politics, ethics, history, and a thousand other aspects of modern life. A design writer who is not aware of design's interconnectedness, can't hope to make a meaningful contribution to the discourse.

It's long been a criticism of designers that they are apolitical. I'd argue that, thanks to the way design is taught in schools around the world, this is less true today. As an educator, the other trend I see is a growing interest amongst design students in having writing as a core component of their creative practice. You don't have to be able to write to be a good graphic designer but the ability to write effective prose is a skill worth having. As Norman Potter says in his book, *What Is a Designer*, "an ability to use words clearly, pointedly, and persuasively is at all times relevant to design work." Amen to that.

Q. *Is it best not to be a designer when writing about design or does this not matter?*

There are two dominant routes from which to approach design writing. The first is as a practitioner. Richard Hollis is a good example of someone who writes primarily as a practicing designer. He has a deep-rooted interest in process, and in his view, a functioning designer is best placed to write about process and the technical minutiae of making design. The second angle is as an informed observer—in other words, a critic. This objective view, divorced from the need to be concerned with what clients and peers might think, is essential for a healthy discourse around the subject.

CHAPTER 9

When I first started writing about design, I was running a studio, and I was aware of a mental handbrake preventing me from saying what I really wanted to say. What would my clients think? If I was critical of another designer's work, would that be seen as professional jealousy? But after giving up studio life, my writing became less constrained.

There are other categories of design writing: professional guidance, business advice, design history, academic writing, and of course the language designers use to talk about their work—usually not much better than dull PR speak. Today we should probably include social media commentary as a category.

Q. *What differentiates reportage from commentary from punditry?*

Most design reportage is not much more than regurgitated press releases—uncritical and compliant. Commentary has been captured by social media. Sometimes enlightening. Sometimes mere snark. Design punditry is less easy to define. The opportunities for lengthy critical analysis are diminishing. But I see signs of hope. The Dutch publisher Set Margins is doing a good job of publishing polemical texts on design.

Q. *Do you draw a distinction between professional and creative design writing?*

I came to design writing through writing professionally, by which I mean writing proposals, website text, and the occasional bit of copywriting for clients. I was aware that written proposals were often overlooked in favor of the instant hit of visuals, so my goal was to make my writing as sharp and as engaging as possible. This helped me when I eventually graduated to writing about design.

Q. *Are design writing and editing viable disciplines?*

Depends on what is meant by "viable." If you want to earn a living solely by writing about design, you'd better have a trust fund behind you. We only have to think about the way the design press has contracted to see how opportunities for paid writing have dried up. Most design writers I know have other jobs. But if you mean, is it intellectually viable, then my answer is yes. To be part of the discourse is rewarding, and to know that something you wrote has had an impact, brings its own reward. I'd also say that writing about design opened doors for me that were closed when I was purely a designer.

WHERE, WHEN, HOW, AND WHY I WRITE

ALL ROADS LED TO "PRINT"

★ JOYCE RUTTER KAYE ★

**Former editor-in-chief *Print* magazine,
Director of Communications, SVA**

Q. *How and why did you become interested in editing design writing?*

It was a process. As a kid and teen in the 1970s-early-'80s, I was an avid reader and aspiring writer smitten by consumer culture and the media, from *MAD* magazine and Archie Comics to Topps' "Wacky Packs" stickers, candy wrappers, Sid and Marty Krofft TV shows, and album covers for Fleetwood Mac, Stevie Wonder, Talking Heads, and others. My father was a longtime subscriber to *The New Yorker* and reader of the Sunday *New York Times*, and he and I would pore over Al Hirschfeld's caricatures in the Arts section to find the hidden "NINA"s.

While studying magazine journalism at Syracuse University, I would go to Bird Library to read *Advertising Age* for new product rollouts. A few years after graduating in 1985, I was thrilled to work there as a reporter for *Ad Age/Creativity*, and discovered an affinity for identifying the inspirations and artistic influences of the people who made design and advertising. As a storyteller, I realized what a goldmine of interesting stuff could come from exploring these unique creative motivations. This is how I came to the field as a generalist writer and stayed as an editor with a specific focus that suited my own creative interests.

Once on that path, all roads for me led to *Print* magazine. Under editor in chief Martin Fox and managing editor Julie Lasky, the magazine produced thoughtful reporting and commentary operating under a very broad definition of what design and visual culture is. After six years working with the wonderful editor Margaret Richardson at the type publication *U&lc*, where I developed a deeper understanding of editor-designer collaborations and freelanced on the side for *Print*, in 1998 Julie departed the magazine, Marty hired me and immediately told me he wanted me to be his successor. Five years later, in 2003, I became editor in chief of *Print*, the first new editor in 40 years and first woman to hold the position since its founding in 1940.

Q. *Can any writer write about design, or is there a singular talent or skill one must have?*

Design touches everything, so the best design writers can write confidently about a wide range of subjects while also being able to view any subject through the lens of design. Finding the best angle is where the secret sauce lies. Take the graphics related to the war in Gaza, for example—there is rich material to be explored in communications directed at Palestinians in the form of leaflets and signage; in the signs pleading for the return of Israeli hostages and in the students' protest banners on college campuses and on social media. Having a well-developed vocabulary around aesthetics—how to relate to art, art history, design, and images—is useful because you need to be able to describe the work in detail and explain why a particular design solution is effective for an audience. An excellent writer can learn to develop that vocabulary if they are truly interested in engaging with those angles on a subject. If they're not interested, it shows.

Q. *What constitutes effective design reporting and writing?*

Tackling a difficult issue or being critical without being concerned about how it's going to land with someone. Design is an insular industry and some outlets or writers lose sight of the obligation to be objective. At *Print* we weren't catering to advertisers' demands or playing favorites with the people we covered. Our goal was to explain design's role in the world using the best writers we could possibly find and reach as broad an audience as we could in the process. We were a general-interest magazine about design, not a trade magazine for design. For the last issue of *Print* (Winter 2017/2018), the editors at that time blanketed the cover with many names of prominent designers who had been covered in the magazine over the years. My choice would have been to instead list the talented writers, editors, and art directors who worked over the decades to make the magazine a respected and beloved outlet for design journalism over those seventy-nine years.

At its essence, effective reporting and writing for design is not that different than any other reporting and writing. Do your research. Interview multiple sources. Regard online citations with skepticism. Think about the best way to shape the story—maybe a Q&A would be better as a straight narrative. Don't go into a story with preconceived notions about what it's going to be. Your sources may surprise you. The best parts of interviews tend to happen before they formally start and after they're supposed to be over. Record it all (with permission, of course). And take notes. Recordings do fail.

Q. *Is it best not to be a designer when writing about design or does this not matter?*

It depends. Some of our best writers at *Print* were designers. Paul Shaw is a tremendously talented type designer, calligrapher, historian, and educator and those skills make him a fantastic writer about type. However, just being a good designer and writer doesn't automatically make you the best writer for the publication you're pitching. You have to be able to understand the outlet's voice and point of view and be able to take direction and accept edits from the assigning editor.

Q. *What differentiates reportage from commentary from punditry?*

Reportage is journalism, it's objective, it's a telling of facts. Commentary is a personal opinion on something and clearly identified as such. Punditry is a range of writing intended to inform but also entertain.

Q. *Do you draw a distinction between professional and creative design writing?*

I think what you're getting at is voice. A skilled writer and editor can read the room and know how to adjust the writing's voice to suit a particular audience. That can mean being buttoned up (professional) or creative (something more free-form or conceptual).

Q. *Are design writing and editing viable disciplines?*

There will always be a need for writers and editors to explain the role and impact of design and visual culture in our lives, from "shrinkflation" in food packaging, to discerning AI-generated images from real ones to living a sustainable lifestyle and even casting votes in an election. People appreciate being literate about design and want to feel good about the choices they make daily.

CHAPTER 9

CHRONICLING BLACK AMERICAN GRAPHIC DESIGN

✴ SILAS MUNRO ✴

Artist, designer, writer, curator, and the founder of Poly-Mode

Q. *You are a key researcher of and writer on BIPOC design and designers. What influenced you to write commentary and history?*

I became a researcher and writer about BIPOC design because, as a designer and design student, I found it hard to find references and histories within a sea of practices and pedagogies that don't represent me, my lived experience, or that of kindred spirits. This is true for African American and African design as it is for LGBTQIA2S design and designers. A big challenge across all fields of design and for those of us who want to know and tell its history are the limited pathways for BIPOC designers and design students. The rich resources, references, methods, and potential mentors are teaming in classrooms, studios, corporations, museums, publications, archives, and in family lineages, chosen or otherwise. And yet BIPOC and QTPOC (Queer and Trans People of Color) designers make up a fraction of design programs and professions. We have been historically repressed, held back, omitted, or undervalued. As a result, I have committed to redirecting and centering art and design BIPOC voices and scholarship in making, writing, and education as a transformational process.

WHERE, WHEN, HOW, AND WHY I WRITE

Q. *What aspect of writing and editing is best for expressing your points of view? Is it through academic, critical, expository, or a combination of approaches?*

I've always found my writing and editing practices to be very fluid. As an educator who has been part of rank and promotion systems, I've felt the academic pressure to "publish or perish" in academic venues and publications. At the same time, I'm sometimes more comfortable with and enjoy the oral traditions of sharing my scholarship through public lectures, workshops, roundtables, and podcasts than writing a text out in prose. I think this comes from being a poet as much as an essayist. One of the most successful pieces of design writing that I'm proud of is the writing for *W. E. B. Du Bois's Data Portraits: Visualizing Black America* in 2018. It was a short essay but then a long series of extended captions. It really felt like constructing an argument and set of observations through fragments. There was something about the call and response between my text and Du Bois and his student visualization that really worked as a format for me. I think this is because my design and art history training was happening in parallel with my learning as an artist and designer.

In 2021, I co-facilitated with my design studio Polymode, *Black Design in America: African Americans and the African Diaspora in Graphic Design 19th–21st Century*, part of a larger project called BIPOC Design History. That entire body of research was created and centered around an oral tradition that was very collected and co-authored—not just with the speakers but with the students in the audience. Each class produced its own archive of references, which form open-ended sets of syllabi that are free and open to the public. Since then, I have continued researching, lecturing, and exploring a generation of Black Grids connecting dots in my meandering search to see myself as a Black and queer designer, artist, and unexpected design historian.

That means some of the writing exists in the form of posters, paintings, wall drawings, videos, and other formats that employ art and design as vehicles for distribution as much as a printed or digital publication.

Q. *How do you define effective design writing?*

Effective design writing is anything that makes you (or an audience) want to look at design differently. That could mean a more informed way for practicing designers or a more "informing" way for those who live with design (which is practically everyone). I'm drawn to design writing that is vivid and brings design to life in a way that is almost more visual, even though it is not an image. Again, I think this is because I often arrive at my arguments, opinions, or points of view about design through a visual mode.

271

CHAPTER 9

Q. *Do you have an agenda in terms of writing about design?*

The former Poet Laureate of the United States of America, Tracy K. Smith, has a quote where she talks about the best poets and poems being changed by their own poems along with their readers. I really think that is my agenda for writing about design. It's often to learn more about design and design history for my own learning, to do some kind of healing, reframing, or refracting of a lineage to an audience who is also in need, want, or curious about something that they have been missing from design or design history—even if they hadn't realized it just yet. Much of the design writing I do is reparative in some way—a way to center references, designers, or designs that have been marginalized or left out.

Q. *You are also an editor. How does an editor improve your writing?*

I was raised by editors. This is both metaphorical and literal. My dad, Stephen B. Munro, was an editor and producer for over three decades at National Public Radio (NPR), primarily on the show *Morning Edition*. He was the one who really edited my text for the Du Bois book I mentioned. He taught me to pay attention to details, to read out my text to myself aloud as a way of scrubbing for errors, omissions, or a better way to say something—to render an idea with more clarity. He passed in the pandemic, and it wasn't just the grief of losing him as a loved one, I had to learn, and am still learning to write and edit my own writing in a new way. Sometimes I imagine what he might think of my writing when I sit down at the page or screen. I often ask for some kind of guidance or to send me a sign. Weirdly, I can hear his voice as a kind of guide, or sometimes I will hear a song or piece of music that makes me think of him—sometimes days after or before I write something, often at a moment of synchronicity.

One of my first design jobs was as a Design Fellow at the Walker Art Center. At the Walker, the design and editorial departments were essentially one department. There was even a long-running joke that called the department "Designatorial." There I learned about proper editing markups to layouts to designs I was working on. Through that back and forth with Kathleen McClean and Pamela Johnson, I really learned the importance of micro-adjustments to a particular word or placement of punctuation. I learned how important it was to take care and craft language and typography as a connected package.

More recently, in 2020–2022, I had the opportunity to co-create and co-curate the exhibition and publication *Strikethrough: Typographic Messages of Protest* with Stephen Coles. Stewf, as his friends and colleagues call him, has a background in journalism (like my dad), and I learned so much from working, researching, and writing with him. His attention to detail and speed of output were inspiring. Our process was highly collaborative, extending our teams at Polymode and the Letterform Archive. We also had a number of designers and the design scholar Colette Gaiter contribute or commissioned them to be part of the show and catalog. This required editing—both text and image, but also what objects would be included and where they would live. Hats off to Lucie Parker's invaluable guidance as a book editor there. I celebrate this kind of collaborative scholarship.

One of the people I write with the most is Brian Johnson, my partner in the studio Polymode. It's one of the strangest sensations to write with him. When we are working together, we literally finish each other's sentences, but more than that, it's like the lobes of our brains merge. It's one of those times where 1 + 1 really does = 3.

Q. *Do you distinguish between writing for designers and the general public?*

In a word, yes. When I write for designers I often feel I can have a kind of freedom to use terms and language that might be seen as jargon or "deep nerd" to a layperson. At the same time, it can be intimidating to write for my peers or those who have a perspective informed by skill or hard-earned time at the task of designing. On the flip side, sometimes, when I try to write for a design audience, I can sometimes suffer from being a bit insular in how I frame my approach. A lot of times, I have this implicit pressure in my head to conform to some kind of design cognoscenti in the sky. Maggie Nelson, the multi-hyphenate writer and a former writing teacher of mine at CalArts, called these "The Cops in my Head," an adaptation from the writings of experimental Brazilian playwright Augusto Boal.

I find that more often, I am writing for a general public. Or at least I hope that my writing can appeal to one. Though the more I write the more I realize that this idea of a general audience doesn't really exist. That is actually true of a design audience as well. I often try to write for the nineteen-year-old version of myself. Sometimes I try to get in the mindset of design writing, taking the form of a letter to my mother or grandmother. How might I be more kind? More real? What would a design essay feel like pended to a best friend, nerds on the internet, or a long-lost lover?

CHAPTER 9

Q. *What more do you want to do as a writer and editor?*

The what I want to do is to continue and finish work on a forthcoming publication version of *Black Design in America*, based on the BIPOC Design History course. This book will revisit and rewrite the course of design history that centers on previously marginalized designers' cultural figures—and particularly Black, Indigenous, and People of Color (BIPOC) and Queer, Trans, People of Color (QTPOC). This is one of the hardest projects I've had to write because the multitude of voices involved, and the sweeping arc of the material. It's also a challenge to take something that existed in an oral space and then translate it into a written, graphic, and typographic space.

Black Design in America topics include the ancient origins of African alphabets, innovative mathematics in African architecture, systemic racism of the transatlantic slave trade, W. E. B. Du Bois's innovative information diagrams in 1900, the aesthetics of Eugenics and its science of racial profiling, the Harlem Renaissance and other queer Blackness, the grassroots network of Victor Hugo Green's Motorists books, urgent Civil Rights protest movements, the rise of hip hop's graphic language, histories of Black liberation from Afrofuturism to the Black Lives Matter movement, and methodologies of Black design education.

It's being co-written with Tasheka Arceneaux-Sutton and Pierre Bowins and edited with Brian Johnson, and being published with Michelle Komie editing at Princeton University Press. The primary text is interwoven in a call-and-response with additional texts adapted from the guest speakers' lectures.

The how of what I want is to write with more freedom and ease, try not to take myself so seriously, and let go of a sense of perfectionism that can have a white supremacist history and bog down design and design writing.

WHERE, WHEN, HOW, AND WHY I WRITE

STARTING A NEWSLETTER

★ DEROY PERAZA ★

Principal, Hyperakt Design

Q. *How and why did you become interested in writing about design?*

I'd say that I've been interested in writing about design for years, but never really had the time or courage to do so. Knowing that there are so many great design writers like you, Michael Bierut, Debbie Millman, and many more, I definitely felt a bit of impostor syndrome. Fortunately, over the years we've managed to surround ourselves with some great consultants, coaches, and editors at Hyperakt who pushed me to put "on paper" what I found much easier to go on about in conversation. This wasn't something that just happened on a whim. It required restructuring and reprioritizing my role to buy me the time I needed to write. I'm not a particularly fast writer, so this was essential. I won't lie, it was a scary shift. It felt like I was giving up precious design time for something I wasn't yet fully confident in. But it wasn't long before I realized that writing was actually just the end product of thinking. Seems obvious, but that's where the biggest value is—it's all about building discipline around organizing thoughts. This has been incredibly valuable for us and has helped us build much more confidence in our expertise. It also didn't hurt to get some encouragement along the way from people I have a lot of respect for.

CHAPTER 9

. . . it wasn't long before I realized that writing was actually just the end product of thinking.

Q. *Can any writer write about design, or is there a singular talent or skill one must have?*

I can't speak for any writer, but I know that in my case, I really needed to write from experience to feel like I had any kind of authority to share my point of view. My writing is based on my understanding of the role of design and branding and learnings from work working with our clients. These experiences help me connect ideas together. But, this might not be how everyone's brain works.

Q. *What constitutes effective design writing?*

The standard I hold myself to is: make things easier to understand; share relevant, useful knowledge others can apply to make their lives easier; and have a clear point of view. If I'm doing that, I feel like I'm being effective.

Q. *You publish your writing, much of it about working the non-profit arena, in a newsletter. Why did you choose this platform?*

Our goal in writing was to demonstrate that we have built up extensive expertise over more than two decades of work. Designers have a tendency of showing results in the form of beautiful visuals. We do this, and it's great, but it's only one dimension of design. Design and branding are intellectual, stra-tegic activities that exist to advance the mission of real world organizations, with real world people. The more we can talk about design in ways that are relevant and accessible to our clients, the better.

Q. *Should all design writing be "entertaining"?*

It shouldn't be boring, but my goal isn't really to entertain. It's to clarify, communicate, teach, facilitate. If it also happens to be entertaining, great.

Q. Are there subjects you prefer or do you think of yourself as a generalist?

These days I'm interested in writing about two things:

1. Explaining and demonstrating the value and the role of branding for nonprofits. They sell ideas instead of things, but they still need to communicate and persuade. They still need to build and encode their reputations.

2. Sharing practical knowledge about how to approach and execute every part of the branding process—from change management to execution to rolling out and activating a brand, to then managing its growth in support of organizational strategy.

Q. Is it best not to be a designer when writing about design or does this not matter?

It depends what you're writing about. If the writing is a critique of design as it relates to the broader world or culture, I don't think it's necessary to be a designer. If the writing requires technical design knowledge and experience to lend it credibility, then I think it's helpful to be a designer. But we write about the role of branding and design from multiple perspectives at Hyperakt. Sometimes it's from the point of view of strategists, others from the perspective of client experience folks. It really depends what the angle is.

CHAPTER 9

AN HONEST ASSESSMENT

★ ROB WALKER ★

Journalist and author of *Significant Objects*

Q. *How and why did you become interested in editing design writing?*

I backed into it, actually. I was doing a lot of work around consumer culture and marketing, and of course that naturally intersects with design. But it also overlapped with a particular design moment—the field was getting mainstream (and business) attention, and absolutely *clamoring* for even more attention. That seemed interesting, so I started trying to develop contacts with smart people in what I came to think of as designworld. I wasn't interested in becoming a design "expert" myself, but I was interested in the way some of these people thought, and how they fit into the bigger themes I was exploring. It wasn't that more people needed to take an interest in design stories; it was that design stories needed to be framed in ways that interested more people.

In those days, the dominant narrative out of designworld was: Design is underrated, doesn't get enough attention (credit), should be taken more seriously, etc. That led to a certain amount of cheerleading. But I think that story is over. Design has long since arrived as a popular subject matter. The necessary narrative(s) now are about accountability, consequences, and recognizing limits—all the things that come with a discipline being widely recognized as powerful and influential. This is good news. It opens up all sorts of new opportunities to define what "design writing" can be.

WHERE, WHEN, HOW, AND WHY I WRITE

Q. *Can any writer write about design, or is there a singular talent or skill one must have?*

I don't think there's one right answer here. The core skills are the skills of any good writer: observation, curiosity, empathy for the reader, a strong point of view. Sometimes it's helpful to have a writer who is deeply grounded in design and design history, but sometimes a more outsider perspective is actually more productive. I think we need to be open and creative about what a design story is, and that argues for opening the subject up to writers with different specialties and interests.

Q. *What constitutes effective design reporting and writing?*

Finding answers to the questions readers may have, before they even have them. Getting as many perspectives as possible. Finding the details behind the official story. Surprising us.

Q. *Is it best not to be a designer when writing about design or does this not matter?*

This can be an advantage, if the knowledge and perspective that comes from that experience is used to benefit the reader. The danger is that it could result in a skewed agenda. And maybe the bigger danger is that it could result in assuming too much about what the reader knows, believes, wants to know, or should believe. But that can be addressed if the writer is self-aware and working to serve the reader. You just have to be honest about how that designer status may influence your perspective—honest with the reader, and honest with yourself.

Q. *What differentiates reportage from commentary from punditry?*

The value of reportage is in the gathered facts, especially facts that were previously obscured. Commentary, when done well, makes us see new ideas and meanings within those facts. Punditry, which is hard to do well and easily to do badly (which is why there's so much of it), consists of reacting to reportage and commentary. At least that's how I'd think of it. I've certainly done all three.

Q. *Are design writing and editing viable disciplines?*

Oh absolutely! As long as we're telling readers things they want to know (even if they didn't know they wanted to know them). We serve our readers. As long as we do that, we're viable.

CONTRIBUTORS

Alicia Olushola Ajayi is an architectural designer, researcher, writer, and (still trying to figure it out) based in NYC. After receiving a dual master's degree in architecture and social work from Washington University in St. Louis, Alicia worked as an associate designer at MASS Design Group. There she contributed to the Equal Justice Initiatives Soil Collection exhibition and the ground-breaking Memorial to Peace and Justice in Montgomery, Alabama, a site dedicated to the racial terror and lynching throughout US history. She graduated from the School of Visual Arts MA Design Research, Writing and Criticism program in 2020. At SVA, she refined her research practice to be rooted in historical research and cultural theory applications. Ajayi is currently documenting and researching Brooklyn, IL, the first Black American town to be incorporated by 1829.

Sarah Boxer is a cartoonist, essayist, and critic from Colorado who often writes on the relationship between word and image. She's the author of two Shakespearean Tragic-Comics, *Hamlet: Prince of Pigs* and *Anchovius Caesar: The Decomposition of a Romaine Salad*, as well as two psychoanalytic comics, *In the Floyd Archives*, based on Freud's case histories, and its sequel, *Mother May I?* Her essays and criticism appear in *The Atlantic*, *The New York Review of Books*, *The Comics Journal*, *The NYT Book Review*, *Artforum*, and numerous anthologies, including *The Peanuts Papers*, *Rereading America*, *You Are Here: NYC*, *The Best American Comics Criticism*, and *On the Couch: Writers Analyze Sigmund Freud*.

Akiko Busch writes about design, culture, and nature for a variety of publications. Her most recent book, *Everything Else Is Bric-a-Brac*, was published by Princeton Architectural Press in September 2022. Her collection of essays, *How to Disappear: Notes on Invisibility in a Time of Transparency*, was published by Penguin Press in 2019. The Incidental Steward, her essays about citizen science and stewardship, was published by Yale University Press in 2013 and awarded an Honorable Mention in the Natural History Literature category of 2013 National Outdoor

Book Awards. She is also the author of *Geography of Home: Writings on Where We Live*, *The Uncommon Life of Common Objects: Essays on Design and the Everyday*, and *Nine Ways to Cross a River: Midstream Reflections on Swimming and Getting There from Here*. She was a contributing editor at *Metropolis* magazine for twenty years, and her essays have appeared in numerous national magazines, newspapers, and exhibition catalogs. She has been a visiting teacher at Bennington College and was on the faculty of the MA Design Research Program at the School of Visual Arts from 2009 until 2020. Her work has been recognized by grants from the Furthermore Foundation, NYFA, and Civitella Ranieri.

Lauren Cantor is a multi-disciplinary strategist with a focus on venture design and innovation. She is an accomplished management executive in the financial industry, who decided to change gears and focus on her passion for design after working on Wall Street for close to 20 years. She has held a number of senior positions, including COO and Trading Manager of a proprietary hedge fund, Strategist to the CEO, and a Product Manager for an Innovation Consultancy. She holds an MFA as Designer + Entrepreneur from the School of Visual Arts, an MBA from the Wharton School of Business, and a BA magna cum laude from Columbia University in Astrophysics. Lauren currently runs her own creative consulting firm, Field & Edge, where she works with companies to create new business strategies by tackling issues of human-centered design.

Ken Carbone is an artist, designer, musician, author, and educator. From 1976 to 2020, he was the Principal Creative Director of the Carbone Smolan Agency and collaborated with top-tier brands internationally. As a columnist, he has written for *Fast Company*, *HuffPost*, *Ad Age*, *CA*, and *Print*.

Liz Danzico is Founding Chair of the MFA in Interaction Design Program. Previously, she was Acting Senior Vice President of Digital and Vice President of Design for NPR, overseeing digital and guiding both the visual and user experience across NPR-branded digital platforms and content. She has written for design-minded publications, including *Eye* Magazine, *Fortune* Magazine, *Interactions* Magazine. She's co-edited or contributed to books, including *LEAP Dialogues: Career Paths in Social Innovation*, *How They Got There: Interviews with Digital Designers about their Careers*, *The Shape of Design*, *Communicating Design: Developing Web Site Documentation for Design and Planning*, *Writing and Research for Graphic Designers: A Designer's Manual to Strategic Communication and Presentation*, and *Becoming a Digital Designer: A Guide to Careers in Web, Video, Broadcast, Game and Animation Design*. She writes part of her time at bobulate.com.

Pune Dracker is a writer, editor, and activist in New York City. She holds an MA in Design Research, Writing & Criticism from School of Visual Arts, and her lyric essays have appeared in *Hyperallergic* and *Oculus* Magazine. She teaches dance and yoga, and her current PhD work at CUNY Graduate Center focuses on 1970s teen idols through a lens of fashion and gender. Her art practice is inspired by The Situationists and the Fluxus movement.

Frederico Duarte studied communication design in Lisbon and worked as a designer in Malaysia and Italy. He holds an MFA in design criticism from the School of Visual Arts and a PhD in design curating from Birkbeck College, University of London and the Victoria & Albert Museum. As a design critic and curator he has written articles and essays, contributed to books and catalogs, given lectures and workshops, curated exhibitions and organized events on design, architecture and creativity since 2006.

Chappell Ellison is Director of Strategy at Launch by NTT Data. Before moving into software development, she led the content strategy discipline at Huge, a Brooklyn-based creative agency. She was also a civil servant for the New York City government, where she learned the importance of design as a service job and why your vote always, always matters. Chappell is proud to be part of the founding class of the Design Writing, Research, & Criticism MFA program at the School of Visual Arts, where she began her longstanding commitment to writing about design.

Jarrett Fuller is a designer, writer, educator, editor and podcaster. He is an assistant professor of graphic design at North Carolina State University; director of the design and editorial studio twenty-six; and host of the design podcast *Scratching the Surface*. He has written for a variety of publications and books. He was a contributing editor at AIGA Eye on Design and the editor or co-editor of four books, including *What It Means To Be a Designer Today* (co-edited with Liz Stinson), *Where Must Design Go Next?, 1, 10, 100 Years of Form, Typography, and Interaction at Parsons,* and *Culture Is Not Always Popular* (co-edited with Michael Bierut and Jessica Helfand).

Colette Gaiter, Professor Emerita in the Departments of Africana Studies and Art & Design at the University of Delaware, is a writer, artist, and designer. Her essays appear in *Black Panther: The Revolutionary Art of Emory Douglas*, *Wonder City of the World: New York City Travel Posters*, and *The Black Experience in Design: Identity Expression and Reflection*, among other books and publications.

Rick Griffith is a graphic designer and master letterpress printer. His work is an exploration of language, history, politics science, music, and ethics—typographically-focused and relevant. Rick was born and raised in Southeast London and immigrated to the U.S. in the late '80s. He had a (short) freelance career on Madison Avenue which funded his first practice, RGD (Rick Griffith Design). With his partner Debra Johnson, Rick cofounded the design practice MATTER, which has grown into an ambidextrous design consultancy, print shop, workshop, and retail bookstore. As Design Director at MATTER, Rick works across all media for business, culture, and civic engagement.

Eva Hagberg is an author, educator, historian, and media strategist. Her writing on architecture and design has appeared in *The New York Times*, *Metropolis*, *Wallpaper*, and more. She holds degrees in architecture from Princeton and UC Berkeley, and a PhD in Visual and Narrative Culture from UC Berkeley. She is the author of the memoir *How to Be Loved* (2019) and *When Eero Met His Match: Aline Louchheim Saarinen and the Making of an Architect* (2022).

Molly Heintz is the chair of the MA in Design Research, Writing and Criticism program at the School of Visual Arts and an Editor at Large at *Architectural Record* magazine. She is a co-founder of the editorial consultancy Superscript and has collaborated on strategy, research, and writing projects for a range of design organizations and institutions, including Pentagram, the Museum of Modern Art, and Rockwell Group, in addition to producing conversation series for the Museum of Arts and Design, the Venice Architectural Biennale, and the Oslo Architecture Triennial. She has edited and contributed to multiple books and magazines, including *Spectacle* (Phaidon 2006), *Design Observer*, *Fast Company*, *The Art Newspaper,* and *The Architect's Newspaper*, among others. From 2018–2022, she was the editor in chief of *Oculus,* magazine for the American Institute of Architects New York chapter. In 2023, she received a special citation for contributions to the profession from AIANY.

Steven Heller is currently the co-chair and co-founder Emeritus of the MFA Design: Designer as Entrepreneur program at the School of Visual Arts, SVA / NYC. He was the art director of the *New York Times Book Review* for 30 years and author, co-author, and editor of over 200 books on the history and practice of graphic design, illustration, and satiric art, most notably *Iron Fists: Branding the Twentieth Century Totalitarian State* (Phaidon). He is a recipient of the Smithsonian National Design Award for "Design Mind," AIGA Medal for Lifetime Achievement; an inductee into the Art Directors Club Hall of Fame and the One Club Educators Hall of Fame and received two honorary PhDs from The College for Creative Studies in Detroit and University of West Bohemia in the Czech Republic. He is the author of *Growing Up Underground: A Memoir of Counterculture New York* (Princeton Architectural Press 2022).

Jennifer Kabat is a writer and educator. Her book *The Eighth Moon* (Milkweed Editions 2024) is the story of an 1840s socialist uprising in her town. Half of a diptych, the second volume, *Nightshining*, will come out in 2025. Her work has been supported by numerous grants including a Silvers Foundation Grant and a Warhol Foundation Arts Writers Grant for her criticism. Her essays have appeared in *BOMB, Granta, Frieze, McSweeney's, The Believer, Virginia Quarterly Review, LARB, New York Review, 4 Columns*, and the *White Review* and been anthologized in *Best American Essays*. She often collaborates with artists and contributes to museum catalogs. She teaches writing in the MA Design Research, Writing and Criticism program at the School of Visual Arts. An apprentice herbalist, she lives in rural upstate New York and serves on her volunteer fire department.

Karrie Jacobs is a professional observer of the man-made landscape. Her recent writing has appeared in Curbed, *The New York Times*, and the *MIT Technology Review*. She has been a columnist for *Metropolis* and a contributing editor for *Travel + Leisure, Architect, House + Garden* and *Metropolitan Home*. Jacobs was also the founding editor-in-chief of *Dwell*, the architecture critic of *New York Magazine*, and the founding executive editor of Benetton's *Colors*. She is the author of *The Perfect $100,000 House: A Trip Across America and Back in Pursuit of a Place to Call Home* (Viking 2006).

Joyce Rutter Kaye is a writer, editor, and communications strategist currently leading the communication office for the School of Visual Arts. She is the recipient of multiple industry awards, including four National Magazine Awards for General Excellence for *Print* magazine during her tenure as editor-in-chief and managing editor.

Mark Kingsley is a designer, creative director, strategist and author with a wide range of experience and recognition. His client list ranges from John Coltrane to the Guggenheim Museum; and he has held positions at Ogilvy, Landor, and Collins. In 2001, his work for Blue Note Records received a Grammy nomination. He is a long-time faculty member in the School of Visual Arts Masters in Branding program and previously held the Melbert B. Cary Professorship at the Rochester Institute of Technology. His book, *Universal Principles of Branding*, was published in 2023.

Julie Lasky is a journalist, editor, and critic best known for her writings on design. She has been the deputy editor of *The New York Times*'s weekly Home section, the editor-in-chief of *I.D.* and *Interiors* magazines, and the managing editor of *Print* magazine. She contributes to *The New York Times, Wall Street Journal, Architectural Digest, Elle Decor, Travel & Leisure*, and other publications. She teaches in the graduate industrial design program at Parsons School of Design.

Warren Lehrer is a writer and artist/designer known as a pioneer in the fields of visual literature and design authorship. His work explores the vagaries and luminescence of character, the relationships between social structures and the individual, and the pathos and absurdity of life. His books, acclaimed for capturing the shape of thought and reuniting the oral and pictorial traditions of storytelling with the printed page, include: *A Life in Books: The Rise and Fall of Bleu Mobley* (Goff Books); *Ouvert Oeuvre: Openings* with Adeena Karasick (Lavender Ink); *Five Oceans in a Teaspoon* with Dennis J. Bernstein (Paper Crown Press); *Crossing the BLVD: strangers, neighbors, aliens in a New America* (W.W. Norton) with Judith Sloan; *The Portrait Series: a quartet of men* (four book series, Bay Press); *GRRRHHHHH: a study of social patterns* (EarSay/Center for Editions) with Sandra Brownlee and Dennis Bernstein; *FRENCH FRIES* with Dennis Bernstein (Visual Studies Workshop); *i mean you know* (Visual Studies Workshop), and *versations* (EarSay).

Adam Harrison Levy is a writer, interviewer, filmmaker, and teacher based in New York where he specializes in the art of the interview. For the BBC he has interviewed a range of actors, writers, and musicians. He has produced/directed two films and his writing has appeared in *The Guardian* and Design Observer. He was a Poynter Fellow at Yale University and has taught at Wesleyan University. He currently teaches at the School of Visual Arts in New York.

Angelina Lippert is the Chief Curator and Director of Content of Poster House, the first and only museum in the United States dedicated to the art and history of posters. She has been a poster historian for 16 years, focusing on printing techniques, major movements, and styles of graphic communication around the world.

Tod Lippy is the creator of the nonprofit arts publication *Esopus* (2003–2018) and executive director of The Esopus Foundation Ltd.; the editor and cofounder of *Scenario: The Magazine of Screenwriting Art* (1994–97); and the founder, designer, and coeditor of *publicsfear* magazine (1992–94). His 2000 book, *Projections 11: New York Film-Makers on Film-Making*, was published by Faber & Faber. His design work has also been featured in a number of books—including the *Graphis*

Design Annual, Print Design Annual, Essentials of Visual Communication (Laurence King, 2008), and *Art Direction + Editorial Design* (Abrams, 2007).

Christopher Long is a professor of architecture at the University of Texas, Austin. His interests center on modern architectural history, with a particular emphasis on Central Europe between 1880 and the present. He is the author of *Josef Frank: His Life and Work* (2002), co-editor of *Josef Frank: Writings* (2012), and author of *Lucian Bernhard* (2024) about the influential German graphic designer, in addition to dozens of other books, exhibition catalog essays, scholarly articles, and reviews.

Ellen Lupton is a writer, curator, educator, and designer. Lupton is the Betty Cooke and William O. Steinmetz Design Chair at MICA (Maryland Institute College of Art) in Baltimore, where she has authored numerous books on design processes, including *Thinking with Type, Graphic Design Thinking, Graphic Design: The New Basics*, and *Type on Screen*. She is curator emerita at Cooper Hewitt, Smithsonian Design Museum in New York City, where her exhibitions included *Herbert Bayer: Bauhaus Master, Face Values: Understanding A.I., The Senses: Design Beyond Vision, Beauty—Cooper Hewitt Design Triennial, How Posters Work*, and *Beautiful Users*. Her book *Design Is Storytelling* was published by Cooper Hewitt in 2017. She received the AIGA Gold Medal for Lifetime Achievement in 2007. She was named a Fellow of the American Academy of Arts & Sciences in 2019.

Andrew McQuiston is a graphic designer and educator practicing in Philadelphia and New York. A multidisciplinary approach informs his work in brand identity, print, and digital design with clients and collaborators in industries ranging from music and technology to hospitality and commerce. Beyond these projects, Andrew researches the political, aesthetic, and environmental contexts and consequences of design. He holds an MA in Design Research, Writing & Criticism from the School of Visual Arts and a BFA in Graphic Design with a concentration in Book Arts & Printmaking from the University of the Arts.

Susan Merritt is a graphic designer; design educator; design researcher, writer, and curator. During her 30-year tenure at SDSU's School of Art + Design, Merritt developed a comprehensive curriculum in Graphic Design and taught a range of graphic design courses, eventually focusing on typography and graphic design history—all the while maintaining a professional practice. She completed postgraduate study in graphic design at the Basel School of Design and earned an MA in Design Research, Writing and Criticism from the School of Visual Arts in New York.

Mark Mothersbaugh is a prolific conceptual artist and composer. He is co-founder of the influential rock group DEVO and parlayed his avant-garde musical background into a leading role in scoring for filmed and animated entertainment, interactive media, and commercials. He has scored 150 films, television shows, video games, and hundreds of commercials through his multimedia company, Mutato Muzika. He has had 165 visual and audio art shows, including his retrospective traveling museum exhibition *Myopia*. He has a doctorate in Humane Letters at Kent State University.

Silas Munro is an artist, designer, writer, and curator engaging multi-modal practices that inspire people to be the best versions of themselves in order to effect positive change on society as a whole. He earned his BFA from Rhode Island School of Design and holds an MFA from California Institute of the Arts. He is the founder of Poly-Mode, the LGBTQ+ and Minority-owned design studio primarily working with cultural institutions and community-based organizations including collaborations with The City of LA, The Phillips Collection, The Center for Urban Pedagogy, Housing Works, MoMA, MOCA, The New Museum, Walker Art Center, Cooper Hewitt Smithsonian Design.

Deroy Peraz is a Cuban-American designer, a partner and creative director at Hyperakt, a design studio dedicated to helping nonprofits and foundations build courageous brands from the inside out.

Zachary Petit is editor of The Daily Heller, a contributing writer for *Fast Company* and the former editor-in-chief of *Print* magazine. He is the author of *The Essential Guide to Freelance Writing* and, most recently, *The Moon & Antarctica* for Bloomsbury's 33 ⅓ series.

Virginia Postrel is a contributing editor to *Works in Progress*, and the author most recently of *The Fabric of Civilization: How Textiles Made the World*. Her previous books include *The Power of Glamour*, *The Substance of Style*, and *The Future and Its Enemies*. Follow her on Instagram @vpostrel, subscribe to her YouTube channel, and like her on Facebook.

Todd Pruzan is a longtime editor and writer on design, business, and culture whose work in magazines and digital media include several years as managing editor of *Print*. His writing has appeared in publications including *The New Yorker*, *The New York Times*, and *The Believer*. He's the author of the 2005 book *The Clumsiest People in Europe*.

Anne Quito is a journalist and design critic whose writing appears in *The Atlantic*, *CNN*, *Metropolis*, *Fast Company*, and *Architectural Digest* among other publications. She wrote *Mag Men: Fifty Years of Making Magazines* (Columbia University Press, 2019), a book about the glory days of magazine design as told by Milton Glaser and Walter Bernard. Anne is the first recipient of the Steven Heller Prize for Cultural Commentary.

Anjulie Rao is a journalist and critic covering the built environment. Based in Chicago, much of her work reckons with the complexities of post-industrial cities; explores connections to place and land; and exposes intersections between architecture, landscapes, and cultural change. She is the founder and editor of *Weathered*, a Graham Foundation-awarded publication focused on cities and landscapes in the wintertime. Her bylines can be found in *Dwell*, *The Architect's Newspaper*, *The Architectural Review*, *The New York Review of Architecture*, and *Landscape Architecture Magazine*, among others.

Alan Rapp is an editor, writer, and visual book packager. His writings have appeared in numerous publications and he has organized graduate-level seminars in Design Writing at Pratt Institute and thesis development at Rhode Island School of Design.

Angela Riechers is a writer, editorial art director, and design educator. Her first book, *The Elements of Visual Grammar,* was published in February 2024 by Princeton University Press. A native New Yorker, she served as Program Director of Graphic Design at the University of the Arts in Philadelphia from 2018–2024. Angela received her BFA from the Rhode Island School of Design and her MFA from the School of Visual Art.

Adrian Shaughnessy is a graphic designer, writer, publisher, and educator. He co-founded Unit Editions in 2009 and has been on the teaching staff at the Royal College of Art since 2010.

Edward Tenner is an independent writer and speaker holding the titles of Distinguished Scholar in the Smithsonian's Lemelson Center for the Study of Invention and Innovation, and Visiting Scholar in the Rutgers University Department of History. He is the author of *Our Own Devices* and *Why Things Bite Back*. His new book, *The Efficiency Paradox: What Big Data Can't Do,* is published by Alfred A. Knopf and Vintage Books. In 2020–21 he was a visiting scholar in the Program in Interdisciplinary Studies at the Institute for Advanced Study.

Roshita Thomas is a writer and creative operations manager from Mumbai. She currently works with the Talent Operations team at Buck. She previously worked with Porto Rocha as the Operations and New Business Associate and as the Editorial Assistant for *Oculus* Magazine with the American Institute of Architects New York. She graduated with a Master's Degree in Design Research Writing and Criticism from the School of Visual Arts.

Kim Tidwell is the managing editor for *Print* Magazine and an independent writer and creative strategist living in Austin, Texas. During her three-decade career, Kim has been a photo editor, graphic designer, retail brand manager, and brand and content marketer. She brings everything together with her master's in art history and a fundamental love of our aesthetic world.

Véronique Vienne has edited, art-directed, and written essays for numerous design publications in the USA and in Europe (*House & Garden, Emigré, Communication Arts, Eye, Graphis, Aperture, Metropolis, Etapes, Print,* and more). Her book, *100 Ideas that Changed Graphic Design,* co-authored with Steven Heller, has been translated in 10 languages.

Alissa Walker is a freelance writer who lives and works in Los Angeles. She is a former senior writer at Curbed, where she covered cities, transportation, and architecture for seven years. She was a 2021 recipient of the Steven Heller Prize for Cultural Commentary for her writing on cities and transportation.

Rob Walker is a journalist covering design, technology, business, the arts, and other subjects. He writes the "Branded" column for *Fast Company* and has contributed to *The New York Times, Bloomberg Businessweek, The Atlantic,* NewYorker.com, *Design Observer, The Organist,* and many others. His latest book is *The Art of Noticing* (Knopf). He is on the faculty of the Products of Design MFA program at the School of Visual Arts.

Michele Y. Washington is a designer, researcher, black memory worker, podcaster, and writer. Her writings have been featured in *The Black Experience in Design, Wonder City of the World: Travel Posters of New York City, Everlasting Plastics: Evoking Objects of Change, Special Issue on The Films of Camille Billops and James V. Hatch.* In her free time, she loves making collages, knitting quirky objects, screen printing, and taking long naps.

ACKNOWLEDGMENTS

In every Allworth Press/School of Visual Arts collaboration we must give our sincere gratitude for the continued support of Tad Crawford, publisher, and David Rhodes, president of SVA; without them this and other books in this series would be impossible.

Thanks to our editor Sarah Janssen at Allworth, whose patience, excitement, and expertise have been invaluable to us during the course of this project.

To Alexandra Mooney we owe a debt for a cover design that influenced the overall design of this book. And to Rick Landers for doing such a great job of designing and producing the interior pages.

All the contributors generously allowed us to use their writing and interviews as case studies. Their works are exemplary; we wish them evermore success as design commentators and writers.

Steven Heller and Molly Heintz

INDEX

#

19th Century Ornamented Typed Faces (Gray), 127
1001 Voices: Symphony for a New America, 28
1619 Project, 141
1990s, 146–150

A

Abloh, Virgil, 212–214
abstraction, 210–211
Admassu, Emanuel, 216
advertisements, 113–117, 147–150, 203–204
Air India, 234–236
Albers, Josef, 178
Allen, Woody, 232
Anderson, Sean, 215
"Anecdote of the Jar" (Stevens), 9
Anthem for a New America (Lehrer), 28
anxiety, in interviews, 79
Arendt, Hannah, 42

artificial intelligence (AI), 102–107, 109, 247, 269

B

Baer, Jo, 211
Balenciaga, Cristóbal, 220
Balzac, Honoré de, 127–128
Bambi, 114–115
Barnes, Germane, 216–217
Bayer, Herbert, 41–42, 178
Beaux, Cecilia, 211
Bell Gothic, 132
Bernhard, Lucian, 85–86
Bernhard, Ruth, 86
Bernstein, Dennis, 19, 21
Bierut, Michael, 130, 132, 275
Billiet, Alain, 138
biography, as genre, 8–9
Black, Rick, 37
BLACK city (Daniels), 217
Black Lives Matter, 218, 274
Black Panthers, 139–141, 143, 216, 257

Blokland, Petr van, 137
Brand, Stewart, 191
Breier, Lo, 135
Brownlee, Sandra, 21
Buchenwald concentration camp, 41–42
"Building Dwelling Thinking" (Heidegger), 9–10
Burt, Ronald S., 152

C

Calm Tech movement, 226
Cantor, Lauren, 102–107
capitalism, 19, 43, 220, 227, 230–231, 239
Caraba, David, 181
Carter, Matthew, 131
Case, Amber, 226
Cassandre, A.M., 180
Chalmers, Matthew, 225
Chantry, Art, 60
character, 22
Chwast, Seymour, 178
cities, 215–218

Claude: A Narrative Portrait of Claude Debs (Lehrer), 22–23

clichés, 54–55

clutter, 66–69

Coles, Stephen, 273

Collins, John, 133

communities, 215–218

Constable, Arnold, 63–64

contemplation, 9

content creation, 223–226

conversation, 15–16

Cooke, Sekou, 216–217

copy editing, 13. *See also* editing

corporeality, 195

counterfeits, 154–163

Covarrubias, Miguel, 143, 257

COVID-19 pandemic, 35

Critical Race Theory, 141

criticism, 206–209

Crossing the BLVD: Strangers, Neighbors, Aliens in a New America (Lehrer and Sloan), 25–28

Csikszentmihalyi, Mihaly, 68

D

Dair, Carl, 127

Daniels, J. Yolande, 216–217

Daniels, Simon, 137

Danzico, Liz, 244–247

Darling, Michael, 212

Davenport, Bob, 166–167

Davis, Felecia, 216

Design with Type (Dair), 127

developmental edit, 12. *See also* editing

Dewey, John, 245

Dewey, Melvil, 152

Dolce Vita, La (film), 197–200

Douglas, Aaron, 143

Douglas, Emory, 140, 143, 257–258

Douglas, Mary, 197

Dupas, Jean, 63

E

Eames, Charles, 46

Eames, Ray, 46

editing, 11–13, 247–252, 254–255, 261–269, 271–272, 274, 278–279

ego, in interviews, 80–81

Ehrlich, Franz, 42

Ekberg, Anita, 197–199

emojis, 51–53

empathy, 39

Esopus (magazine), 242–243

essays, 48–50

Estrada, Joseph, 160

Euro (currency), 134–138

Evil Eye, 120–121

exclamation points, 51–52

exclusion, 7

Eyben, Bruno Ninaber von, 135

F

Family of Man (Steichen), 42–43

Farocki, Harun, 8–9

fashion, 219–222

Figgins, Vincent, 127

Figura, Starr, 210

Figures of Speech (exhibition), 212

Fitzpatrick, Robert, 91

Five Oceans in a Teaspoon (Bernstein and Lehrer), 34–35

Floyd, George, 144

Follis, John, 89–90, 97, 100

fonts, 15–16, 41–42, 86, 116–117, 126–133, 137, 142, 203–204, 212–213, 227–229, 256

forgeries, 154–163

Fox, Martin, 267

Frankenthaler, Helen, 211

French Fries (Bernstein and Lehrer), 19–20

Frere-Jones, Tobias, 131–132

Fuller, Buckminster, 191

G

Gaiter, Colette, 256–260

Garamond, Claude, 40–41

Garnett, Blake, 127

Gattinoni, Fernanda, 197

Gehl, Paul F., 228–229

Gentileschi, Artemisia, 211

Giovanni, Nikki, 253

Glaser, Milton, 178, 258

Glenn, Joshua, 69

Globalization: Preventing the Sameness of the World, 27

Gobé, Marc, 136
Goebbels, Joseph, 41
Gooden, Mario, 216
Goodman, Charles, 165–166
Goodspeed, Elizabeth, 236
Gray, John, 138
Gray, Nicolete, 127
Greenberg, Stanley, 4–5
Griffin, Andrew, 39
GRRRHHHH: A Study of Social Patterns (Lehrer), 21
Gunn, James Newton, 152–153
Gutenberg, Johannes, 40, 126
Gutenberg Galaxy, The: The Making of Typographic Man (McLuhan), 126

H

Hartt, David, 216
Heads Together: Weed and the Underground Press Syndicate, 1965–1973 (Kramer), 237–239
Heck, Bethany, 232
Heidegger, Martin, 9–10
Heller, Steven, 11, 13, 257
Hess, Amanda, 224
Higham, John, 152
historical context, 7
history, as genre, 8–9
Hoefler, Jonathan, 131–132
Hollin Hills, 164–138
Hollis, Richard, 263
Hood, Walter, 216

I

IBM, 43–47
Igarashi, Takenobu, 177–179
i mean you know (Lehrer), 17–18
inclusion, 7
Indiana, Robert, 178
International Style, 165–166
interrupting, in interviews, 79–80
interviewing, 78–81
Ive, Jony, 206
Iyengar-Lepper study, 225

J

Jayne, Sam, 233
Jeyifous, Olalekan, 216
Johnson, Pamela, 272

K

Kalina, Robert, 135
Kandalgaonkar, Neil, 137–138
Karasick, Adeena, 35
Kaufmann, Edgar, Jr., 43–47
Kaye, Joyce Rutter, 267–269
Koda, Harold, 222
Kondo, Marie, 67
Kooka, Bobby, 234
Koshalek, Richard, 90
Kramer, David Jacob, 237–239
Krasner, Lee, 211
Kusama, Yayoi, 211

L

Langer, Ellen, 3–4
language, 14–15
Lasky, Julie, 267–268
Leary, Timothy, 237
legibility, 41
Leman, Andrew, 132–133
Letter Box: The Geometry of Loss (Lehrer), 37–38
Liberation News Service (LNS), 239
Licko, Zuzana, 59
Life in Books, A: The Rise and Fall of Bleu Mobley (Lehrer), 29–33
Lippy, Tod, 242–243
listening, in interviews, 79
literacy, 40
LNS. *See* Liberation News Service (LNS)
Lokko, Lesley, 253
London, Frank, 35
Long, Christopher, 85–86
Loy, William E., 231
Lupton, Ellen, 261–263
Luycx, Luc, 135

M

mail art, 83
Making Space: Women Artists and Postwar Abstraction (exhibition), 210–211
Malhotra, Manish, 236
Manutius, Aldus, 40
Marshall, Kerry James, 145
Martin, Agnes, 211
Mason, Bridget, 217
materialism, 67–68

MC5, 238
McClean, Kathleen, 272
McEwen, Mitch, 216–217
McLuhan, Marshall, 126
McMakin, Roy, 184–188
McMurtrie, Douglas C., 228–229
Meister, Sarah Hermanson, 210
Middleton, Robert Hunter, 228–229
migration, 25–28
Millman, Debbie, 275
mindfulness, 3–6
minimalism, 67–68
Mitchell, Joan, 210–211
Miyake, Issey, 199
modernism, 165–166, 201, 227–229
Monroe, Marilyn, 194–197, 200
Moreira, Victor, 122–123
Mori, Haruki, 177
Morrison, Toni, 253, 257
Moscoso, Victor, 180–181
Mothersbaugh, Mark, 82–84
Mungo, Ray, 239
Munro, Silas, 270–274
Munro, Stephen B., 272
Munter, Gabriela, 211
MyFonts.com, 133

N

narratives, 8
Nazis, 41–42, 46–47
Negrin, Llewellyn, 195
Nevelson, Louise, 211
Newton, Huey, 141

New Typography, 228
Nicky D. from LIC (Lehrer), 23–24
Nietzsche, Friedrich, 7
Nomiyama, Sakura, 177
North, Michael, 220
nostalgia, 201–203
Noyes, Eliot, 44–47

O

Olivetti, Adriano, 44
Ouvert Oeuvre: Openings (2023) (Karasick and Lehrer), 35
Oxenaar, R.D.E., 135

P

pandemic, 35
Pechey, Elisha, 231
Peraza, Deroy, 275–277
Picard, Max, 4
posters, 118–119
Prisco, Michael, 179
proofreading, 13. *See also* editing
punctuation, 51–53
punditry, 262–263, 266, 279

Q

questions, interview, 78–79
quotations, 108–111

R

race, 139–145, 270–274
racism, 142–143, 215–218
Rand, Paul, 44–47

Rao, Umesh, 234
Rapp, Alan, 254–255
Reconstructions: Architecture and Blackness in America (exhibit), 215
Recto, Claro M., 155
Reder, Hillary, 210
Refusal of Space, The (Gooden), 216
Renner, Paul, 8
Republica: Temple of Color and Sound (Robinson), 217
Reynolds, Debbie, 195
Richardson, Margaret, 267
Riveted in the Word (Lehrer), 39
Robinson, Kristina Kay, 217
Rochberg-Halton, Eugene, 68
Rodriguez, Quique, 179
Rowin, Michael Joshua, 197
Runyan, Robert Miles, 89
Ruskin, John, 2–3
Ryan, Anne, 211

S

Salten, Felix, 114–115
Satisfaction (font), 133
sensationalism, 8
Seventy-nine Short Essays on Design (Beirut), 130
shadowed typefaces, 128–129
Shaughnessy, Adrian, 264–266
silence, in interviews, 80
Sinclair, John, 238

Sloan, Judith, 25–28
Smith, Tracy K., 272
Soleri, Paolo, 191
"Some Memories of the Glorious Bird" (Vidal), 109
speech, 17–18
Steele, Valerie, 220–222
Steichen, Edward, 42
Stevens, Wallace, 9–10
Strikethrough: Typographic Messages of Protest (Coles), 273
Stuart, Dan, 89
Sussman, Deborah, 87–101
systems, 72
Sywalski, Helen, 179

T

tabs, 151–153
theses, 48–50
Thompson, William, 142
Thorowgood, William, 127
"Three Academic Pieces" (Stevens), 10
Tidwell, Kim, 248–251
Tillett, D.D., 173
Tillett, Leslie, 173
Tillett, Linnaea, 172–176
Torday, Piers, 114–115
Travilla, William, 194
Truitt, Anne, 211
Typefounders and Typefounding in America (Loy), 231
typography, 15–16, 41–42, 86, 116–117, 126–133, 137, 142, 203–204, 212–213, 227–231, 256

U

Underground Press Service (UPS), 238
Universal font, 41–42
UPS. *See* Underground Press Service (UPS)
user experience (UX), 223–226
utterances, 17–18

V

versations (Lehrer), 15–16
Vidal, Gore, 109
Vignelli, Massimo, 135–136
"Visual Poetry in Vacant Storefronts," 29
Vogue (magazine), 144–145
Vonnegut, Kurt, 245
Vreeland, Diana, 201

W

Walker, Rob, 278–279
walking, 5
Washington, Michele Y., 252–253
Watson, Thomas, Jr., 43–44, 47
Watson, Thomas, Sr., 44, 47
W. E. B. Du Bois's Data Portraits: Visualizing Black America (Munro), 271
whiteness, 144
white supremacy, 142–144
Whole Earth Catalog, 189–193, 230, 232
Williams, Amanda, 216
Williams, Tennessee, 109

Wilson, Mabel O., 215
Windsor (typeface), 230–233
Windsor, Kenneth R., 136–137
Wintour, Anna, 219
Wolper, David, 93–94
women, 210–211
World of Silence, The (Picard), 4
Worth, Thomas, 142–143
Wright, Mary, 165
writing, 15–16, 48–50, 61–65, 245–252, 254–269, 271–274, 276–279. *See also* editing
"writing for the ear," 58–60

Y

Young, Iris Marion, 195

Z

Zintzmeyer, Jorg, 135
Zipes, Jack, 115

Books from Allworth Press

About Design by *Gordon Salchow, foreword by Michael Bierut, afterword by Katherine McCoy*
(6⅛ × 6⅛, 208 pages, paperback, $19.99)

Advertising Design and Typography by *Alex W. White*
(8½ × 11, 224 pages, paperback, $29.99)

The Black Experience in Design edited by *Anne H. Berry, Kareem Collie, Penina Acayo Laker, Lesley-Ann Noel, Jennifer Rittner, Kelly Walters*
(6 × 9, 312 pages, paperback, $19.99)

Brand Thinking and Other Noble Pursuits by *Debbie Millman*
(6 × 9, 256 pages, paperback, $19.99)

Citizen Designer (Second Edition) by *Steven Heller and Véronique Vienne*
(6 × 9, 312 pages, paperback, $22.99)

Designing for People by *Henry Dreyfuss*
(6 × 9, 288 pages, paperback, $19.99)

Design School Reader by *Steven Heller*
(6 × 9, 264 pages, paperback, $24.99)

Editing by Design (Fourth Edition) by *Jan V. White and Alex W. White*
(8 × 10, 232 pages, paperback, $29.99)

The Elements of Logo Design by *Alex W. White*
(8 × 10, 224 pages, hardcover, $34.99)

For the Love of Design by *Steven Heller*
(6 × 9, 168 pages, paperback $26.99)

Graphic Design Rants and Raves by *Steven Heller*
(7 × 9, 200 pages, paperback, $19.99)

How to Think Like a Great Graphic Designer by *Debbie Millman*
(6 × 9, 248 pages, paperback, $24.95)

Line Color Form: The Language of Graphic Design by *Jesse Day*
(7 × 8½, 144 pages, paperback, $19.95)

Listening to Type: Making Language Visible by *Alex W. White*
(8 × 10, 272 pages, paperback, $29.99)

The Swastika and Symbols of Hate by *Steven Heller*
(6 × 9, 216 pages, hardcover $24.99)

Teaching Graphic Design (Second Edition) by *Steven Heller*
(6 × 9, 312 pages, paperback, $39.99)

Teaching Graphic Design History by *Steven Heller*
(6 × 9, 312 pages, paperback, $24.99)

Vintage Graphic Design by *Steven Heller & Louise Fili*
(8 × 10, 208 pages, paperback $24.99)